THE UPROOTED

THE UPROOTED

Second Edition

OSCAR HANDLIN

PENN

University of Pennsylvania Press
Philadelphia

Originally published 1951 by Little, Brown and Company
Published by arrangement with Little, Brown and Company (Inc.).
Copyright © 1951, 1973, 2002 Oscar Handlin
Printed in the United States of America on acid-free paper

10   9   8   7   6   5   4   3   2   1

Published 2002 by
University of Pennsylvania Press
Philadelphia, Pennsylvania 19104-1011

LIBRARY OF CONGRESS CATALOGING-IN-PUBLICATION DATA

Handlin, Oscar, 1915–
    The uprooted : the epic story of the great migrations that made the
American people / Oscar Handlin
        p.   cm.
    ISBN 0-8122-1788-8 (pbk. : alk. paper)
        1. Immigrants—United States—History. 2. Acculturation—United
States—History. 3. United States—Emigration and immigration—
History. I. Title
JV6450 .H35   2001
304.8'73—dc 21   2001048096

To
Mary
with love

CONTENTS

Author's Note

THE UPROOTED WAS NOT THE first of my works to find its way into print. Its three predecessors had earned modest scholarly success though no great monetary rewards. Still, the fact that they had long remained in print provided sufficient satisfaction.

Nor was I aggrieved by the ambiguous academic status of untenured assistant professor though member of three departments: history, sociology, and psychology. Only much later did I learn of the byzantine plots that had shunted me into that situation. Meanwhile I scrabbled through my notes to stitch together coherent courses, among them one on immigration to the United States — more general, more theoretical than that I offered in the History Department. I drew upon the materials I had long assembled, much of it bequeathed to the Harvard College Library by the Immigration Restriction League a quarter of a century earlier. But the guiding theme came from a book by Mario Praz that had lingered in my mind for decades. *The Romantic Agony* had traced the undercurrent of pain in the thought of eighteenth-century enlightenment writers. In a vague way I sensed an analogy to the reaction of immigrants to their American promised land. I had no wish to encase these insights in formal academic language, but sought a style more appropriate to the subject.

Fortunately, I had no need to invent or imagine data. Although the book dispensed with conventional scholarly apparatus, it rested on a solid foundation of materials drawn from letters, journals, and contemporary observations. It made no effort to distinguish among the various groups involved in the migration, but focused on the common human elements evident in them all.

The Uprooted made no big splash upon publication, inspired few reviews, but steadily gained a widening circle of appreciative readers. A half century later it is gratifying to find that circle still expanding.

PREFACE TO THE SECOND EDITION

THE TEXT STANDS AS WRITTEN.

It is the product of another time, written from the perspective of earlier years. What value it has for future readers derives in part from the understanding afforded by the outlook of the 1930's and 1940's.

The author of this book recalled in 1971 the painful process by which it took form and sorted out in memory and notes the elements which entered its composition. But he could not exclude impressions left by the intervening twenty years—years of change in the people of the country who were the subjects of his study, years too in which other scholars had added to the knowledge about the subject he had treated. Though the structure of the work as complete in 1950 left no space for their incorporation, the newer visions called for reflection and commentary.

The manuscript that went to its first printer closed with a set of questions and affirmations which probed the meaning of the immigrant experience. The questions expressed doubts, the affirmations hopes, about the altered relationship of the individual and the community that affected immigrants most directly, but other Americans also. Two decades later, the issue deserves reconsideration in the light of further changes in that relationship; a new chapter therefore picks up where the book formerly ended and extends the quest for meaning into the very recent past.

Reexamining what had been written — and a long lapse separated the writing and rereading — the author become reviser asked, how had he known what was true? And was it still true what he thought then was true, since other findings over the years had added to the available information? To still those doubts required another kind of reexamination — of the methods and evidence originally used, of the new data and variant opinions since published. The results appear in a commentary which leaves intact the original text with its own integral character. The corrections necessary, the modifications desirable, the reappraisals and the reaffirmations form the closing chapter of this version.

Perhaps the message of this book will prove as unwelcome to some readers in 1972 as its earlier version did. Two decades ago, at the height of American postwar euphoria, it seemed to some critics to offer an unduly harsh view of the national experience. Now, at the depth of American pessimism, the view may seem unduly roseate.

It is neither. The book tells an epic story. At the time of writing there was a possibility that it, like other epics, would have a tragic conclusion. Twenty years later, there is still a possibility that it might not.

THE UPROOTED

Introduction

ONCE I THOUGHT to write a history of the immigrants in America. Then I discovered that the immigrants *were* American history.

For almost fifteen years now, I have searched among the surviving records of the masses of men who peopled our country. As I worked, the conviction grew upon me that adequately to describe the course and effects of immigration involved no less a task than to set down the whole history of the United States. That is not a burden I can now assume.

My ambitions in this volume are more modest. I hope to seize upon a single strand woven into the fabric of our past, to understand that strand in its numerous ties and linkages with the rest; and perhaps, by revealing the nature of this part, to throw light upon the essence of the whole.

Choice of the strand about which this book was written had particular significance for me, for it called for a radical reversal of perspective. I had written, as others had written, of the impact of the immigrant upon the society which received him, of the effect upon political, social, and economic institutions of the addition of some thirty-five million newcomers to the population of the United States in the century after 1820.

[3]

It was not surprising that these aspects of the subject should have received earliest treatment. Towns that suddenly grew into cities and found themselves engulfed in slums, overwhelmed with problems of pauperism and relief; the governmental system that swiftly changed under the control of voters with new conceptions of politics — these drew immediate attention to the consequences of injecting alien elements into our society. These were practical problems in the face of which there was no forgetting the importance of immigration.

In retrospect too the effects of the movement of population upon the new continent were the most striking. The arrival of a labor force that permitted the expansion of industry without the pauperization of the native workers; the fact that costs of production could fall while the capacity to consume continued to grow; the remarkable fluidity of a social system in which each new group pushed upward the level of its predecessors — these were the phenomena that gave immigration a prominent role in the development of the United States.

In this work, however, I wished to regard the subject from an altogether different point of view. Immigration altered America. But it also altered the immigrants. And it is the effect upon the newcomers of their arduous transplantation that I have tried to study.

My theme is emigration as the central experience of a great many human beings. I shall touch upon broken homes, interruptions of a familiar life, separation from known surroundings, the becoming a foreigner and ceasing to belong. These are the aspects of alienation; and seen from the perspective of the individual received rather than of the receiving society, the history of immigration is a history of alienation and its consequences.

I have tried historically to trace the impact of separation, of the disruption in the lives and work of people who left one world to adjust to a new. These are the bleaker pages of our history. For the effect of the transfer was harsher upon the people than upon the society they entered.

The experience of these men on the move was more complex than that of eighteenth-century Negroes or of seventeenth-century Englishmen or of eleventh-century Normans. The participants in the earlier mass migrations had either wandered to unoccupied places, where they had only to adjust to new conditions of the physical environment, or they had gone under the well-defined conditions of conquering invader or imported slave.

It was the unique quality of the nineteenth-century immigration that the people who moved entered the life of the United States at a status equal to that of the older residents. So far as law and the formal institutions of the nation were concerned, the newcomers were one with those long settled in the New World. The immigrants could not impose their own ways upon society; but neither were they constrained to conform to those already established. To a significant degree, the newest Americans had a wide realm of choice.

Therein lay the broader meaning of their experience. Emigration took these people out of traditional, accustomed environments and replanted them in strange ground, among strangers, where strange manners prevailed. The customary modes of behavior were no longer adequate, for the problems of life were new and different. With old ties snapped, men faced the enormous compulsion of working out new relationships, new meanings to their lives, often under harsh and hostile circumstances.

The responses of these folk could not be easy, automatic, for emigration had stripped away the veneer that in more stable situations concealed the underlying nature of the social structure. Without the whole complex of institutions and social patterns which formerly guided their actions, these people became incapable of masking or evading decisions.

Under such circumstances, every act was crucial, the product of conscious weighing of alternatives, never simple conformity to an habitual pattern. No man could escape choices that involved, day after day, an evaluation of his goals, of the meaning of his existence, and of the purpose of the social forms and institutions that surrounded him.

The immigrants lived in crisis because they were uprooted. In transplantation, while the old roots were sundered, before the new were established, the immigrants existed in an extreme situation. The shock, and the effects of the shock, persisted for many years; and their influence reached down to generations which themselves never paid the cost of crossing.

No one moves without sampling something of the immigrants' experience — mountaineers to Detroit, Okies to California, even men fixed in space but alienated from their culture by unpopular ideas or tastes. But the immigrants' alienation was more complete, more continuous, and more persistent. Understanding of their reactions in that exposed state may throw light on the problems of all those whom the modern world somehow uproots.

ONE

Peasant Origins

THE IMMIGRANT MOVEMENT started in the peasant heart of Europe. Ponderously balanced in a solid equilibrium for centuries, the old structure of an old society began to crumble at the opening of the modern era. One by one, rude shocks weakened the aged foundations until some climactic blow suddenly tumbled the whole into ruins. The mighty collapse left without homes millions of helpless, bewildered people. These were the army of emigrants.

The impact was so much the greater because there had earlier been an enormous stability in peasant society. A granite-like quality in the ancient ways of life had yielded only slowly to the forces of time. From the westernmost reaches of Europe, in Ireland, to Russia in the east, the peasant masses had maintained an imperturbable sameness; for fifteen centuries they were the backbone of a continent, unchanging while all about them radical changes again and again recast the civilization in which they lived.

Stability, the deep, cushiony ability to take blows, and yet to keep things as they were, came from the special place of these people on the land. The peasants were agriculturists; their livelihood sprang from the earth. Americans they met later would have called them "farmers," but that word had a different meaning in Europe. The bonds that held these men to their acres were not simply the personal ones of the husbandman who temporarily mixes his sweat with the soil. The ties were deeper, more intimate. For the peasant was part of a community and the community was held to the land as a whole.

Always, the start was the village. "I was born in such a village in such a parish" — so the peasant invariably began the account of himself. Thereby he indicated the importance of the village in his being; this was the fixed point by which he knew his position in the world and his relationship with all humanity.

The village was a place. It could be seen, it could be marked out in boundaries, pinned down on a map, described in all its physical attributes. Here was a road along which men and beasts would pass, reverence the saint's figure at the crossing. There was a church, larger or smaller, but larger than the other structures about it. The burial ground was not far away, and the smithy, the mill, perhaps an inn. There were so many houses of wood or thatch, and so built, scattered among the fields as in Ireland and Norway, or, as almost everywhere else, huddled together with their backs to the road. The fields were round about, located in terms of river, brook, rocks, or trees. All these could be perceived; the eye could grasp, the senses apprehend the feel, the sound, the smell, of them. These objects, real, authentic, true, could come back in memories, be summoned up to rouse the curiosity and stir the wonder of children born in distant lands.

Yet the village was still more. The aggregate of huts housed a community. Later, much later, and very far away, the Old Countrymen also had this in mind when they thought of the village. They spoke of relationships, of ties, of family, of kinship, of many rights and obligations. And these duties, privileges, connections, links, had each their special flavor, somehow a unique value, a meaning in terms of the life of the whole.

They would say then, if they considered it in looking backward, that the village was so much of their lives because the village *was* a whole. There were no loose, disorderly ends; everything was knotted into a firm relationship with every other thing. And all things had meaning in terms of their relatedness to the whole community.

In their daily affairs, these people took account of the relationships among themselves through a reckoning of degrees of kinship. The villagers regarded themselves as a clan connected within itself by ties of blood, more or less remote. That they did so may have been in recollection of the fact that the village was anciently the form the nomadic tribe took when it settled down to a stable agricultural existence. Or it may have been a reflection of the extent of intermarriage in a place where contact with outsiders was rare. In any case, considerations of kinship had heavy weight in the village, were among the most important determinants of men's actions.

But the ties of blood that were knotted into all the relationships of communal life were not merely sentimental. They were also functional; they determined or reflected the role of individuals in the society.

No man, for instance, could live alone in the village. Marriage was the normal expected state of all but the physically deformed. If death deprived a person of his marriage partner, all the forces of community pressure came into play to supply a new helpmate. For it was right and proper that each should have his household, his place in a family.

The family, being functional, varied somewhat to suit the order of local conditions. But always the unit revolved about the husband and wife. The man was head of the household and of its enterprises. He controlled all its goods, made the vital decisions that determined its well-being, had charge of the work in the fields, and was the source of authority and discipline within the home. His wife was mother, her domain the house and all that went on in and about it. She was concerned with the garden and the livestock, with domestic economy in its widest sense — the provision of food, shelter, and clothing for all. The children had each their task, as befitted their age and condition. Now they herded the cattle or assisted in the chores of cleaning and cookery; later they would labor by the side of mother and father, and prepare to set up families of their own. Other members too had their allotted and recognized roles. Grandparents, aunts and uncles, sometimes cousins up to the fourth degree with no establishments of their own, found a place and a job. The family felt the obligation of caring for all, but also knew that no one could expect food and a corner in which to sleep while doing nothing to earn it. In this respect such collateral relatives did not differ in condition from the hired servants, where they existed, who were also counted members of the family.

The family was then the operating economic unit. In a sense that was always recognized and respected, the land on which it worked was its own. The head of the household, it was true, held and controlled it; legally, no doubt, he had certain powers to waste or dispose of it. But he was subject to an overwhelming moral compulsion to keep it intact, in trust for those who lived from it and for their descendants who would take a place upon it.

The family's land was rarely marked out in a well-defined plot. The house, the garden, and the barnyard with its buildings were its own, but the bulk of agricultural lands were enmeshed in a wide net of relationships that comprehended the whole community.

Once, it seems, the village had held and used all the land communally; until very recent times recognizable vestiges of that condition persisted. The pastures and meadows, the waste, the bogs and woodlands, existed for the use of all. It hardly mattered at first that the nobility or other interlopers asserted a claim to ownership. The peasants' rights to graze their cattle, to gather wood for building and peat for fire, in practice remained undisturbed. In some parts of Europe, even the arable lands rested in the hands of the whole village, redivided on occasions among its families according to their rights and condition.

Even where particular pieces of land were permanently held, it was rarely in such consolidated plots as the peasants might later see on American farms. A holding consisted rather of numerous tiny strips that patched the slopes of the countryside in a bewildering, variegated design. A Polish peasant, rich in land, could work his nine acres in forty different places.

Agriculture conformed to the pattern of landholding. By long usage, the fields almost everywhere were divided into thirds, a part for winter crops — wheat, rye; another for summer crops — barley, oats, and potatoes; and another to lie fallow. Since no man's lands were completely apart from his neighbor's there was no room for individuality in working the soil. Every family labored on its own and kept the fruit of its own labors. Yet all labor had to be directed toward the same ends, in the same way, at the same time.

Many important aspects of agriculture, moreover, were altogether communal. The pastures were open to all villagers; in the common fields, the boys tended the cattle together or a hired herdsman had their oversight. Women, working in groups at the wearisome indoor tasks, spinning or plucking cabbage leaves, could turn chores into festive occasions, lighten their labors with sociable gossip. The men were accustomed to give aid to each other, to lend or exchange as an expression of solidarity. After all, folk must live with each other.

So the peasants held together, lived together, together drew the stuff of life from an unwilling earth. Simple neighborliness, mutual assistance, were obligations inherent in the conditions of things, obligations which none could shirk without fear of cutting himself off from the whole. And that was the community, that the village — the capacity to do these things together, the relationships that regulated all.

Their all-embracing quality gave peasant ways a persistent quality, forced each generation to retrace the steps of its predecessors. Family and land in the village were locked in an unyielding knot. And the heart of the bond was the marriage system.

Marriage affected not only the two individuals most directly involved; it affected deeply the lives and the lands of all those related to them. Marriage destroyed the integrity of two old productive units and created a new one. The consummation of the union could be successful only with provisions for the prosperity of both the new and the old families, and that involved allocation of the land among the contracting parties in a proper and fitting manner.

Long-standing custom that had the respect and usually the effect of law regulated these arrangements, and also determined the modes of inheritance. Almost everywhere the land descended within the family through the male line, with the holding passing as a whole to a single son. But provision was also made for the other children. The brothers had portions in money or goods, while substantial amounts were set aside as dowries for the sisters.

The marriage of the oldest son was the critical point in the history of the family. The bride came to live in her father-in-law's home in anticipation of the time when the old man would retire and her husband become the head of the household. In a proper marriage, she brought with her a dowry profitable enough to set up the younger brothers in the style to which they were accustomed and to add to the dowries of the daughters of the family.

No marriage was therefore isolated; the property and the future welfare of the whole family hung in the balance each time an alliance was negotiated. And not only the family's;

the whole community was directly concerned. Naturally matters of such importance could not be left to the whim of individuals; they rested instead in the hands of experienced, often of professional, matchmakers who could conduct negotiations with decorum and ceremony, who could guarantee the fitness of the contracting families and the compatibility in rank of the individuals involved.

The whole family structure rested on the premise of stability, on the assumption that there would be no radical change in the amount of available land, in the size of the population, or in the net of relationships that held the village together. Were there daughters without dowries or sons without portions, were no lands made vacant to be bought with dowry and portion, then a part of the community would face the prospect of economic degradation and perhaps, even more important, of serious loss in status.

Not within the village, but beside it, were mushrooming treacherous growths that would jeopardize all that assumed stability.

The village loomed so large in the peasants' consciousness that they were tempted to think it the whole of their society, to behave as if it were entirely self-sufficient and self-contained. The family worked to cover its own needs and expected to subsist by consuming what it produced. But the actual functioning of village life contradicted that assumption and the strain of that contradiction weakened the peasants' whole place on the land.

Is was true that the peasant could adjust his consumption to the level of his productivity, eat more in good times, less in poor. But in practice he found himself compelled to produce a disquieting surplus upon which he could not reckon and which regularly upset his scheme of life. To create that surplus he had either to raise his productivity or to divert a part of his produce away from his own consumption. Neither alternative was easy or pleasant.

After all, much as he disliked to consider the fact, the peasant was not alone in his society. Superimposed upon the ranks of the husbandmen was a formidable array of groups that lived by his labors. Beside the village and the village lands were the manor house and the manor lands. That imposing structure, those extensive tracts bespoke the power and wealth of the landlords, nobility or gentry, in peasant eyes equally lords. He who lived within the manor gates was not a part of the village; but his will had a profound effect upon it. The lord owned all about him, land and water and even wind (for only he could build a mill). The lord was strong. On horse, with sword, he wielded power.

The sword of the lord protected the peasant, gave him peace against hostile strangers. The sword of the lord did justice among peasants, interceded in quarrels, and supported right against wrong. But the sword of the lord also took days' work from the peasant, collected rents and dues from the tillers of the soil. These payments constituted a first charge against the income of every household in the village; failure to pay entailed the danger of losing the land. The peasant could meet these charges only by deductions from his own consumption or by producing a surplus.

Apart from the village was also the priest's house. Its occupant, the church over which he presided, and the essential services he performed, were also supported by the peasant. Almost everywhere compulsory dues of some sort recurred year after year and special contributions marked the critical points of every man's life. In kind or in cash there were gifts to bring at holidays and festivals and fees at birth, marriage, and death. It was the good peasant's duty to pay as well for memorials for his dead, for thanksgiving at special good fortune, or for prayers against particular calamities. Those who labored in the fields sometimes grumbled that it was easier to grow rich by plowing with a pen, but they dutifully provided such unavoidable expenses out of a surplus laid by for the purpose.

Yet these were not all the peasant bore on his back. Some tasks he could not perform for himself or even with the aid of his fellows. His work often brought him to the point at which he needed the paid services of a specialist endowed with unusual skill or possessed of unusual equipment; such were the smith's work, the miller's work, and the weaver's. Or there were things — butchery, for instance — not reckoned proper for a man to do, obnoxious, loathsome tasks undertaken by someone else for a fee.

There were also services the peasants were obligated to perform for each other without charge, but services so expensive that fulfillment of the obligation would be ruinous to the conscientious individual. Conventionally such services were transferred to an outsider who could take payment. Peasant solidarity thus demanded that loans be without interest and hospitality without cost; "Am I a Jewess or a trader, to take money for a little fire and water?" asked the goodwife.

Yet nothing in this world, she knew, was given for nothing and the burden of the obligation could only rarely be suffered by any man. Hence the resort to moneylenders and innkeepers, neutral outsiders not expected to conform to the peasant requirements of solidarity. These too drew support from the peasant's surplus.

Furthermore, the village ideal of self-sufficiency could not protect it against the temptation of dealing in the markets of the outside world. Some things it had to buy: always salt, but later also some luxuries become necessities, as tea. From time to time peddlers passed the peasant's door, tantalized his women with offerings of cloth and ribbons, teased away coin, egg, or fowl. Peddlers of another sort bought and sold horses, bartered livestock. Wandering tinkers periodically made the circuit of the villages, willing for a consideration to sell or repair utensils of kitchen or field. All brought to his very threshold wares tempting enough to induce the peasant to accumulate a surplus.

And that was not all. Seasonally there were fairs, booths crammed into the market place, spilling over with attractions. Who was so dull as to stay away from these festive occasions, or to leave at home the pig, cow, and handful of accumulated silver? And who was so stern, once there, to resist the pleas of women and children, of his own longings for some indulgence away from the necessities of his everyday life?

In the sober reckonings of the morrow, there was a double significance to all these demands upon the peasant's surplus. In the first place, they tempted him to expand his production in the hope that the ever-growing populations of the towns would take off his hands ever larger quantities of agricultural goods. At the same time, the dealing in surpluses made room for many strangers, people who were not peasants, yet who lived side by side with the peasants and played an important part in the peasant world. The nobility and clergy had long been there. But there were, as well, Jews to carry on the functions of trade, to act as innkeepers and moneylenders, to serve as middlemen between lords and peasants. Gypsies dealt in horses and livestock, worked as blacksmiths and tinsmiths. There were places where outlandish Italian masons, Slovak besombinders, Hungarian bricklayers, made each their appointed appearance to do their appointed tasks. Of these groups, some were of necessity itinerant; no single village could support them the year round. Others settled in the village, though not part of it, or lived in the little towns in close proximity to it. And not distant in miles, though worlds removed, were the cities, regions of total strangeness into which the peasant never ventured, where not the people alone, but the very aspect of the earth was unfamiliar.

The peasant, as an individual, welcomed the strangers. These were not wild men of the woods, but for generations planted in his midst, and in an immediate way, they made his life easier. But as a member of the community the peasant disapproved, knowing that these outsiders were a threat to the stability of the village. The myth of the gypsies who ran off with the child had a literal and a figurative meaning. The wanderers brought with them the heady smell of wonderful distances, now and then lured to city or to the open road those impatient with family burdens or with the stolid peasant ways.

The figurative snatching was more dangerous. More often than the gypsy stole the child, he stole the birthright. For in these strangers was incarnated the temptation to acquire a surplus beyond the needs of the peasants' livelihood and that temptation was feared lest it some day destroy the delicate balances by which the village held together.

The drive for a surplus was dangerous because it was difficult to expand the volume of production without an enormous strain upon the whole village. Only with difficulty could the peasant, later in America, describe the smallness of his holdings, not only because size varied so much in time and place, but because the scale of things was so inconceivably different. Anywhere at any time, in the Old World, a family that held twelve acres was incredibly well off. In areas particularly poor, in nineteenth-century Galicia for instance, a plot as large as five acres was not usual; and nowhere would that have been reckoned too small. From such tiny acreage the peasant had to draw the sustenance of all the souls dependent upon him. It was certainly difficult to draw from it also enough to leave a surplus.

Furthermore, the techniques of production were inefficient and it was difficult to make changes. Since so much of the work of the fields was communal, innovations had to wait upon the conversion to the new idea of the whole village, and that meant indefinite postponement. Radical departures from traditional, that is, from safe, ways of acting were not introduced without long, acrimonious debate. Naturally there was no room for risky experimentation. The gamble was too great, for failure meant starvation, not for an individual alone, but for his whole family, and perhaps for the whole village.

A large part of the productive land lay idle; who would give up the fallow year on the guess that there were other means of restoring fertility? Who would venture to turn woodland and pasture into arable land for the possibility of gains necessarily remote? The scrawny peasant animals could never grow fat. There were neither enough acres in the fields nor enough hands in the family to raise fodder to feed them. The beasts were allowed to fare for themselves as best they could in the meadows and, in winter, were either slaughtered or grew lean — visible evidence of the peasants' inability to lay aside a surplus.

In every phase of their labor the peasants ran headlong into the same difficulty. They could never get together capital, turn accumulations into further production. Every fragment of income, long before they had it, was dedicated to some specific end and was not to be used for any other purpose. Indeed money, when they laid hands on it, was never regarded as capital. It made no peasant sense to think of gold and silver, even of tools, as themselves productive. The precious metals could be hoarded up against the expected needs, against the recurrent disasters that were not long absent in their lives; they had no other use, were merely provisional substitutes for the goods or services they would ultimately buy — rent money, shoe money, salt money, funeral money. So many previous immediate claims ate up the little extras good fortune occasionally left that nothing could be laid aside. These people could not plan for the proximate future; it would be foolish to give the grass time to grow while the steed starved. This was their plight, always to be eating up their seed corn.

It was against these rigid limits of production that the demands for a surplus pushed. There was the danger. Squeezed by the pressure of rising charges and fixed income, the peasant could see in the offing the greatest disaster of all, loss of his land, the sole measure of his worth in the community.

For the peasant loss of the land was a total calamity. The land was not an isolated thing in his life. It was a part of the family and of the village, pivot of a complex circle of relationships, the primary index of his own, his family's status. What was a man without land? He was like a man without legs who crawls about and cannot get anywhere. Land was the only natural, productive good in this society.

Within the village economy there was little the landless could do. Paid labor was degrading. The demand for any kind of work for others was slight. Those who sought such labor had to enter service — in a measure, they surrendered their freedom, their individuality, the hope of establishing families of their own. They lost thereby the quality and rank of peasants. That was why the peasant feared to encumber his land with mortgages, preferred to pay high interest for personal loans. That was why he hesitated to divide his holding, felt threatened by every new charge against it.

Yet time in its changes had made it difficult for some men to assume the position and maintain the station of peasants. Son after son found that modifications in the pattern of land ownership prevented him from taking the place his father had held.

By the beginning of the nineteenth century the effects were noticeable in almost every part of Europe. As landlords, eager to consolidate holdings, combined the old strips into contiguous plots, the peasant suffered. Whether he emerged with the same or lesser acreage, the creation of larger productive units put him at a competitive disadvantage in the market place. He could thrive only if he managed to become a farmer, that is, managed to rent a large plot under a long-term lease, perhaps for life, or for several lifetimes, or without limit of term. (Some indeed were fortunate enough to become proprietors.)

Consolidation widened the differences among peasants. A few grew wealthy as they rose to the status of farmers (*gospodarze*, the Poles called them; *bøndar*, the Norwegians). Many more became poor, were completely edged off the land, and sank helplessly into the growing class of landless peasants, ironic contradiction in terms. Cottiers they were named where English was spoken, *husmaend* in Norwegian, *Häusler* in German, *komorniki* in Polish. The designation described their condition. Their only right was to rent the cottage in which they lived. By sufferance they used the common fields. But their livelihood they earned by day labor for others or by renting small plots under short-term leases or from year to year.

Their livelihood! Such huts they lived in as they themselves in a few days could build. Such clothes they wore as their wives alone could make. Food was what the paid rent left. In Ireland the annual expenditures of a family of cottiers ran not above thirty-two shillings a year. Calculate a shilling how you will, that is still a grim standard of living.

Could anything be worse? Indeed it could — the times disaster struck, broke in upon the even tenor of these plowmen's ways. Within the rigid, improvident system of production, no reserve absorbed the shock of crop failures. No savings tided him over whose roots rotted in the hostile ground. The very idea was a mockery; if he had had those coins, to what market would he turn? Trade took food from the village, never brought it back. When the parched earth yielded only the withered leaves of famine, then, alas, conditions were somewhat equalized. Farmer and cottier looked to their larders, already depleted since the last year's harvest, and, reconciled, delayed the day the last measured morsel would disappear. Many then reached in vain, found starvation in the empty barrels. No power could help them.

Calamity was familiar. If not the ill-favor of nature, then the caprice of human beings could give her entree to the peasant household. The whims, the incomprehensible needs and interests of landlords created crises for whole villages. Wars came, taxes, laws. The roll of drums desolated fields. Resentful, silent eyes watched the men in uniform drive off the beasts, enlist sons who might never come back, pour out the winter's stored-up grain in heedless waste.

Disaster chained the peasant to his place. The harshness of these burdens immobilized those upon whom they fell, made the poor also poor in spirit. Revolt, escape, were not the stuff their dreams were made of as they paused in the sickle's swing or leaned back in the shadows of the long winter evening. It was for an end to all striving that their tired hearts longed.

While there was no surcease, they would hold on. Peasant wisdom knew well the fate of the rolling stone, knew that if it remained fixed, even a rock might share in growth. The unwillingness to move reflected, in part, a stubborn attachment to that fierce mistress, the land. It expressed also a lethargic passivity in which each man acquiesced in the condition of his life as it was.

Long habit, the seeming changelessness of things, stifled the impulse to self-improvement. In the country round (the parish, *okolica*) each village had a reputation, a pack of thieves, a crew of liars, a lot of drunkards, fools, or good husbandmen, thrifty, prosperous. Within the village, each family had its place, and in the family each individual. Precisely because the peasant thought only in terms of the whole, he defined his own station always by his status within the larger units. The virtue of one brought benefits, his sin, shame to the whole.

The efforts of man were directed not toward individual improvement but toward maintenance of status. It was fitting and proper to exact one's due rights, to fulfill one's due obligations. It was not fitting to thrust oneself ahead, to aspire to a life above one's rank, to rebel against one's status; that was to argue against the whole order of things.

The deep differences among peasants and between the

peasants and the other groups were not a cause for envy. This was the accepted configuration of society. The lord was expected to be proud and luxurious, but humane and generous, just as the peasant was expected to be thrifty and respectful. Even bitterly burdensome privileges were not open to dispute. All knew that to him that can pay, the musicians play. The peasant did not begrudge the magnates the pleasures of their manor houses; let *them* at least draw enjoyment from life.

Acceptance of status stifled any inclination toward rebelliousness. There were occasional peasant outbursts when the nobility deviated from their expected role or when they tried to alter traditional modes of action. The Jacquerie then or Whiteboys, the followers of Wat Tyler or of Pugachev, savagely redressed their own grievances. But apart from such spasmodic acts of vengeance there were no uprisings against the order within which peasant and noble lived. The same docility blocked off the alternative of secession through emigration. If disaster befell the individual, that was not itself a cause for breaking away. It did not become so until some external blow destroyed the whole peasant order.

The seeds of ultimate change were not native to this stable society. They were implanted from without. For centuries the size of the population, the amount of available land, the quantity of productive surplus, and the pressure of family stability, achieved together a steady balance that preserved the village way of life. Only slowly and in a few places were there signs of unsteadiness in the seventeenth century; then more distinctly and in more places in the eighteenth. After 1800, everywhere, the elements of the old equilibrium disintegrated. The old social structure tottered; gathering momentum from its own fall, it was unable to right itself, and under the impact of successive shocks collapsed. Then the peasants could no longer hang on; when even to stay meant to change, they had to leave.

Earliest harbinger of the transformations to come was a radical new trend in the population of Europe. For a thousand years, the number of people on the continent had remained constant. From time to time there had been shifts in the areas of heaviest density. In some centuries famine, plague, and war had temporarily lowered the total; in others, freedom from famine, plague, and war had temporarily raised it. But taken all in all these fluctuations canceled each other out.

Then in the eighteenth century came a precipitous rise, unprecedented and, as it proved, cataclysmic. For a hundred years growth continued unabated, if anything at an accelerating rate. Between 1750 and 1850 the population of the continent leaped from about one hundred and forty million to about two hundred and sixty, and by the time of the First World War to almost four hundred million. In addition, by 1915 some two hundred and fifty million Europeans and their descendants lived outside the continent. Even taking account of the relief from emigration, the pressure on social institutions of this increase was enormous. The reckoning is simple: where one man stood in 1750, one hundred and sixty-five years later there were three.

This revolutionary change came under the beneficent guise of a gradual decline in the death rate, particularly in that of children under the age of two. Why infants, everywhere in Europe, should now more often survive is not altogether clear. But the consequences were unmistakable; the happy facility with which the newborn lived to maturity put a totally unexpected strain upon the whole family system and upon the village organization. The new situation called into question the old peasant assumption that all sons would be able to find farms capable of maintaining them at the status their fathers had held. As events demonstrated the falsity of that assumption, stability disappeared from peasant life.

The eldest sons waited for their inheritance. They married, brought children into the world, and still had only a place in the parental home. Until the old men died the middle-aged heirs could not assume the station of house-holders. Impatient, weary of being commanded, the sons saw the years of their best powers go by and themselves, with no land of their own, deprived of the dignity and authority of the head of a family. Tense in the fear of unfulfillment, they urged the fathers to retire, to surrender possession, to make room.

Against the claims of a crowding new generation, the elders stubbornly held to their own. If they were to yield, move off to a corner, learn to take orders, cease to be productive, could they count on respect to leave them more than the crumbs of family income when already the grandchildren were there to be provided for? Turn over the property, and to what rights could they lay claim — to a rope with which to hang themselves, to a stone to tie around their necks!

Then too, a father's obligations were more onerous now. It was more difficult to provide for the younger sons and for the daughters. An ironic providence had, in the old days, made sure that not too many boys would reach an age to claim a man's estate. The same kind fate that kept more children alive complicated the problem of their settlement. Few holdings fell vacant through want of heirs; few peasants had so much land they would willingly part with some of it. Dowries were increasingly inadequate to settle the young bride-grooms. A class of men grew up for whom there was no longer room within the constricted acreage of the village. Dissatisfied and unhappy, peasants' sons looked ahead to a bleak degradation, to a final loss of status in the community.

The available expedients were pitifully inadequate to meet the needs of the desperate situation. Only a few found hired work or learned to draw an income from other than agricultural pursuits. More delayed marriage to an unseasonable age, not having the means to undertake it properly.

But the presence in the village of unmarried adults was itself a danger. Most often, the seeming solution was subdivision of the old plots, the creation of two holdings from one to serve the more numerous families. Within a single man's lifetime, in Poland, the fifteen farms of one village grew to twoscore; in another place two hundred and ninety-four households came to work the land that had fifty years earlier held forty-two. Land was then indeed scarce, divided again and again; its price rose steadily whether for purchase or rent, and each rise diminished further the margin left for the peasant's subsistence. Now, whether the harvest be rich or poor, the folk found themselves always poorer.

So the peasants learned that poverty was a dog whose teeth sank deep. The struggle for existence grew fiercer; yet there was no halt to the steady recession in standard of living. The mark of that deterioration was the uninterrupted advance across Europe of the cultivation of the potato, the cheapest of foods, the slimmest sustenance to keep bodies alive. In place after place, the tillers of the soil came to rely for their own nourishment upon this one crop, while their more valuable products went to markets to pay rents, to maintain the hold upon the soil. The peasant diet became monotonously the same — potatoes and milk. Meat was a rare luxury, and even tea. The housewife found there was never enough for the mouths to be fed; and those whom the constricted acreage condemned to idleness were not likely to be left a share. Often the old folk were sent out in winter to beg for the bread of God's giving, only to come home like the birds to their nests in the spring.

To hold to the land, those strong in arm would also sometimes venture away, roam the countryside in search of a hirer, move in ever-wider circles away from the home, for which they still labored and to which they seasonally returned. In time these migratory workers became familiar to every part of Europe.

The Irish spalpeen somehow made his way to the sea, crossed to Liverpool, to toil for a spell in the fertile English Midlands. On the same errand, Italian peasants drifted across the border to Austria, France, and Switzerland, then moved still deeper into Germany. Polish peasants became known in the wheat fields of Prussia, in the beet fields of the Ukraine, or as drivers on the barges that moved down the river to Danzig. Thus they bent their backs over alien soil, tended the crops of strangers, to the end that enough would be paid them, while the family got on at home, to hold their own dear land which alone could no longer sustain them and meet as well the other charges against it.

Of these migrants, some sought refuge in the growing cities, perhaps like the others, with the intention of making the stay temporary. For to accept permanent residence there was truly the last resort; only those thought of it who gave up entirely the struggle for the land, who surrendered ancestral ways and the hope of maintaining status. Every instinct spoke against that course; the peasant knew well that he "who rides away from his lands on a stallion will come back on foot a tatterdemalion."

Much safer at any cost to hold on! So the whole peasant order came to live under the sense of a desperate tension to retain a grip on the land. As against that predominant consideration all other problems receded in importance. With every energy mobilized against this one overwhelming strain, men regarded every other attendant difficulty with apathy — the wretched diet, occasional periods of starvation, squalid quarters, blank future. Within the closed horizons of this perspective was not much scope for aggressive venturesome action, only a plodding determination to resist further changes; for all that changed changed for the worse.

But already a far-reaching transformation in the organization of European agriculture and industry was beginning to turn these strains into the causes for emigration.

The calls on the land for its produce grew more insistent as the eighteenth century drew to a close and continued as the nineteenth century advanced toward its middle. It was not only that the population as a whole grew, but particularly that the urban population grew. The peasants could not know it, but those who went to the cities, in effect, increased the pressures on those who stayed behind. Townsfolk could not raise their own food; more numerous at the market place, they multiplied the demands upon agriculture.

You cannot make the land to stretch, the peasants said; and that was true enough in their own experience. But others witnessed with impatience the multitude of buyers, calculated the advance in prices and the prospect of profit, and disagreed. What if the land could be made to stretch under a more efficient organization of production? In the more advanced, that is, the more densely settled, areas of the continent there were significant attempts to answer that question. In the Netherlands and in England experiments tested the utility of new crops. Perhaps there were ways of eliminating the fallow year that had kept one third of the land annually out of production. Perhaps it was possible to bring more meat to the butcher not only by increasing the number of beasts, but also by increasing the weight of each through scientific breeding.

Landlords everywhere were quick to sense the potentialities. In region after region, England, Ireland, France, the Rhineland, Italy, Prussia, Hungary, Poland, Russia, there were excited speculations, eager efforts to apply the new developments.

But everywhere the old wasteful peasant village stood in the way. In these minuscule plots too many men followed stubbornly their traditional communal ways. As long as they remained, there could be no innovations. Sometimes the landlords tried to introduce the changes on their own lands, using outsiders as intermediaries, English farmers in Ireland, for instance, or Germans in Poland. But such compromises left untouched the great common meadows and forests, to say nothing of the arable lands in the grip of the peasants themselves. The ultimate solution, from the viewpoint of efficient exploitation, was consolidation of all the tiny plots into unified holdings and the liquidation of the common fields.

Only the power of government could effect the transition, for the dissolution of vested rights, centuries old, called for the sanctions of law. From England to Russia, in the century or so after 1750, a series of enactments destroyed the old agricultural order. The forms were varied; there were statutes by parliament, decrees from the Crown. The terms varied — enclosure, reform, liberation. But the effect did not vary.

Men drove into the village. They had the appearance of officers and the support of law. They were heavy with documents and quick in reckoning. They asked questions, wished to see papers, tried to learn what had been in time beyond the memory of man. There came with them also surveyors to measure the land. Then the peasants were told: they were now to be landowners, each to have his own farm proportionate to his former share and in one piece. The communal holdings were to disappear; every plot would be individual property, could be fenced around and dealt with by each as he liked.

Whether or not strict justice was done the peasant depended upon local circumstances and the conscience of the executing officials; it was not always possible to supply precise legal proof for property traditionally held. But in every case, the change undermined the whole peasant position. They were indeed now owners of their own farms; but they were less able than ever to maintain their self-sufficiency. The cost of the proceedings, in some places the requirement of fencing, left them in debt; they would have to find cash to pay. When the wastes disappeared there disappeared also the free wood for fire or building; there would have to be cash now to buy. If there were no longer common meadows, where would the cows graze?

All now found themselves compelled to raise crops that

could be offered for sale. Confined to their own few acres and burdened with obligations, the peasants had no other recourse. The necessity was cruel for these were in no position to compete on the traders' market with the old landlords whose great holdings operated with the efficiency of the new methods and ultimately of the new machinery. Steadily the chill of mounting debt blanketed the village. Like the chill of winter, it extinguished growth and hope, only worse, for there seemed no prospect of a spring ahead.

The change, which weakened all, desolated those whose situation was already marginal. The cottiers, the crop-sharers, the tenants on short-term leases of any kind could be edged out at any time. They had left only the slimmest hopes of remaining where they were.

Some early gave up and joined the drift to the towns, where, as in England, they supplied the proletariat that manned the factories of the Industrial Revolution. Others swelled the ranks of the agricultural labor force that wandered seasonally to the great estates in search of hire. Still others remained, working the land on less and less favorable terms, slaving to hold on.

A few emigrated. Those who still had some resources but feared a loss of status learned with hope of the New World where land, so scarce in the Old, was abundantly available. Younger sons learned with hope that the portions which at home would not buy them the space for a garden, in America would make them owners of hundreds of acres. Tempted by the prospect of princely rewards for their efforts, they ventured to tear themselves away from the ancestral village, to undertake the unknown risks of transplantation. The movement of such men was the first phase of what would be a cataclysmic transfer of population.

But this phase was limited, involved few peasants. A far greater number were still determined to hold on; mounting adversities only deepened that determination. In addition, the costs of emigration were high, the difficulties ominous;

few had the energy and power of will to surmount such obstacles. And though the landlords were anxious to evict as many as possible, there was no point in doing so without the assurance that the evicted would depart. Otherwise the destitute would simply remain, supported by parish charity, in one way or another continue to be a drain upon the landlords' incomes.

Soon enough disaster resolved the dilemma. There was no slack to the peasant situation. Without reserves of any kind these people were helpless in the face of the first crisis. The year the crops failed there was famine. Then the alternative to flight was death by starvation. In awe the peasant saw his fields barren, yielding nothing to sell, nothing to eat. He looked up and saw the emptiness of his neighbors' lands, of the whole village. In all the country round his startled eyes fell upon the same desolation. Who would now help? The empty weeks went by, marked by the burial of the first victims; at the workhouse door the gentry began to ladle out the thin soup of charity; and a heartsick weariness settled down over the stricken cottages. So much striving had come to no end.

Now the count was mounting. The endless tolling of the sexton's bell, the narrowing family circle, were shaping an edge of resolution. The tumbled huts, no longer home to anyone, were urging it. The empty road was pointing out its form. It was time.

He would leave now, escape; give up this abusive land his fathers had never really mastered. He would take up what remained and never see the sight of home again. He would become a stranger on the way, pack on back, lead wife and children toward some other destiny. For all about was evidence of the consequences of staying. Any alternative was better.

What sum the sale of goods and land would bring would pay the cost. And if nothing remained, then aid would come from the gentry or the parish, now compassionate in the eagerness to rid the place of extra hands, now generous in the desire to ease the burden on local charity. So, in the hundreds of thousands, peasants came to migrate. This was the second phase in the transfer of a continent's population.

It was not the end. Years of discontent followed. The burdens of those who stayed grew no lighter with the going of those who went. Grievances fed on the letters from America of the departed. From outposts in the New World came advice and assistance. Across the Atlantic the accumulation of immigrants created a magnetic pole that would for decades continue to draw relatives and friends in a mighty procession. This was the third phase.

With the peasants went a host of other people who found their own lives disrupted by the dislocation of the village. The empty inn now rarely heard the joy of wedding celebrations. The lonely church ministered to a handful of communicants. The tavernkeeper and priest, and with them smith and miller, followed in the train of those they once had served. There was less need now for the petty trade of Jews, for the labor of wandering artisans, for the tinkering of gypsies. These too joined the migration.

And toward the end, the flow of peoples received additions as well from the factories and mines. Often these were peasants or the sons of peasants whose first remove had been to the nearby city, men who had not yet found security or stability and who, at last, thought it better to go the way their cousins had earlier gone.

So Europe watched them go — in less than a century and a half, well over thirty-five million of them from every part of the continent. In this common flow were gathered up people of the most diverse qualities, people whose rulers had for centuries been enemies, people who had not even known of each other's existence. Now they would share each other's future.

Westward from Ireland went four and a half million. On

that crowded island a remorselessly rising population, avaricious absentee landlords, and English policy that discouraged the growth of industry early stimulated emigration. Until 1846 this had been largely a movement of younger sons, of ambitious farmers and artisans. In that year rot destroyed the potato crop and left the cottiers without the means of subsistence. Half a million died and three million more lived on only with the aid of charity. No thought then of paying rent, of holding on to the land; the evicted saw their huts pulled down and with bitter gratitude accepted from calculating poor-law officials the price of passage away from home. For decades after, till the end of the nineteenth century and beyond, these peasants continued to leave, some victims of later agricultural disasters, some sent for by relatives already across, some simply unable to continue a way of life already thoroughly disrupted.

Westward from Great Britain went well over four million. There enclosure and displacement had begun back in the eighteenth century, although the first to move generally drifted to the factories of the expanding cities. By 1815, however, farmers and artisans in substantial numbers had emigration in mind; and after midcentury they were joined by a great mass of landless peasants, by operatives from the textile mills, by laborers from the potteries, and by miners from the coal fields. In this number were Scots, Welsh, and Englishmen, and also the sons of some Irishmen, sons whose parents had earlier moved across the Irish Sea.

From the heart of the continent, from the lands that in 1870 became the German Empire, went fully six million. First to leave were the free husbandmen of the southwest, then the emancipated peasants of the north and east. With them moved, in the earlier years, artisans dislocated by the rise of industry, and later some industrial workers.

From the north went two million Scandinavians. Crop failures, as in 1847 in Norway, impelled some to leave. Others found their lots made harsher by the decline in the fisheries and by the loss of the maritime market for timber. And for many more, the growth of commercial agriculture, as in Sweden, was the indication no room would remain for free peasants.

From the south went almost five million Italians. A terrible cholera epidemic in 1887 set them moving. But here, as elsewhere, the stream was fed by the deeper displacement of the peasantry.

From the east went some eight million others — Poles and Jews, Hungarians, Bohemians, Slovaks, Ukrainians, Ruthenians — as agriculture took new forms in the Austrian and Russian Empires after 1880.

And before the century was out perhaps three million more were on the way from the Balkans and Asia Minor: Greeks and Macedonians, Croatians and Albanians, Syrians and Armenians.

In all, thirty-five million for whom home had no place fled to Europe's shores and looked across the Atlantic.

What manner of refuge lay there?

TWO

The Crossing

EMIGRATION WAS THE END of peasant life in Europe; it was also the beginning of life in America. But what a way there was yet to go before the displaced would come to rest again, what a distance between the old homes and the new! Only the fact that these harried people could not pause to measure the gulf saved them from dismay at the dizzy width of it.

Perhaps it is fortunate that, going onward, their sights are fixed backward rather than forward. From the crossroad, the man, alone or with his wife and children, turns to look upon the place of his birth. Once fixed, completely settled, he is now a wanderer. Remorseless circumstances, events beyond his control, have brought him to this last familiar spot. Passing it by, he becomes a stranger.

Sometimes, the emigrants at that moment considered the nature of the forces that had uprooted them. All the new conditions had conspired to depress the peasants into a hopeless mass, to take away their distinguishing differences and to deprive them, to an ever-greater extent, of the capacity for making willful decisions. The pressure of the changing economy had steadily narrowed every person's range of choices. Year by year, there were fewer alternatives until the critical

[34]

day when only a single choice remained to be made — to emigrate or to die. Those who had the will to make that final decision departed.

That man at the crossroads knew then that this was a mass movement. Scores of his fellows in the village, hundreds in other villages, were being swept along with him. Yet he moved alone. He went as an individual. Although entire communities were uprooted at the same time, although the whole life of the Old World had been communal, the act of migration was individual. The very fact that the peasants were leaving was a sign of the disintegration of the old village ways. What happened beyond the crossroads, each would determine by himself. It was immensely significant that the first step to the New World, despite all the hazards it involved, was the outcome of a desperate individual choice.

He who turned his back upon the village at the crossroads began a long journey that his mind would forever mark as its most momentous experience. The crossing immediately subjected the emigrant to a succession of shattering shocks and decisively conditioned the life of every man that survived it. This was the initial contact with life as it was to be. For many peasants it was the first time away from home, away from the safety of the circumscribed little villages in which they had passed all their years. Now they would learn to have dealings with people essentially different from themselves. Now they would collide with unaccustomed problems, learn to understand alien ways and alien languages, manage to survive in a grossly foreign environment.

Later, the memories of old men would blur all that had happened between departure and arrival, make it difficult to remember the proper sequence of events. Recollection would bring back the numbing uncertainty of the way, confuse all the incidents of the journey into a single nightmare of hostile encounters. Yet the crossing was not one, but a combination of five traumatic experiences, each with the dangers of its own strangeness, each with the consequences of its own pit-falls.

Coming away from the village, the emigrant pushed toward a seaport. Surely in the beginning it was a task sufficiently difficult just to know the road. For guides there were only the remembered tales of pilgrims, of beggars, and of peddlers, the habitual wanderers of the peasant world. After a time there would be letters from America or guidebooks that gave foreknowledge of the route, but these, when available, were only.the dimmest marks for those who, uncertainly, sought the proper paths.

Conveyances varied with conditions. On the continent, travel was most commodious by river or canal; but few poor folk could pay the heavy tolls with which such streams were charged. In some places there were public stages. These too were out of reach, prohibitively expensive, meant for the gentry who alone, in more normal times, had occasion to use them. Here and there was a fortunate fellow with a cart. More rare was a beast to pull it; both would be sold at the destination. But not many peasants had been able to hold on to horse and wagon when all else in their world disappeared from around them. Mostly the emigrants relied on the power of their own legs and began the crossing with a long journey on foot.

In the 1830's they become familiar figures on Europe's highways; in the 1840's and 1850's and long thereafter they are still a common sight: little groups of tired men and women, with their children, raising puffs of dust from the dry summer roads. Sometimes, the trek would cover three hundred miles or more; it might consume a precious month, two. And all the while, every turn in the way ahead concealed its own peculiar dangers — misinformation, blunders, cheats, exposure to the elements, assaults by humans and by beasts.

On the move, existence is ever precarious. Cash is scarce, so the emigrant must find shelter where he may, try to subsist on what he brings with him. If that fails he has no recourse but to live off the land, only not as a conqueror who takes what he needs, rather as a supplicant who works for what he can get.

The miles took heavy payment in human energy, a payment not all the peasants could make. Many were left at the wayside who had resolutely set forth in the spring but could not carry on and succumbed to hunger, illness, and incapacitating mischance. The others, at whatever cost, held to the uncertain way, passed through other men's fields where other men's crops thrived, passed through strange villages where other fathers' children laughed at play. And in whose fellowship did the wanderers now find themselves? They were now of the company of pilgrims, beggars, peddlers, itinerant tinkers, and laborers; and there was cold comfort in the bitter thought that all were now alike, outcasts in the world of settled men.

With such the journey, who would linger on it? Better, at whatever risk, to get to any harbor as soon as possible. Until the middle of the nineteenth century, the difficulty of moving about on land induced the emigrants to make for the nearest point on the coast — which port was secondary; the need for reaching any destination was too great.

In England one could move to London, Plymouth, Liverpool, Bristol; in Scotland, to Greenock or Glasgow; in Ireland, to Dublin, Belfast, Cork, Limerick, Sligo, or the smaller harbors on the Shannon. On the continent the places of departure were yet more numerous. The valley of the Rhine was a great open channel through which a flow of Germans from many states drifted to the ocean, to Rotterdam and Antwerp and other Low Country cities. Other Central Europeans sought the sea at Hamburg and Le Havre, and Scandinavians at Stavanger, Bergen, and the many tiny havens of their indented shore.

By midcentury, however, the focal points toward which the emigrants moved became fewer and larger. Everywhere transatlantic trade slipped out of the hands of the old individual merchant shipowner and fell into those of great companies, which confined their operations to a single port. So, in England, commerce with America concentrated more and more heavily in Liverpool; indeed that city more and more engrossed the carrying business even of Ireland, to which it was linked by regular cheap packet lines. On the continent, transatlantic business drew irresistibly to Bremen and Le Havre, to a much lesser extent to Antwerp and Hamburg, as wheat and cotton from the United States determined what course shipping would take. As the activity of the few great ports snowballed, the emigrants increasingly found it advantageous, even at the cost of a longer trip by land, to make their way to a place where they would be sure of accommodations. Increasingly they converged upon the major cities from which vessels sailed frequently, preferring thus to minimize the risk of being stranded in smaller, nearer harbors from which departures were infrequent and unpredictable.

The shipping lines had also the means and the interest to spread information. In distant villages the placards went up at the chapel gate or by the side of the inn; and Liverpool and Bremen somehow became familiar places, drew nearer, in anticipation at least, to the homes of many peasants from Ireland to Germany.

The emigrants who left other parts of the continent after 1870 fell heir to the same routes. Only the Italians and some of the Balkan peoples, who could take advantage of Mediterranean trade, helped to develop new ports in this traffic at Naples, Genoa, and Trieste. But some of these too, and the great mass of Russians, Poles, and Austrians of diverse nationalities, found more attractive the facilities that already existed in England and Germany. By this time, of course, the midcentury expansion of the railroad network all over Europe eliminated some of the harsher physical difficulties of the journey by land. For the first time, transportation was available at a price the emigrants could pay and that undoubtedly made them more willing to travel long distances to the great ports.

But, as if to make sure that the crossing would never become too easy, new problems arose to harass the wanderers. Distance was less frightening. Time spent in travel fell to a few days. Physical hardships were less likely to be disastrous. But man-made hardships now became imposing.

National boundaries, at first of very slight importance, suddenly were substantial obstacles. All sorts of complicated border regulations developed. It became difficult to secure the right of transit through intermediate foreign countries. There were checks of identity and of citizenship, examinations to discover whether taxes had been paid or military service evaded, inspections for disease and disability. Soon the traveler was loaded down with mysterious bits of paper, stamped cards, precious official documents he must clutch to get by the hazards of the course. At every border station came the risk of being stranded in a strange place, of separation from family, and of disastrous interruptions in the journey. They were fortunate who had funds enough to enlist the aid of the knowing characters one met by the way, sly people who, for a price, would reveal the unguarded spots, the secret ways of slipping by the control points. That is, mostly they were fortunate; but sometimes, caught, they would find their destinations sadly altered. What emigrant had the money for bribes enough?

Eventually those who survived got through. The early comers passed wearily into the straggling suburbs. Cautiously, they saw the now familiar road turn into a crowded street. Between the houses, the green spaces grew smaller, then disappeared. Multitudes of men appeared around them.

Carts and coaches ran all about. Tall buildings consecrated to unknown uses hemmed them in. The sun was darkened. The noises of nature were stilled. All direction was gone. This was the city.

This is a place full of wonders for those who never have seen a city before. Amazement, the shadow of so much newness, covers them. Their minds rush to find a known comparison. But this is like nothing else in the world; no town, no fair, no market place was ever like it. And the new men, who very likely will spend the rest of their lives in a city, pause. They look at the life of the city, take in the myriad of impressions, and begin to shape their attitudes toward urban society through residence in the seaport.

Already in 1800 the seaport was a large place; and it swelled thereafter with the growth of trade. As the harbor deepened and the wharves spread out about it, as the warehouses shot up and the numerous countingrooms that managed the flow of goods through them, scores of new men were drawn in to buy and sell, to reckon and carry, to make and repair. This permanent population, mounting in numbers, found room for itself only with difficulty. What resources of space then would await the hordes of transient emigrants whose means were limited and who, to boot, were often foreigners?

Where should the peasant go in the city but to the redeeming sea from which new life will come? He makes his way to the crowded quays, among the lowered casks to the ships tied by. Here will be captains, agents; here he will negotiate for passage. And until he sails, here he will stay, or close nearby. Now he belongs with those whose home is on the ocean, for the ocean will lead him to the unknown home he hopes to have.

Meanwhile his home is of another sort. In the harbor district are temporary lodgings that will serve while he waits. Side by side with the boardinghouses that cater to the sailors there emerge special quarters devoted to the emigrants. Here a man can sleep for a penny a night. True, it is straw he will sleep on, and as many as forty in a room twelve feet by fifteen. But if low price is the only virtue of these lodgings, that is still virtue enough.

So the peasants began their urban careers. Living in this manner was difficult. Isolated in complete strangeness, they could scarcely accommodate themselves to the quick succession of new situations; even the simple matter of victualing a family out of the dwindling supply of remaining cash was exasperatingly hard. If, in addition, the areas in which these people lived were also slums, were also centers of vice and gambling, that only introduced the emigrants the sooner to problems they would continue to face for the rest of their lives. Not that they could be philosophical about the prospect; on the contrary, the only consolation was that the stay was not permanent.

But permanence and impermanence were only relative. Sometimes these temporary stays stretched out for weeks or months. In the early nineteenth century the craft on which the emigrants traveled did not operate on schedule. Passengers had no way of knowing in advance when a ship would sail. They could only come to port, trust that chance would bring them to a captain ready to depart and willing to take them. Even then, when passage was arranged, there could still be weary spells of waiting while the cargo was completed. Meanwhile the earnestly hoarded resources ran out to the last penny.

The desire to limit this uncertainty and to get out of the city as quickly as possible helped account for the concentration of emigrants, as time went on, into the few large ports where the routes of trade converged. But that concentration only put additional strains on the housing facilities of cities already full to overcrowding.

The experience of the later traveler was, therefore, not essentially different from that of his predecessors. The crowded train expelled him in a cavernous station amidst thousands of rushing people. Surrounded by his baggage and his family, he was very likely approached by a glib stranger, free with offers of help. But how could a man tell whether this was an official, a representative of one of the philanthropic societies that were reputed to ease the emigrants' way, or one of that dread tribe of cheats that was known to trick away the last coin with false counsel? It was better to go alone, alone find the way through the maze of streets and accept the lodgings to which fortune led.

Only toward the end was the strenuous quality of life in the ports alleviated. Then regular sailing schedules announced well in advance ended the need for lengthy stays in the city, and government intervention protected the emigrants in quarters specially set aside for them. Some, in that happier period, would still find unpleasant the barrack-like structures in which they were then housed. But these could have no inkling of the misery of life in the early boarding-houses.

The difficulty of residence in the ports complicated the problems of securing passage. The overpowering desire to get away as soon as possible took precedence over every other consideration. The temptation was to regard the ship quickest found, the best. Haste often led to unexpected and tragic consequences.

Until after the middle of the nineteenth century, the emigrants were carried in sailing vessels, few in number, irregular in the routes they followed, and uncertain as to their destination. Often the masters of these craft did not know for which port they would head until the sails were set; generally the cargo dictated the course. But there was no assurance, even after the ship was under way, that wind or weather would not induce a change. Only rarely could the passengers protest or, as on the *Mary Ann* in 1817, actually revolt. The generality did not expect to be able to choose a precise place of landing in the New World; if they reached shore somewhere in America that was enough.

Nor could they be overly fastidious about the character of their conveyance. Reckoning up the sum of guarded coins, the emigrants knew how little power they had to command favorable terms. The fare could, of course, be haggled over; there were no established rates and those who shared the same steerage would later discover that the charge varied from two to five pounds, depending upon the bargaining power of the various parties. But in the long run the shipmasters held the more favorable situation and could push the rate nearer the higher than the lower limit.

Indeed, as the volume of traffic mounted, the captains no longer had to trouble with these negotiations themselves. The business fell into the hands of middlemen. Enterprising brokers contracted for the steerage space of whole ships and then resold accommodations to prospective travelers. As might be expected, avarice magnified the fancied capacity of the vessels to an unbearable degree, in fact, to a degree that provoked government intervention. But even when the American and British governments began to regulate the number of passengers and, after 1850, even began to enforce those regulations, the emigrant was but poorly protected. The brokers continued to sell as many tickets as they could; and the purchasers above the legal limit, denied permission to board, could only hope to hunt up the swindler who had misled them and seek the return of their funds.

In time, at last, the day approached. On the morning the fortunate ones whose turn it was worriedly gathered their possessions, hastened from lodginghouse to ship's side. The children dragged along the trusses of straw on which they would sleep while the men wrestled onward with the cumbrous barrels that would hold their water, with the battered chests crammed with belongings. Not into the ship yet, but into a thronging expectant crowd they pushed their way, shoving to keep sight of each other, deafened by their own impatient noises and by the cries of peddlers who thrust at them now nuts and taffy for the moment, now pots and provisions for the way.

Some, having waited so long, would wait no more and tried to clamber up the dangling ropes. The most stayed anxiously still and when the moment came jostled along until they stood then upon the ship. And when they stood then upon the ship, when the Old Land was no longer beneath them, they sensed the sea in uneasy motion and knew they were committed to a new destiny. As they lined up for the roll call, their curious gaze sought out the features of this their unfamiliar home — the rising masts, the great folds of sail, the web of rigging, and the bold, pointing bowsprit. Silenced and as if immobilized by the decisiveness of the moment, they remained for a while on deck; and some, raising their eyes from examination of the ship itself, noticed the shores of the Mersey or Weser move slowly by. There was time, before they passed through the estuary to the empty ocean, to reflect on the long way they had come, to mingle with the hope and gratitude of escape the sadness and resentment of flight.

In the early days there was leisure enough for reflection on these matters. The journey was long, the average from Liverpool to New York about forty days. Favorable weather might lower the figure to a month, unfavorable raise it to two or three. The span was uncertain, for the ship was at the mercy of the winds and tides, of the primitive navigation of its masters, and of the ignorance of its barely skilled sailors.

These unsubstantial craft sailed always at the edge of danger from the elements. Wrecks were disastrous and frequent. A single year in the 1830's saw seventeen vessels founder on the run from Liverpool to Quebec alone. Occasional mutinies put the fate of all in dubious hands. Fire, caused by the carelessness of passengers or crew, added another hazard to the trials of the journey. At a blow, such catastrophes swept away scores of lives, ended without further ado many minor histories in the peopling of the new continent.

Other perils too, less dramatic but more pervasive, insidiously made shipwreck of hopes. In the slow-elapsing crossing, the boat became a circumscribed universe of its own, with its own harsh little way of life determined by the absence of space. Down to midcentury the vessels were pitifully small; three hundred tons was a good size. Yet into these tiny craft were crammed anywhere from four hundred to a thousand passengers.

These numbers set the terms of shipboard life. If they talked of it later, the emigrants almost forgot that there had also been cabins for the other sort of men who could pay out twenty to forty pounds for passage. Their own world was the steerage.

Below decks is the place, its usual dimensions seventy-five feet long, twenty-five wide, five and a half high. Descend. In the fitful light your eye will discover a middle aisle five feet wide. It will be a while before you can make out the separate shapes within it, the water closets at either end (for the women; the men must go above deck), one or several cooking stoves, the tables. The aisle itself, you will see, is formed by two rows of bunks that run to the side of the ship.

Examine a bunk. One wooden partition reaches from floor to ceiling to divide it from the aisle, another stretches horizontally from wall to aisle to create two decks. Within the partitions are the boxlike spaces, ten feet wide, five long, less than three high. For the months of the voyage, each is home for six to ten beings.

This was the steerage setting. Here the emigrants lived their lives, day and night. The more generous masters gave them access to a portion of the deck at certain hours. But bad weather often deprived the passengers of that privilege, kept them below for days on end.

Life was hard here. Each family received its daily ration of water, adding to it larger and larger doses of vinegar to conceal the odor. From the limited hoard of provisions brought along, the mother struggled to eke out food for the whole journey. She knew that if the potatoes ran out there would be only the captain to turn to, who could be counted on mercilessly to extort every last possession in return; some masters, in fact, deliberately deceived the emigrants as to the length of the journey, to be able to profit from the sale of food and grog. Later, at midcentury, the government would specify the supplies that had to be taken for each passenger. But there remained ways of avoiding such regulations; tenders followed the ships out of the harbor and carried back the casks checked on for the inspector.

It was no surprise that disease should be a familiar visitor. The only ventilation was through the hatches battened down in rough weather. When the close air was not stifling hot, it was bitter cold in the absence of fire. Rats were at home in the dirt and disorder. The result: cholera, dysentery, yellow fever, smallpox, measles, and the generic "ship fever" that might be anything. It was not always as bad as on the *April*, on which five hundred of eleven hundred Germans perished in the crossing; the normal mortality was about 10 per cent, although in the great year, 1847, it was closer to 20.

It was perhaps no consolation to these emigrants, but they were not the worst off. Among the Irish before 1850 there were some who had not the paltry price of a steerage passage, yet for whom there was no return from Liverpool. They had to find the means of a still cheaper crossing.

From Canada came awkward ships built expressly to bring eastward the tall timbers of American forests, lumbering vessels with great open holds not suited for the carriage of any west-bound cargo. From Nova Scotia and Newfoundland came fishing boats laden with the catch of the Grand Bank;

these craft also could be entrusted with no cargo of value on their return. Formerly both types went back in ballast. Now they would bring the New World to Irishmen. The pittance these poor creatures could pay — ten to twenty shillings — was pure gain. As for the passengers, they would camp out in the empty stinking space below decks, spend an uneasy purgatory preparatory to the redemption by America.

From the harshness, the monotony, the misery of the journey, there was no effective relief. Government protection came late, was minimal, and lacked effective means of enforcement. After all, as the shipping agents argued, the emigrant had never known what it was to sleep in a bed. Give him pork and flour and you make the man sick. Let him lie on a good firm deck, eat salt herring, and he'll be hale and hearty.

Against the open brutalities, against the seamen who reckoned the women fair game, against the danger from within of petty theft and quarrels, the passengers formed spontaneous organizations of their own. The voluntary little associations were governed by codes of agreement, enforced by watchmen appointed from among themselves. But there was no power in these groups, on major matters, to resist the all-powerful captain and crew.

So they'd lie there, seafaring adventurers out to discover new continents, amidst the retching, noisome stench, the stomach-turning filth of hundreds of bodies confined to close quarters. Many nights, and many days that were indistinguishable from nights, they could see, by the sickly light of swinging lanterns, the creaking ugly timbers crowding in about them; they could hear the sounds of men in uneasy silence, of children in fitful rest; everywhere they could sense the menace of hostile winds and waves, of indifferent companions, of repressed passions.

There are times when a man can take no more. Incidents occur: ugly noises of childbirth; sopping disorder when the sea seeps in in a storm; unsuccessful rat-hunts; the splash of burials under a dark sky and without the consolation of a priest. *Ah, we thought we couldn't be worse off than we war; but now to our sorrow we know the differ; for supposin we war dyin of starvation, it would still not be dyin like rotten sheep thrown into a pit, and the minit the breath is out of our bodies, flung into the sea to be eaten up by them horrid sharks.* And a red rage takes hold of the sufferers, of their survivors. They pace about in the warm sticky passage. They clench fists. But against whom shall they raise them? Indeed they are helpless, and they fall into meaningless arguments among themselves. Furious blows are given by the wrestling mass of men in the narrow spaces; until, exhausted, they stand back, angry, ashamed, pick up the pitiful belongings kicked loose, broken, wet from the bilge water oozing up through the spaces of the floor boards. They laugh only at the greater misery of others.

Substantial improvements in the conditions of the crossing came only as indirect results of changes in the techniques of ocean travel. The introduction of steam in the transatlantic service in the 1840's was the first step. The Cunard Line and its imitators pre-empted the high-class passenger business and drove the sailing ships back upon the immigrant trade. Competition for that trade lowered the costs and improved the accommodations. By 1860 it was possible to buy reasonably priced prepaid tickets and to travel on a reliable schedule.

After 1870 the situation was even better. The new era in international relations emphasized navalism and drew the major European nations into a warship building race. Great merchant fleets seemed the necessary complements. England, France, Germany, and Italy hurried to build up their tonnage. Toward that end they were willing to grant heavy subsidies to the operators of the lines bearing their flags. Under those circumstances the price of steerage passage on a steamship fell to as little as twelve dollars, and included food. By the end of that decade, steam had displaced sail in the emigrant-carrying business. Now the duration of the journey fell until it took ten days or less. Comfort and safety increased also. By 1900, the traveler could count on a crossing of little more than a week in vessels of ten to twenty thousand tons. It was still no easy trip, however. There remained the discomfort of crowded quarters, the lack of privacy, the isolation among dense masses of human beings, and the pangs of seasickness. The incongruous mixture, in these latter years, of emigrants of diverse nationalities created perplexing problems of communication: Jews and Greeks, Finns and Poles, Irishmen and Italians had difficulty sharing the same steerage. Yet the enormous lightening of the physical difficulties and the shortening of the time span by the end of the century enabled the later comers to survive the journey in much better condition than had their forerunners.

Earlier or later, all emigrants entered upon a fourth stage of the crossing — a residence of some duration in the American port of arrival. Now were repeated, in reverse, the conditions of the stay in the European port of departure. Now the sea led in, not out; the road away, not toward. Now too the voyagers were the weaker for the effects of the ocean journey; to compensate for the loss of energies and of resources on the way they had only the advantage of wisdom earned in the first urban experience.

Still, many a new arrival who thought simply to pause in the place where he landed was entrapped and never escaped. Some had exhausted all their funds in the coming and were already paupers when they came off the ship; these were unlikely ever to earn enough to take them away. Others simply stumbled in the unsuccessful struggle to overleap the hurdles of city life.

The low-hilled harbors seemed friendly enough to men

and women who had spent the weeks before aboard the emigrant ships. The long American coast dawned unnoticed by those who had waited weary days for it; like the gift delayed in coming which arrives when hope is almost gone, as the travelers came on deck this unexpected vision gladdened all hearts, not only with the pleasure intrinsic to it, but also with the reassurance that no hostile element had intervened to snatch it away.

There is still an interval before the final landing; often the little vessels may spend days beating down the rocky shore to their destined harbors. Sometimes there are heartrending shipwrecks in the treacherous and foggy waters. But the sense of sight, at least, can fasten on to the New World, bring expectation into some contact with reality.

A feverish bustle of preparations sweeps the steerage as the ship clears the headlands of the bay, as land appears on both sides and narrows toward the port, as the pilot comes on board. Clothes are washed and children put in order. All is arranged. Anxious eyes already make out the approaching cluster of spires that marks the place, when everything comes to a halt. This is quarantine.

Although, in the beginning, the pause was usually perfunctory, there was always the possibility of some dangerous new obstacle. The authorities surveyed the assembled passengers, asked if they were well, examined the record of the vessel, and allowed it to dock if there were no signs of contagion. If there were? In 1847, eighty-four ships were held at Grosse Isle below Quebec. Of the Irish immigrants who sought shelter beneath the flimsy exposed sheds, ten thousand died, three thousand so alone that their names were never known. *I have seen them lyin on the beach, crawlin on the mud, and dyin like fish out of water.*

Facilities in the United States were somewhat better and improved with time. On Staten Island, outside New York, was a marine hospital — supported by a tax on the immigrants themselves — which held out at least the hope of recovery. But with time also regulation of the process of landing became more precise and more exacting. The states demanded guarantees lest they be burdened with the support of paupers; many immigrants were asked to give bond, as a condition of admission, that they would not become dependent upon charity. In practice, this requirement, obviously impossible of literal fulfillment, was satisfied by the payment of a fee to a professional bondsman and ultimately was converted into a commutation tax levied by the state.

As the century advanced, the items of inspection grew more numerous. To the old questions of health and the capacity to labor were added new ones that probed into the newcomer's morals and character (Did he believe in polygamy? Had he committed a crime?) ; into his political convictions (Did he advocate anarchism or the overthrow of government by force?) , and into the possibility that he had agreed in advance to take some job in violation of the contract-labor law. By then the Federal government had taken over the whole machinery of admission and control, employing for the purpose the services of a large corps of functionaries, but a corps never adequate enough to handle the ever-increasing masses of men who stood at the gates.

As the volume of traffic rose and as the process of admission grew more elaborate and more complicated, it became less possible to release the immigrants directly after the end of the quarantine period. They were instead directed to new receiving stations created for them. There the final act of admission was consummated. In 1855 Castle Garden, at the tip of Manhattan Island, lost its operatic glitter; the drama of the stage gave way to that of selection, for here the fortunate would now be sorted from the unfortunate. Three decades later the old building could not hold the throngs the steamers brought it. In 1891 a whole island in New York Harbor was given over to their reception; millions here would look from the red brick buildings across the bay for a first glimpse of the promised land. Along the coast from Portland to New Orleans were dotted similar, smaller stations. The immigrants would debark here, not at the piers with the favored occupants of cabins.

Men, women, and children come off their floating homes. They are arranged in lines cut off from each other by wooden barriers, and they begin wearily to tread an incomprehensible maze. Officials in uniform survey them, look at the already large collection of papers, peer at eyes, down throats, thump chests, make notes on cards, and affix tags of various colors to the hesitant bodies that pass uneasily along before them. Now and again one of the fellow travelers is separated out from the rest — to go who knows where.

After a while, and it can be a long, eventful while, there come questions. How can a simple man understand the language? The clever gentleman, smooth-shaven and freshly washed, conducts the interrogation, but speaks down only through the aid of an interpreter. (One knows the type, a fellow who gains the good graces of the authorities by trapping his unfortunate countrymen.) One must answer cautiously, reveal not too much, lie if need be. Keep in mind: *destination, funds on hand, relatives, work.* These are tricky matters. The law says you must not have contracted for your job, also that you must be not likely to become a public charge. How can you demonstrate that you will not become a public charge? It is said a show of money, say ten dollars, will do it. But caution.

Where did you get this money you have just shown us?
In Liverpool.
Who gave it to you?
The man in the office.
What office?
I don't know the name, where I took the boat.
What did you give him for it?
Two English pounds.

Where did you get those?
In Cork.
From whom?
In the bank.
How did you get them in the bank?
I gave them some sovereigns.
Where did you get these from?
I earned them. . . .
There are the right words at last. Magically you are through.

Anyway, most are lucky and do get through. The handful of inspectors are too few to permit more than a perfunctory examination. They look for surface disabilities (trachoma, an infection of the eyelids, is one; favus, a skin disease, is another), for obvious deformities, and for signs of idiocy or insanity. On the hot summer days which see the peak load, the impatient officials, starched collars wilting under the heavy serge, now and then single out for more than casual study a case from the long rows that move stolidly before them. The rest get by. They escape to the free American air and leave behind the luckless who must still face medical boards of review, hearings, and appeals, perhaps soon to be sent back from whence they came or to spend more months in the confinement rooms of the station while distant powers thumb through the dossiers that pile up on Washington desks.

Not here, though, where the ferry left them from Ellis Island or East Boston, was the end of the journey. There was still a way to go. In the earlier years, it was not uncommon that the exhausted newcomer, weak and penniless, sometimes one survivor of a numerous family, should stagger away and wander about till some kindly passer-by directed him to the almshouse. Later, trouble took another form, perplexity in the face of the simple tasks of unloading baggage, of finding temporary lodgings, of transporting trunks and boxes to the boardinghouse, of getting to the railroad station, of purchasing tickets to the interior. All about indeed were obliging men, eager to assist, men who offered a bit of whisky to mark the elation of the landing, men who snatched at the immigrants' baggage and pointed out the places to stop. Sometimes these runners were fellow countrymen who spoke the old language and sprung the treacherous trap in the accents of friendship. Thousands were thus lost toward the end who had survived the more obvious perils, who had walked days by land, braved the dangers of the sea but were vulnerable to those of the city. They were stranded in the seaport and never reached their destinations. Only toward the end, when runners were barred from the vicinity of the receiving stations and when most immigrants were met by friends or relatives, could the newcomers relax their vigilance, cease to fear the danger of being fleeced at the threshold.

By comparison with what had come earlier, the difficulties of the journey into the interior were comparatively simple. For some there were strenuous days of travel on foot; by this means the Irish made their way southward from Canada and the Maritime Provinces to New England and New York. By foot or by wagon, too, immigrants of many nationalities joined the general movement of Americans westward. But even in the earlier days, it was not expensive to go by water, sloops up the Hudson, barges on the lakes and canals, boats carrying plaster of Paris down from New Brunswick. And after 1830, the railroads that webbed the map of the nation helped to ease the hardship of this phase of the crossing.

After the Civil War the efforts of the transcontinental railroads further improved the condition of the immigrant travelers. Financed in good part by government land grants, these corporations were less concerned with collecting fares than with settling their holdings with industrious farmers who would turn out a constant supply of products to keep the freight cars full. Some roads arranged for special low-rate immigrant trains; others sold through tickets in Europe that carried the voyager all the way from his native village to his future home and that eliminated the hazards and uncertainties of bad connections and arrangements made on the spot. By the twentieth century, the general improvement in transportation in America had done much to relieve the physical tensions of the journey. The greatest obstacle then was a pervasive, biting fatigue. That existed from the start and persisted to the end, despite the advances in means of communication. Having come thus far, there was often no energy to go any farther. This was America; there was the temptation to stop off by the way, perhaps for a time, they thought, to recuperate, to take some temporary job and earn some money. For these, the stay was usually permanent. Many remained at the junction points on the route to which, but not beyond which, their tickets carried them. In Buffalo, Cleveland, Pittsburgh, Chicago, St. Louis, and Milwaukee there were thousands of immigrants whose destinations were elsewhere, but who each found some final insurmountable hurdle that kept him immobilized where he was.

The crossing in all its phases was a harsh and brutal filter. On land in Europe, in the port of embarkation, on the ocean, in the port of arrival, and on land in America, it introduced a decisive range of selective factors that operated to let through only a few of those who left the Old World. In part these factors were physical; the hardier survived the dangers and the difficulties, the weaker and more dependent fell by the side. In part, however, these factors were more than physical, for they measured also the power of adaptation: only those who were capable of adjusting from peasant ways to the needs of new conditions and new challenges were able to absorb the successive shocks of migration.

For the crossing involved a startling reversal of roles, a radical shift in attitudes. The qualities that were desirable in the good peasant were not those conducive to success in the transition. Neighborliness, obedience, respect, and status were valueless among the masses that struggled for space on the way. They succeeded who put aside the old preconceptions, pushed in, and took care of themselves. This experience would certainly bring into question the validity of the old standards of conduct, of the old guides to action.

Perhaps that was the most luminous lesson of the crossing, that a totally new kind of life lay ahead. Therein was the significance of the unwillingness of the peasants to undertake the journey in the old traditional communal units. Despite the risks entailed, they preferred to act as individuals, each for himself. Somehow they had been convinced that the village way which had been inadequate to save them at home would certainly prove inadequate away from home.

Not that they derived much joy or comfort from the conviction. In any case they suffered. The separation itself had been hard. The peasants had been cut off from homes and villages, homes and villages which were not simply places, but communities in which was deeply enmeshed a whole pattern of life. They had left the familiar fields and hills, the cemetery in which their fathers rested, the church, the people, the animals, the trees they had known as the intimate context of their being.

Thus uprooted, they found themselves in a prolonged state of crisis — crisis in the sense that they were, and remained, unsettled. For weeks, and often for months, they were in suspense between the old and the new, literally in transit. Every adjustment was temporary and therefore in its nature bore the seeds of maladjustment, for the conditions to which the immigrants were adjusting were strange and ever changing.

As a result they reached their new homes exhausted — worn out physically by lack of rest, by poor food, by the constant strain of close, cramped quarters, worn out emotionally by the succession of new situations that had crowded in upon them. At the end was only the dead weariness of an excess of novel sensations.

Yet once arrived, the immigrants would not take time to

recuperate. They would face instead the immediate, pressing necessity of finding a livelihood and of adjusting to conditions that were still more novel, unimaginably so. They would find then that the crossing had left its mark, had significantly affected their capacity to cope with the problems of the New World they faced.

THREE

Daily Bread

LET THE PEASANT, now in America, confront his first problem; time enough if ever this is solved to turn to other matters.

How shall a man feed himself, find bread for his family? The condition of man is to till the soil; there is no other wholeness to his existence. True, in retrospect, life on the soil in the old home had not yielded a livelihood. But that was because there was not there soil enough. In consequence, the husbandmen, in their hundreds of thousands, have left their meager plots. They have now come to a New World where open land reaches away in acre after acre of inexhaustible plenty. Arrived, they are ready to work.

Yet only a few, a fortunate few, of these eager hands were destined ever to break the surface of the waiting earth. Among the multitudes that survived the crossing, there were now and then some who survived it intact enough in body and resources to get beyond the port of landing and through the interior cities of transit. Those who were finally able to establish themselves as the independent proprietors of farms of their own made up an even smaller number.

All the others were unable to escape from the cities. Decade after decade, as the Federal government made its count, the census revealed a substantial majority of the immigrants in the urban places; and the margin of that majority grew steadily larger. Always the percentage of the foreign-born who lived in the cities was much higher than that of the total population.

Yet the people who were to live the rest of their days amidst a world of steel and stone and brick were peasants. If they failed to reach the soil which had once been so much a part of their being, it was only because the town had somehow trapped them.

All those who could not immediately move into the interior, purchase at once a farm, and settle down as agriculturists without delay, spent some period as residents of one of the great cities. Here they worked in preparation for the moment when they might leave. Working as they did in a new fashion and in a strange place, it took time to find a way around, to begin to learn the operations of the productive system of which they had become a part.

The difficulty was that a man could live years in an American city without coming to understand the mainsprings of its economy. In the period before the Civil War, before this very tide of immigration began to condition the development of these places, they served a distinctive and narrow function. The cousin, friend, or acquaintance who wished to enlighten the newcomer would have to explain that Boston and New York, that Philadelphia, Baltimore, and New Orleans, were commercial points of exchange. These were valves situated along the coast through which was pumped the flow of goods between the Old World and the New. Here, and at the internal market towns — at Albany, Buffalo, Cleveland, and Chicago, at Pittsburgh, Cincinnati, and St. Louis — commodities were exchanged, were repacked, and were transshipped from one conveyance to another. This was the function of the American city in the early nineteenth century; whoever sought employment there had to find it within this trading structure.

The old resident, leading the immigrant about, could readily show visible evidence of the town's role. The important places were the piers and markets; the critical buildings were the exchange and the shops and countinghouses of the merchants. The weightiest people were those engaged in buying and selling.

What could the peasant do here? He could not trade or do much to help the traders. There was some room for petty shopkeepers; he lacked the training and the capital. Some handicraftsmen supplied clothes and furniture and a variety of other products to the townsfolk; he lacked the skill and tools. Back on the docks at which he had landed were a number of casual jobs with the stevedores. Here and there in the warehouses and stores were calls for the services of porters. But there was a limit to the amount of lifting and carrying to be done. Wandering about in the first days of their arrival, these immigrants learned that beyond these few opportunities there was, at first, no demand for their capacities.

As time went by, they became restless seekers after employment. Yet many remained unsuccessful in the quest or, drifting about, picked up odd jobs that tided them over from week to week. They joined a growing army of the anxious for work, for they could certainly not remain long without income. Perpetually on the verge of destitution, and therefore of starvation, eager to be hired at any rate, these redundant hands accumulated in a fund of available but unused labor.

No wonder that the newcomer was somewhat incredulous when he finally learned that outside the city there were jobs, that his power to toil, here so little valued, elsewhere was urgently needed. Yet advertisements in the newspapers, chalked-up notices in the streets, told him it was indeed so. Was he then likely to quibble over terms, inquire closely as to conditions? At the intelligence bureaus, the employment offices whence all these benefits flowed, he was signed on, gathered up into a gang with others like him, and hurried along to his appointed task.

The jovial fellow who humored the men into agreement and who sealed the contract with a dram of the best was agent of a remarkable construction system that kept pace with the unparalleled expansion of the country through the nineteenth century. With no machines, with only pick, shovel, and sledge for tools, the boss and his gang contrived the numerous links that held the nation whole in these years. Out of their labors came first the chain of canals, and then an intricately meshed network of railroads — by 1910, more than 350,000 miles of them. And these tasks were hardly completed before bicycle riders and motorists began to call for and to get a paved highway system; 200,000 miles were already laid in 1910.

Engineers' estimates reckoned up the immense quantities of unskilled labor these projects would take; surveyors' reports revealed that the lines would run through unsettled or partly settled agricultural regions, places where no supply of such labor was available. To get the jobs done meant bringing in from outside the hands for the doing.

Thus the earliest immigrants find their calling. Desperate in the absence of alternative they leave behind wife and child and go to live the hard life of the construction camp. Exposed to the pitiless assaults of sun and snow and dusty winds, they work long hours, are paid low wages; in the lonely distances, away from all other beings, there is no arguing with a contractor who suddenly, arbitrarily lowers his rates. They may not complain of the degrading quarters — broken-down old freight cars or dilapidated shanties quickly thrown together. They can have nothing to say of the compulsion to buy food and supplies from the company's swindling store. To whom can they turn? It is not the railroad or canal that employs them; an intermediary, responsible to no one, battens off their misery.

In any case, until the laborers paid off the price of bringing them there and until they accumulated the fare to return, they were bound to submit to the unscrupulous exploitation of the boss. In many states, the money advanced to get the worker to the job was considered a debt, and the law condemned the unwitting immigrant to serve out his time for the contractor until the debt was cleared. Not until 1907 did the Federal government intervene to halt this practice as peonage.

Those who sampled the life of the construction gang were, therefore, not likely to wish to repeat the experience. For such men, it was a relief to discover, as time went on, that analogous opportunities were gradually opening up within the city itself. The increase of urban population strained existing housing and created a persistent demand for new construction that kept the building trades prosperous. Everywhere streets pushed out into the suburbs where farms had once been; men's muscles had to grade the way, carry and fit the paving blocks. Each seaport dredged and improved its harbor, built imposing piers to accommodate the larger vessels of nineteenth-century commerce. Intricate systems of aqueducts, of gas pipes, of electric wires, of trolley tracks, supplied water and light and transportation for the new city millions.

Every one of these activities, which occupied the attention of a whole century, depended for its execution upon an ample fund of unskilled labor. The immigrants supplied that fund; and in doing so made for themselves a role that could have been occupied by no other element in American society — no other was so thoroughly deprived of the opportunity for choice. In sad succession, from 1830 to 1930, the Irish, the Bohemians, the Slovaks, the Hungarians, the Italians, and many other peoples less numerous took up for a period the service of the pick and shovel.

It was not likely that any among them, at the time, took much pride in their contribution to the nation. Nor was it likely that many individuals among them would long think such employment a satisfactory solution to the problem of finding a job. These tasks were, in their nature, intermittent and transitory; each project, once completed, left the laborers back where they started, face to face with the necessity of looking for another. Wages hung close to the cost of subsistence, never rose to a point that permitted a man to accumulate the stakes of a fresh start. At the end of a stint the worker was weaker and older, otherwise no different from what he was before. Meanwhile, from day to day he ran the risk of total calamity from illness or disabling injury.

Whatever elements of order appeared in this disorderly system came from the laborers themselves. With no prospect of security and so often incapable of protecting themselves against strange men or hostile events, the immigrants could look only to each other for assistance. Sometimes in the tired dusk of the close of a week's work they would stand by the track's edge against the rolling countryside and hear the clerk read off the notice of some new oppression: dismissals, lower rates, higher store charges. They would wait in the still air, stifle rage in the knowledge of their own impotence, and think to return acquiescent to the dark bunks of their degradation. Then one would speak, give words to their grievances, and be their leader. Sometimes they would watch the gaping ditch where the locks would be, see the line of aliens come up the slope to take their jobs, and one would yell, and urge them on, and lead them down to drive those others off. Or the quarrels would take some other form, rise from intoxication, from resentment at differences in language or manners.

Then men banded together in gangs and worked together under a leader. That was a way that seemed proper to those who had once been peasants. As the scale of hiring was enlarged and as the process became more complicated, management of the labor of the group fell entirely into the hands of the leader — "boss" he was usually called, but "padrone" by the Italians and Greeks. Ultimately he negotiated a single contract for the lot, assuming himself the expense of maintaining them, and retaining for himself a profit from the transaction. Before long, this means of organizing construction labor became so lucrative for the padrone that he turned into a species of subcontractor, built up new gangs on his own initiative, and often also recruited members from his countrymen abroad.

Guidance by the padrone had the virtue of shielding the laborer against the excesses of employers. It had also the advantage of a kind of security; at least there would always be something to eat, a place to sleep, and the company of understanding compatriots. But the padrone system had also this disadvantage, that it left the immigrant helpless against exploitation by the padrone himself. To their sorrow, the newcomers frequently learned that a leader in America was not bound by the patterns of obligation that were sacred in the Old World. Deception and dishonesty penetrated even these relationships and many men discovered that such attempts at self-help only worked into new forms of enslavement.

In no case could construction work, therefore, be ever more than a makeshift. Whether they went as individuals or in gangs, whether in the country or in the city, the peasants regarded this labor in the same light as they had viewed migratory labor in their European homes. This was an expedient taken up as a result of some immediate pressure. This was not a way of life, not a fitting use of man's power to toil, not a dependable source of daily bread. The quest for that, continuing, would take other turns.

In the beginning, the new-built canals served not only to carry the cargoes of commerce, but also to turn the wheels of industry. In those early decades, when manufacturing first became familiar to the American economy, the digging Irishmen often looked up with envy at the imposing new mills. But there was no room within those walls for such as they.

Pitched in small towns wherever the sources of water power happened to be, the factories were as inaccessible to the city-bound as the agricultural West. For the desperate, immobile immigrants in Boston and New York, Fall River and Paterson were as far away as Ohio and Illinois. And those who did manage somehow to get through to the industrial villages knew the likelihood was slight of being taken on by the superintendent or being received as an equal by the other workers.

In the 1820's and 1830's, factory employment was the province of groups relatively high in social status. North of Boston, the bulk of the labor force was made up of respectable young girls, many the daughters of neighborhood farmers, girls willing to work for a few years in anticipation of the marriageable young man. In southern New England the general practice was to employ whole families of artisans. Everywhere, paternalistic organization and the closely knit communal life of the boardinghouses did not allow the easy entrance of newcomers. The only immigrants who then found a place in industry were the few skilled operatives who had already mastered the craft in the Old Country and were hired for the sake of their skills.

The reservoir of unskilled peasant labor that mounted steadily higher in the cities did not long remain untapped, however. In the 1840's and 1850's came a succession of new inventions that enterprising men of capital used to transform the productive system of the United States. The older industries had disdained the immigrants; but the new ones, high in the risks of innovation and heavy initial investments, drew eagerly on this fund of workers ready to be exploited at attractively low wages. The manufacture of clothing, of machines, and of furniture flourished in the great commercial cities precisely where they could utilize freely the efforts of the newcomers, hire as many as they needed when necessary, lay off any surplus at will. A completely fluid labor supply set the ideal conditions for expansion.

Thereafter, whatever branch of the economy entered upon a period of rapid expansion did so with the aid of the same immigrant labor supply. At midcentury the immigrants went to dig in the mines that pockmarked the great coal and iron fields of Pennsylvania, first experienced Welshmen and Cornishmen, later raw Irishmen and Germans, and still later Slavs — a vague term that popularly took in Bohemians, Slovaks, Hungarians, and also Italians. These people spread with the spread of the fields, southward into West Virginia and westward to Illinois, in a burst of development from which impressive consequences followed.

The wealth of new power extracted from the earth, after 1870, set off a second revolution in American industry. Steam replaced water power. Iron replaced wood in the construction of machines. Factories became larger and more mechanized and the place of unskilled labor more prominent. On the payrolls of new enterprises, immigrant names were almost alone; and the newcomers now penetrated even into the older textile and shoe industries. The former peasants, first taken on for menial duties as janitors and sweepers, found themselves more often placed at machines as the processes of production were divided into ever simpler tasks open to the abilities of the unskilled.

By the end of the nineteenth century the national economy had been transformed. Immigrants then still did the burdensome jobs of commerce. They still toiled in construction and maintenance crews. But they had found a larger usefulness in the mines and factories. In the mill towns and industrial cities the availability of their labor had been instrumental in converting production from its old handicraft forms to the mechanized forms of power.

This process, so rich in rewards for the country as a whole, paid mostly dividends of pain for the immigrants involved in it. It cost the peasants this to make the adjustment, that the stifling, brazen factories and the dark, stony pits supplanted the warm, living earth as the source of their daily bread. Year after year they paid the price in innumerable hardships of mind and body.

When he reviewed his grievances the man who went to work said that the conditions of his labor were oppressively harsh. His day was long, he pointed out; not until the 1880's was the ten-hour limit an objective seriously to be struggled for, and for many years more that span remained a pleasing ideal rather than a reality. His week was full, he added; seven days, when they could be had, were not unusual. And, he complained, along with the Sunday there vanished that whole long calendar of holidays that had formerly marked the peasant year. Here the demands of industry and the availability of employment alone determined when a man should work and when he should rest.

These were such wrongs as the ache in his muscles recalled. Others were summoned up by an ache of the spirit. For this matter of time reflected an unhuman lack of concern with human needs that was characteristic of the entire system. In these great concerns, no one seemed troubled with the welfare of the tiny men so cheap to come by who moved uneasily about in the service of the immense expensive machines. A high rate of industrial accidents and a stubborn unwillingness to make the most elementary provisions for the comfort of the employees, to the immigrant were evidence of the same penetrating callousness.

In the terms of his own experience, the laborer could come to understand his total insecurity by recollecting the steady decline in the span of the labor contract. In the Old Country, and in the old America, a man was hired for the year or for the season. But that period was altogether out of place under these conditions. Now it was not even by the month or by the week that the worker was taken on, but by the day or by the hour. Such an arrangement released the employer from the compulsion of paying hands when he had no need of them. But it left the hands uncertain, from moment to moment, as to how much work and how much income they would have.

The ultimate refinement was the shift to piecework in which the laborer, rewarded in accord with his output, received payment only for the instants he was actually at his task. The peasant sometimes conceived of this as an attractive alternative, for he hated the idea of selling his time, of taking directions like a servant, of cringing under the frowns of a foreman who judged all performances inadequate. Piecework brought the consolation of independence — one's time was one's own — and the illusion that additional effort would bring additional returns. But, though the immigrants often clung to the illusion as a token of hope, the reality was inescapably different. There was no independence and rewards would not rise. For the employer who set the rates manipulated them to his own interest while the employee had no choice but to accept. The net effect was to shift from the employer to the employee the whole burden of labor insecurity.

These elements of insecurity, the immigrant learned, were not confined to the conditions of the working day; they pervaded the total relationship of the worker to the economy. The fluid labor supply that gave the employer complete liberty to hire as many workers as he wished, when he wished, also gave him the ability, at will, to dismiss those whose toil he no longer needed. Under such circumstances there were always some men without jobs. Each industry came to have its seasons, peaks and troughs in the level of employment dictated either by the weather as in construction, or, more generally, by the convenience of the managers. It was a rare individual who did not go on the bricks for some part of the year, for periodic unemployment was an expected aspect of the laborer's career.

Then there were the years when unemployment deepened and spread out. The intervals of idleness grew longer and were less frequently interrupted until unemployment was no longer intermittent but continuous. More men appeared on the streets during the day; children were seen, pail in hand, on the way to the police station for the doled-out soup. First in the mill and mining towns where there was only one employer or one industry and where a closing had an immediate cataclysmic effect, then in the cities where the impact was delayed by diversity of occupations, but in time everywhere, the laborer knew a depression was upon him.

At such times, the burdens of his economic role became intolerable. The hunger left behind in Europe was again an intimate of the household, and the cold and raggedness. Endurance stretched to the bursting point, and the misery of regret was overwhelming. It was a golden land here in America as long as there was work, but without work it was worth nothing. In the miry slough of inactivity into which he now sank, the peasant had leisure to meditate upon the meaning of his lot in the New World.

The central condition of that lot was inadequate earnings. Competing with each other in an overstocked market, the unskilled laborers forced down their own rate of pay. As it was lowness of wages that enabled the immigrants to enter industry, the continued development of industry was accompanied by a steady decline in their real remuneration. Statistics were only approximately revealing. But it was significant that the most desirable forms of labor for municipalities in 1900 brought only two dollars a day. And it was characteristic that, about then, for every hundred dollars earned by native wage earners, the Italian-born earned eighty-four, the Hungarians sixty-eight, and other Europeans fifty-four. To tell the truth, few immigrant laborers knew just how much they earned. Pay was uncertain in amount; it came at irregular intervals; and no man could look ahead and predict with security what his next year's income would be. For that matter, few men could look back and reckon with exactitude what the past year's income had been. They only knew, and this was clear enough without computation, that the average earnings of the unskilled were simply not large enough to support a family. Allowing for the inevitable periods of idleness between jobs, even a moderately skilled worker found it difficult to provide for a wife and children.

Only by calling upon the earnings of more than one of its members could the immigrant household make ends meet. Not unless it utilized the efforts of wife and child, as well as those of the husband, could the family be certain that there would always be someone working and that the income of the whole would be large enough, secure enough, to withstand the recurrent shocks of American economic life.

It was not the mere fact that wife and child must exert themselves that was hurtful. These were no strangers to toil in the Old World, or in the New. The degradation lay in the *kind* of work. The boys drifted into street occupations, blacked boots or hawked newspapers, missed thus the opportunity to acquire a trade and fell into all sorts of outlandish ways. Or they, and girls too for that matter, entered the shops, where they did men's work at child's wages. For the women, there was "domestic service" — maid's work in strangers' homes or back-breaking laundering in their own; or, more often as time went on, service to industry in the factory or by homework. If it was characteristic of these families that they somehow found the room for a boarder, that was only another method of adding to their ranks another breadwinner.

But in America bread never came without complications. The peasant, new to the means of earning his livelihood, was also new to the means of spending it. To his misfortune he discovered that he himself added to the difficulties in making ends meet through inability to use efficiently whatever money came to his hands. In his old life, he had thought of objects in their individuality and uniqueness; the chair, the hat, the cow. Here he had to learn to think of them as commodities, subject to a common quantitative standard of price. Without a clear conception of the relationship of money to things, every transaction involved a set of totally new conditions.

What good wife, at home, was so lacking in housewifely skills as to buy food? Only the improvident were incapable of nurturing their families out of their own farms and gardens. But in America every crumb was paid for. The unfamiliar processes of shopping, of purchasing goods from impersonal strangers in stores, led to countless losses and often induced the immigrant, whatever the cost, to deal with peddlers, as in the Old World. Furthermore, lack of funds made it inevitable that these people transact their affairs in a most wasteful manner. There was no margin for stock. They bought bread and potatoes by the pound, rather than by loaf or peck, coal by the basket rather than by ton. (And where would they have put more had they the money to invest in quantity?) Purchasers in such small lots could not choose of whom they should buy, or at what terms. They marketed where they could and were at the mercy of those willing to trouble with their trifling custom.

Frequently, the shortage of cash drove the immigrants into the trap of an expensive credit system. In the bitter intervals between earnings they were compelled to turn to the generosity of the local shopkeeper, who would tide them over to the limit of his own slim resources. (What else could the merchant do when all his customers were in the same miserable condition?) As debts mounted up in the grocer's book, the immigrants lost the freedom to shop and paid, in the price of their food, the interest and more.

For one cause and another, the laborer got pitifully little from his labor. The dollars that seemed large enough from the perspective of Europe shrank with disheartening rapidity under the conditions of America. What was left, every waking hour, was the tormenting need to provide, the nagging need to restrict expenditures. Occasional windfalls, not enough to alter his situation, might be spent in bursts of indulgence — a gold watch, a glittering pin. What difference did that make? Day-to-day existence was still close to the bone.

How could this man, so recently removed from an altogether different life, explain to himself the productive system in which he was enmeshed? Now he was a part of something altogether unnatural. It was that, rather than the length or laboriousness of his work, that was harshest. Indeed the factory was not at all like the field, the field over which he had once bent in piety, the field over which he had once cast forth the sacred seeds that would bring forth God's fruit on a morrow. At best, there was this cardinal fault in the new work, that it was separated from the soil; and, at least, it required this adjustment of the peasant, that he reconcile himself to a life away from the earth, that he cut himself off from the process of birth and death, from the cycle of growth, aging, and regeneration that had once given meaning to his being. Now he was to act within a realm of inanimate things. Senseless iron shapes will everlastingly be about him, and stone will hem him in — on city street, in mill or mine. In his own estimation he would be that much the less a man.

In all matters, the New World made the peasant less a man. Often he toiled at intangibles, labored to produce objects he never would see. In the laborer's perspective, the factory turned out only parts of things: not a shoe, a coat, a plow, a cart — but a sole, a sleeve, a blade, a wheel. Bound to the monotony of a minute task, endlessly repeated, the worker sometimes could not envisage the whole of which his bit would be a part. He through whose hands all of production had then passed, from the dropped seed to the eaten bread, often now could not tell what manner of thing his labor made — its shape, its quality, its function. Such labor was labor for its own sake and meaningless.

Actions no longer related to the rhythms of the soil now seemed related to nothing at all. In the new context, all sorts of old judgments became irrelevant. Formerly the peasant's life had been guided by standards he accepted as fixed and immutable. Now his life made a mockery of those very standards. Could he here, as at home, expect the relationships of reciprocal goodness between master and men, between just employer and true employee? Could he count on neighborly loans, on the mutual help of men working together? Those who thought it were quickly disabused.

As in the crossing, there was a reversal of roles. The loyal dutiful man, faithful to tradition, the man who was the son and grandson of substantial peasants, was reduced to the indignity of hired labor, while shrewd, selfish, unscrupulous upstarts thrived. Clearly the attributes the immigrants held in high esteem were not those that brought success in America. The idea of success was itself strange; to thrust oneself above one's station in life called for harsh competitive qualities the peasant had always despised. Of course there was a satisfaction in the knowledge that even the well-to-do worked here and a man's cap was not worn out from lifting it to the gentry. But the satisfaction was mixed with a sense of impropriety. And to the extent that the immigrant lacked fixity of place, he felt again the less a man for it.

He was not a man at all. Whether he worked or was idle, whether he prospered or starved, was quite unrelated to his qualities as a human being, to his virtues as an individual. The line would move forward by the hiring boss, and then suddenly stop. The rest would be turned away, not through any deficiency of their own, not through lack of skill or will, but because the system operated impersonally. Where the line stopped was unpredictable. Those figures on the line who got in or did not felt part of an entity vast beyond their comprehension, certainly beyond their control. Driven in a helpless alternation of fortunes by the power of remote forces, these were no longer men, not any more men than the cogs spinning in their great machines.

If the system was also wasteful, that only added to the irony of the situation for those entangled in it. The American economy operated in the mass; it was prodigal of resources of human energies and of raw materials; yet it never yielded enough. In the midst of plenty was always want; in the midst of shortages, much that seemed usable continued to be discarded. This the peasant could not grasp, that serviceable articles should not have a market, that other men should throw away what he needed. Buildings razed within the decade of their erection, the immense accumulations of junkyards and dumps, made no sense to him. What he could not understand was not that some were rich while he was poor, but that so much was wasted that he could use.

Yet it did not matter how harsh the immigrants judged their lot. They were inextricably involved in their situation, saw no apparent means of escape, and found no hands extended to assist them. Through most of this period the labor unions either barred the foreign-born from membership or made no effort to organize them. Occasionally radicals, for reasons of their own, provided temporary leadership, as did the I.W.W. at McKees Rocks, Pennsylvania, in 1909 and at Lawrence, Massachusetts, and Paterson, New Jersey, in 1912 and 1913. But the gulf between immigrants and radicals quickly terminated such incongruous alliances. The unskilled laborers never effectively made their voices heard, never discovered a way to help themselves.

[74]

Oh, they longed to get away, longed somehow to shake off the intolerable burdens of the land of opportunity. Tied down as they were, they yearned for other men's ability to move. But the roads that led away were inaccessible. Insecurity reached so deep into their lives that any change involved a risk of incalculable proportions. Living as they did so close to the margin of existence, they never accumulated the modest surplus that might have given them freedom to alter their position. They were permanently immobilized, fixed where they were.

Mostly they worked on; after their fashion, they accepted their place. Only, now and then they would know that heart-weary sense of strain for what it was, recognition that this was the goal of their long coming to the New World.

Yes, but try to get away! Where will you go who have come so far? The way back is closed, barred by too vivid memories of the troubles of crossing. Your prosperous fellows may take it into their heads to return, swing the gold watch of success before the admiring eyes of the village. But you will never again venture the sickening ocean, take failure back to the place of your birth. And it is not Europe of which you dream, but America. Even now your mind glides through opening streets, beyond the last trolley stop, takes in the vision of endless acres that roll empty away to the horizon. There, peasant, the land still awaits the touch of your fructifying hand.

Few got through who longed to mingle their labor with the soil. Some were fortunate from the outset, lived through the passage with funds intact and moved directly to farms in the West. Others were fortunate in their settlement in the city, found jobs in which they could save up the regenerating purchase price. Sometimes these latter formed themselves into land associations, hoping to hasten the process by united action (and as often as not discovered these were schemes of unscrupulous promoters who sucked away the ill-spared dues and gave nothing in return). Still, this was a goal worthy of sacrifices — to be a free farmer, on one's own bit of ground, doing man's work.

With the relief of return after a long absence, the peasant came back to the familiar earth. But he was not here simply to repeat the experiences of the Old Country. The old ways proved ineffective under new conditions and the new life quite different from the old.

The communal qualities of peasant agriculture never took root in America. Attempts to restore the village or to colonize whole groups together failed miserably. The mass of immigrants had no dealings with the utopian socialist experiments; and the philanthropic projects that scattered clusters of Germans, Irishmen, Jews, Poles, Italians, and Bohemians everywhere from Louisiana to Oregon speedily disintegrated, for the successful settlers soon learned it was to their advantage to split away and to farm as individuals. Here and there, under religious auspices, small communities held together for a time. Various schemes created tiny plantations of German and Irish Catholics at Benedicta, Maine, at St. Mary's, Pennsylvania, at Glandorf, Ohio, at Jasper, Indiana, and, most successfully, at St. Nazianz, Wisconsin, where Father Oschwald brought as a nucleus a band of Benedictine monks from the Black Forest.

But the only settlements that held together over long periods were those of the pietistic communist sects, mostly German, in which religious authority furnished the sanctions for rigid control over the private property, the sex life, and the family structure of the members. In these communities, the zealous founders could impose unchangeable ideas upon the generations that followed, enable them to resist the pressure of a hostile American environment. Yet even the fellowships at Amana, Iowa, or Harmony, Pennsylvania, were not simply counterparts of the European villages. They were far closer in spirit and in organization to such native American societies as sprang up at Brook Farm, Massachusetts, at

Oneida, New York, and at Phalanx, New Jersey. The traditional peasant way of life did not develop in the United States; the agriculturist there entered upon an altogether new way of cultivation.

As far as they could, the immigrants tried to find land similar in physical appearance to that they had left; the same combinations of woodland, of fields for tillage, and of meadows for pasture attracted them. To discover such tracts was easy neither in the dense forests of the East nor on the open prairies of the West; and that prejudice alone tended to limit the newcomers to farms already developed. But in addition, the peasants stayed away from the frontier because they lacked the special skills to cope with the unfamiliar conditions with which settlers there were immediately and incessantly confronted. The Europeans did not know how to subsist by fishing and hunting until the first crops were in; the gun, the basic tool of the frontiersman, was strange to their touch. They were ignorant of the tricks for clearing trees rapidly away and were clumsy in getting on with the Indians.

Reluctance to pitch on the cheapest frontier lands, the expensive compulsion to settle on farms already brought under cultivation by others, accounted in part for the inability of immigrants in more substantial numbers to get directly to the West. The usual pattern saw the newcomer, with his city savings or imported capital, move in after the huntsmen and trappers had done their work and after the frontier farmer had made an initial clearing. There were always Americans willing to sell, the improvident fallen into debt or the simply restless itching to move to the advancing edge of settlement. The peasant took over, allowed those impatient with humdrum farming to drift farther westward with the profits of the sale. Meanwhile the new owner set out painfully to rescue what his predecessor had heedlessly exploited.

Painfully, because ancestral wisdom was sadly inadequate

to the needs of this soil which, on approach, also revealed itself strange. Application of well-tried ways was here not enough. The peasant had constantly to consider his steps, to make decisions in matters that had passed without thought in the Old World — what to plant, and when, and how much, and where. To shoulder this burden of choices, the individual had not now the support of a village council. He acted alone.

He had not long to wait before the difficulties were apparent. He found little on his American farm that was familiar. Physical conditions were different; the climate was more strenuous, more capricious, more violent. (Was it so, or did it seem so? . . . It did not matter.) The soil was hard. Untamed, with deep-hidden roots and sun-baked crust, it fought the plow. In the prairies were no trees for fire, fence, or building. Everything had to be created from the beginning and with labor wearying as never before. The tools were not the same, and not so good. Even the farm's large size, it appeared, had disadvantages. These proud acres invited much more toil in the clearing than he expected and, if all went well, demanded machines in cultivation. Hardly conscious of the means by which it happened, the peasant often found himself possessor of intricate, impersonal devices that stood between him and the simple labor on his fields.

It took no longer than the time needed to sow and harvest a crop before the immigrant learned that these differences were not only in the surface appearance of things; they penetrated his whole life as a farmer. It was not the American way, as it had been his in his other life, to grow a variety of plants for subsistence — some wheat, but also barley, potatoes, oats, and vegetables. In the New World there was not much concern even with the care of domestic animals. Americans concentrated on a staple, threw the whole of their energies into raising a single product for sale.

That the focal effort of agriculture should be the market rather than the household was altogether strange to the peasant. A few adjusted by application to specialties in which old skills were valuable — raised hops, planted vineyards, made cheese. But for most, farming became an entirely new pursuit. They were now entrepreneurs, tied to the kaleidoscopic fortunes of a market economy.

The peasants had also known a market at home, a visible place to which they brought their surplus of commodities to be bartered for what pleased them in the array of goods displayed before their eyes. But the American market was of another sort, not a place, but an abstract relationship. Buyer and seller never met to bargain over price. Instead some remote and obscure mechanism set the terms independently of the will, sometimes of the very knowledge of the parties to the transaction. This market was coextensive with the wide world; increasingly fluctuations within it were determined by events in Liverpool, in Australia, in Russia. Prosperity and depression hinged not on the state of production in the neighborhood, but on remote occurrences in remote places. Like the forces of nature, therefore, the market was unpredictable, no more to be known or controlled by the individual than the weather. In the one case as in the other, the farmer could only be reconciled to his helplessness in the swing of such erratic gyrations.

After the Civil War, the sense of helplessness of these farmers grew deeper. With enormously expanded production came a more common use of machines. The scale of operations was larger also, and the size of the crops harvested. Efficiency and volume lowered costs and also prices so that no man could hold out against the trend. All farmers now produced for the same market, competed with each other, and had to match each other's costs. No one could afford not to maintain the pace of expanded production and mechanization. Yet for most agriculturists to do so meant to go into debt. Ominously, through the last decades of the nineteenth century, the amount of farm mortgages rose steadily, as did the percentage of farms operated by tenants.

No peasant could face the prospect of debt and of tenancy with equanimity. Debt and tenancy had been the wedge of ruin in the Old World. Those who had with such difficulty reached the soil again, those for whom the expectation of a further remove to a new frontier offered no consolation, were determined, at any cost, to avoid those fatal pitfalls here. The immigrants of necessity fell in with the commercial agriculture that existed about them. They yielded to the drive to produce staples. But they nevertheless sought anxiously to avoid the vicious cycle that plagued other farmers.

Those succeeded who held on at the expense of their own well-being and of that of their families. The only alternative to debt was not to spend, to buy only what could immediately be paid for, and to avoid capital involvements. Frugality became a fixed principle in the lives of those who wished to get by — except in one thing. Of his own labor the immigrant farmer was prodigal. To compete with the machines of others, he summoned into the fields wife and child; by their exertions and his own avoided any investment that might lead to indebtedness. The expense of survival was unrelenting toil.

The willingness without limit to dig their labor into the earth also accounted for the success of some immigrants in the specialized forms of truck farming. Latecoming Poles and Italians made a go on little hard patches of earth in the outskirts of the great cities, on abandoned holdings in New England and Long Island, on passed-by places in the West, not by virtue of any racial aptitude for these pursuits but by drudgery and self-sacrifice.

These people had come after the initial force of the American expansion in agriculture had spent itself. By their time, neither the Federal government nor the railroads were actively concerned with disposing of large tracts of land cheaply. The price of good farms had risen and continued to rise. It was more difficult than earlier to get to the West, to become established as a commercial farmer. Would-be agriculturists turned then instead to the vicinity of the great cities, found used-up bits of ground about to be surrendered as unprofitable. The newcomers took up the sterile neglected acres, achieved a miracle of redemption through ungrudging fertilization by their own labor.

Here was their only good fortune. The very cities from which these immigrants tore themselves away supplied a market that was the means of their salvation. By the closing decade of the nineteenth century, unbounded urban growth, the irresistible spread of new building, had crowded out the surviving little gardens. There was no longer room to raise at home the perishable foods that played an increasingly prominent part in American diet in those years. The nearby peasant who tended the familiar patches of potatoes and greens found eager purchasers for his produce. Let him but pour enough sweat into the ground and it would yield the fruits of success.

This too they learned who, in the same years, took the American fisheries out of the doldrums into which the Yankees had allowed them to drift.

The main thing was to get away. Those who never left the city found Herculean the task of pulling themselves up within it. For the rank and file of workers in manufacturing, there was almost no possibility of advancement; the organization of the mass-production industries in which they labored stood in their way. There was, in the factories, no hierarchy of skills through which the untrained could progress to ever-higher levels by developing proficiencies. On the contrary, the labor force was decisively divided into self-contained segments of managers, the skilled, and the unskilled. The unskilled had no opportunity for acquiring skill. Completely segregated from those who were more fortunate inside and outside the plant, often barred from the trade unions, they could hardly hope to advance their positions.

Of all the millions employed in industry or in casual labor

there were never more than a handful able to turn some skill or, more likely, some lucky contrivance to their advantage. A restless man like Conrad Huber, who had tried his hand in a cigar store, a restaurant, a boardinghouse, a farm, a milk wagon, could finally hit upon an invention (the flashlight) that would make him a place in manufacturing. But such achievements while individually impressive were insignificant in terms of the mass of immigrants.

A few more could climb by strategically putting to use the labor of their fellow countrymen. The fabrication of clothing, of gloves, of artificial flowers, and of tobacco called for large amounts of relatively unskilled labor, but for only a few simple machines and for very little capital. In these branches of manufacturing the characteristic mode of production was through home rather than through factory work. Intermediary between the plant of the prime producer and the tenements of the workers stood a series of middlemen, contractors who distributed the materials and collected the made-up goods, and in addition assumed the brunt of the difficult relationship with the sewers and stitchers. In the role of contractor the enterprising immigrant had the advantage of intimate acquaintance with the labor force; and through such services some Irishmen, Germans, Jews, and Italians could climb upward to the ranks of the manufacturers.

In other forms of enterprise too there were opportunities in contracting for the use of immigrant workers. Within the building and construction trades, the man who could get most out of his fellows could be foreman or boss or padrone. He could take on jobs on his own, become a person of substance. But he did so by climbing on the backs of those whose toil he managed.

A similar situation obtained in commerce. Newcomers could make a start in petty retailing if they drew support from their Old Countrymen by catering to their special needs. Lack of capital and ignorance of English and of business ways were less imposing obstacles if the aspiring businessman stocked the products others did not handle and if he dealt with the immigrants in the familiar forms of the old village market. The essential problem was to establish confidence, to avoid price comparisons. The shopkeeper extended credit, on the book, to those he knew; he bargained in the old manner, dropping a few cents on one article to make them up on another. He spoke to the women in their own language, made his establishment a neighborhood meeting place where gossip and advice passed with each purchase. Against those attractions, the competition of the chain stores was irrelevant.

On this basis, some immigrants became grocers; that trade was entirely with housewives and was conditioned by the persistent habits of particular diets. Restaurateurs and the purveyors of coffee and other liquors, hard and soft, also operated at an advantage; these services had a ceremonial social quality, best indulged in the company of countrymen. Businesses that involved contacts with the Old World were also open to the immigrants' talents. Did you wish to send a steamship ticket to a cousin or money to the old mother, then better to see the man who still knew the Old World, still spoke the old language, yet miraculously had acquired the skill to manipulate drafts and bills, to talk as an equal to the big companies. The notary's seal on his window was a token of government approval, his enterprise was open evenings and Sunday when the worker had time, and he spared you the need of difficult encounters with strangers in the great marble institutions in town. From the confidence of their compatriots such agents and brokers prospered — a few, enough so they could venture into full banking operations.

So, in their various fashions, immigrants became men of business, some to reach ultimate affluence, others to work all their days with effort and heartache, supporting miserable enterprises out of their bodies' spent energy. For all there was a period of hard beginnings, when they toiled long days in the pursuit of the first stake. The peddler's bag, the cart of goods, the uncertain heaped-up wagon, these were the starting points. Here, capital laboriously come at was first invested, added to with pain, and — in some cases — accumulated into the New World's success.

In the pursuit of this fleeting success, the peasant broke with his past. His constant task here was to transform income, no matter how small, into capital. Only with difficulty, if at all, did these people learn to do so who, at home, had conceived only of the land as property and had been accustomed to consuming all their income. To create capital in America meant a miserly scrimping at the expense of day-to-day consumption. It meant also a slighting of traditional obligations, the exploitation rather than the succor of neighbors.

It was, as a result, less often the conventional peasant who got ahead than an outsider not so limited by the peasant past. The most likely to gain by the new situation were the city folk who emigrated with the peasants and who spoke the same language, and such familiar strangers as the Jews who, even in the Old Country, had learned to reckon, to direct earnings toward a purpose.

For those who were themselves not successful the only hope was to transfer hope to the children, to trust that a second generation would find room where the first had not. Given the constant expansion of the American economy, it was not vain to think that the sons of the immigrants might enter the skilled trades, business, and the professions.

But for that hope there was also a cost. For success, whether at first hand or second, put a distance between the immigrant and the ideals of his former life. One way or another he probed this consequence of separation from Europe: that to live in the old way was to court failure and hardship, while success brought the pangs of unsettled, unrooted values.

FOUR

New Worlds, New Visions

OFTEN, THEY WOULD TRY to understand. They would think about it in the pauses of their work, speculate sometimes as their minds wandered, tired, at the close of a long day.

What had cut short the continuous past, severed it from the unrelated present? Immigration had transformed the entire economic world within which the peasants had formerly lived. From surface forms to inmost functionings, the change was complete. A new setting, new activities, and new meanings forced the newcomers into radically new roles as producers and consumers of goods. In the process, they became, in their own eyes, less worthy as men. They felt a sense of degradation that raised a most insistent question: Why had this happened?

More troubling, the change was not confined to economic matters. The whole American universe was different. Strangers, the immigrants could not locate themselves; they had lost the polestar that gave them their bearings. They would not regain an awareness of direction until they could visualize themselves in their new context, see a picture of the world as it appeared from this perspective. At home, in the wide frame of the village, their eyes had taken in the whole of life, had brought to their perceptions a clearly defined view of the universe. Here the frame narrowed down, seemed to reveal only fragmentary distorted glimpses that were hardly reminiscent of the old outlines.

The peasants brought with them from their life on the soil the preconceptions and basic assumptions that had controlled their attitudes and influenced their actions. Before emigration they had lived in intimate contact with nature, never much removed from the presence of the objects of the physical universe. All around were things not made by men's hands, things that coexisted with men. Between these things and men there were differences. But they were also held together by the most powerful ligatures, for the universe was not made up of entirely disparate, disconnected objects but of elements which varied only imperceptibly from each other. Men and things were alike subject to natural processes, alike responsive to the same moving forces.

Everything the peasant saw about him was, like himself, a being. All the objects of nature, of whatever shape or form or substance, were literally animated, perhaps to greater or lesser degrees, but all were essentially capable of life and growth. All were God's creatures, man and the beasts too, and also the trees, the meadows, the stars, the sun, fire and water, the days of the week and the seasons of the year. Yes, even clods and stones had being.

In all these entities, the characteristics of animation were the same as those among men. All had individuality. So, the animals of the barnyard had each his own name, and those of field and forest — not so intimately known — were represented by imaginary titled heads of their species. Trees, rocks, springs, had also each its appellation, and every day of the year its own designation from the saint or festival that gave it its quality.

With the name went the ascription of personality: each being had character, had the capacity for action, had some degree of volition. All the objects of nature, being animate, had understanding enough to react meaningfully to conditions about them. They had a kind of intelligence which, while different from man's, was not necessarily inferior. In fact, other beings knew things humans did not know: birds and beasts could foretell changes in the weather; at the approach of danger, geese would fall a-clamoring in the enclosures, dogs run nervously about. Animals even had a sense to judge bad action; for instance, bees, it was said, would not stay with a thief.

It was incumbent upon men, dealing with these beings, to be careful, to stay on good terms with them, to give them their due lest they retaliate. Each day thus had its own character and, if not respected, would return after a year to exact vengeance. A violated tree, or one not properly bound with straw, would bear no fruit; neglected land would yield no grain; the mistreated cow would give no milk; an unclean fire would go out. Accidental injuries to these beings, when they occurred, had to be explained and the victims appeased if possible. The utmost caution was worth while, for those who won them over could use the foresight of animals to good advantage. So, the friendly birds, if only rightly understood, could with certainty give the sign for the best time for sowing.

Among all natural beings there existed also the relationship of solidarity. All were so connected with each other that what happened to any one affected every other. If the birds flew away to the woods, then the snow would soon decide to fall. If the sparrows were permitted to eat cherries in the summer that would help the grain to thrive. Such attributes as richness and the capacity for growth were therefore transferable and fecundity could be bestowed by one object on another. The peasant rubbed fertile soil onto his cow to be sure she would bear often.

There were also special kinds of solidarity within species of things. All animals were particularly related and, when danger threatened, warned each other, at times indeed could speak among themselves. There was a more intimate relationship within each class of animals; the cows lowing softly to one another had their own secrets. This was the identical solidarity that men felt for other men. Did not the peasants' lives revolve about their membership in a natural community that cared for them?

To whatever degree it was general, solidarity among all beings sprang from the common situation in which they found themselves. All the objects of nature were engaged in growth. They participated thereby in the same struggle against decay. The solidarity among them was the inner recognition that man and beast, plant and living soil, in some measure fought the same battle. A breach of solidarity was treachery in the face of the enemy of all and merited the severest punishment. To cut down a fruit tree, to kill a stork, to waste, was a hideous disruption of the order of nature, an invitation to calamitous retaliation.

A sacrifice was justified only when it involved a lesser retreat before decay in the interests of greater growth. Thus it was proper to clear trees in order to bring new lands under cultivation; increased production would expiate the destruction. So, also, animals gave up their lives, willingly as it were, to the end that men might eat. But even in such legitimate instances, it was best to be cautious, to act according to appropriate forms. Special rites to ward off unfavorable consequences accompanied the slaughter or any other measure that might involve some hidden breach of solidarity.

If man had to proceed warily in encounters with the world of natural objects, he was compelled to be doubly careful when it came to the mysterious realm of unnatural beings that also existed about him. This realm was not continuous with his own world. It was a dread level of being, inhabited by spirits of many kinds that took many shapes. Fairies, elves, leprechauns might perhaps be visualized, though not reliably; but no mind could conceive of the variety of forms that might be assumed by vampires, specters, souls adrift on earth or released for some special end from hell or purgatory. These beings could enter the natural world, but there was no solidarity between them and the objects of nature.

The affairs of the spirits were ever a source of concern to the peasant. They had powers beyond those of the poor human and could interfere when they liked with his own affairs — sometimes beneficently assisting him, sometimes through malice or mischief bringing utter ruin down upon the unfortunate victim who had offended them. Their imminent presence called for constant caution. They might do no more than make trouble with their pranks; or they might possess the bodies of people and animals; or they might betray men into disastrous temptations. They added an awesome dimension to a universe already terrifyingly vast. Among so many hazardous forces, the peasant had to walk carefully, be constantly alert to the presence of all the elements about him.

The safest way was to know the hidden causal connections among objects and events. Such knowledge gave some persons a measure of control over the activities of the beings about them. Command of magic — that is, of the certain ways, of the certain words, of the certain rites — would appease or neutralize hostile forces, enlist the support of friendly ones. That would give the peasant security.

Only, where was that knowledge found? The wily ones who had it would not share for nothing. In the stress of great need there was no choice but to seek out the witch or wizard who could converse with their familiar spirits. Yet everyone knew what frightful bargains were exacted for such assistance.

It was much safer, when each decision could have incalculable consequences, to follow the traditional time-proven patterns. One could seek guidance from the special vision of pilgrims, seers, and idiots. But the most certain advice came from the wise old ones who knew from the experience of the past what ways were the most reliable. Safety lay in adherence to routines that had been effective before; new actions were doomed to dangerous failure. When all was said and done, all things had their given course, and would follow that course.

Yes, all things follow their course. *We sow to reap, and reap to sow again. And grow to die.* Childhood, youth, maturity, old age, death, come each like the seasons in their destined order. In this endless rotation is the meaning of growth.

Ponder the matter as the face of the earth changes, as the signs of living life give way to the dead emptiness of winter. This season, in its occurrence and recurrence, marks the end and start of the peasant year. This is the time of death and the period antecedent to new births.

A dulling chill creeps across the poorly protected country-side; frequent blasts rip the frozen branches from the trees. In northern places, the still snow hides the land. Everywhere, shortening days give notice of the change in all time. Briefly the peasants hurry out while the sun still shines to perform the necessary tasks, then back to the cold interior.

Within, the precious light is brief. Long dusks sink over the silent village. The open fire or ever-burning gleaming stove throws strange shadows over rooms suddenly become unfamiliar. Later, little islands of brightness around the sput-tering pine knot, the candle, or lamp, give the place a new appearance. Outside is the unknown silence broken by mys-terious creakings, by the rustle of beasts, by sounds whose meaning no man knows.

The few indoor tasks are done and it is not yet the time when sleep will come. The old ones retell the stories that all their listeners know; and reverie sinks down over men's minds. Questions come.

Of what did the peasants think day after day in the winter? Not in those exceptional hours when sudden storms shook the hut and drove the icy cold through its creviced walls; not in the desperate last weeks when stored-up stocks ran low, and hunger waited at the door, but day after day — what did they think in the long cold stillness?

As all living things receded before the winter, their minds turned to the mystery of life which was death. Indeed what was that daily round of deeds of theirs, so dull, so squalid? Like the beasts of burden beneath the yoke they were, caring only for the present task, cut off always by the tedious darkness from the sight of the marvels, of the hidden prodigies beyond their range of vision. Then indeed there was a yearning towards a life uniting all things — fancy and reality, a dream existence for which, under the miserable conditions of their earthly days, their weary hearts insatiably longed.

Strange things happened in the long dead night of winter as men reviewed their lives, remembered. On All Souls' Day there welled up in every heart a pervasive sense of desolation, a distressed silent recollection of those gone to lie beneath the drooping trees and looming crosses of the churchyard, the home of the dead. From place to place, the rites that marked the day were different. But everywhere men felt renewed the consciousness of utter helplessness. Were they more than little twigs, blown about they knew not where in the vastness of the great universe?

Winter confronted the peasants with death in all its hated, feared, despised features. It was as if all the emotions brought forth at a funeral were stretched out, attenuated, prolonged for the season — the sense of irreparable loss, the desolate thoughts of their own inevitable fate. All hopes and joys were vain. They were themselves like stray clouds, drifted from the unknown, destined for the unknown, and moved by unknown impulses.

To what purpose then did men live?

To those who awaited its coming in eagerness and expectation, spring brought back the signs of life. The sun resumed its blessed mastery over the land. The warmth returned and the light played again on walls whitened, or at least cleaned, for the Easter.

In the fields the grain rises again. Again the leaves break forth. These are not the grain and leaves of last year. The new is not the old. Yet the new and the old are related. They are related by the death of the old which was necessary for the birth of new.

Is it not so with men who live to die, and die so that those who come will later live? In dying they do not end, any more than does the cut grain or fallen leaf. All live on, regenerated — in generation after generation.

What is the religion of the men who live through winter and spring? It is the affirmation that life is victorious over death. Though the trees stand bare in winter, yet will they be clothed in spring with green leaves and sweet-scented blossoms. Though a man's life be sown with labor, with hardship, with blood, a crop will come of it, a harvest be reaped.

That affirmation was the peasant's faith, his own explanation of his place in the universe. But overlaid on this natural religion was one taught by the priests, a religion that stemmed from outside the village, from the monasteries, the towns, the nobility. By now Christianity was well-established, in some regions for more than a thousand years. Yet it had by no means destroyed the older order of beliefs. The magical practices and the ideas they embodied held on even in places where the Church made an effort to fight them. And more often than not, the priest was himself rooted in the village and was content to allow the peasants to identify their own notions with elements of Christian doctrine, to effect a practical if not a dogmatic reconciliation.

Christianity did add to the earlier peasant ideas a conception of sin and the faith in a supernatural redemption. The distinction between good and evil he heard reiterated from the pulpit the peasant identified with his own distinction between helpful and harmful forces. In the galaxy of spirits, the peasant found a place for the devil and his imps, operating for their own hellish purposes. To resist their designs he learned to call upon an army of saints, each with its own province and potency. In these terms, he came to think of the world as the field of battle between two spiritual communities, the divine and the demoniacal, which struggled for the soul of man.

The burden of choice, already heavy, thus became heavier. Any act now might be wrong not only in the sense that it could bring on hostile consequences, but also in the sense that it might partake of evil. A bad decision was induced by spirits who were unfriendly and also devilish, was damaging and also sinful. Man bore the weight not simply of his mistakes but of his guilt also. His lot was to suffer and, as well, to expiate.

Yet to him, in his troubled state, Christianity brought also the miracle of redemption. Poor thing that he was, his soul was yet a matter of consequence. For him the whole drama of salvation had been enacted: God had come to earth, had suffered as a man to make for all men a place in a life everlasting. Through that sacrifice had been created a community of all those who had faith, a kind of solidarity that would redress all grievances and right all wrongs, if not now, then in the far more important aftermath to life.

Therefore it is well to look not to the present but to the eternal future, not to this world in which there is nothing but trouble and woe but to the next in which will come ease and consolation. Here evil increases and multiplies like the thistles in the woods. Here all things are vain and to no purpose like the bubbles which the wind tosses up on the surface of the waters. Yet let our souls but fly to Jesus as the birds fly south in winter and they will find comfort and joy and an end to all sorrow.

And in those moments of meditation when the comfort comes, we know this hope is not merely a delusion personal to us. The evidence is in the visible community which together participates in the mystery of salvation. Within the divine universe is this village, and within this village we men. This is our reassurance; thus we know where we are in the world.

These were the contents with which the hearts and minds of the peasants were laden as they came to the New World. This was the stock of ideas on which they drew when they came to account for their situation in America, once they had arrived and were at work and the work they did seemed not fit work for a man. Now there would be new questions. Would the old answers do when these people tried to explain what had happened to them?

They found it difficult, of course, to reconstruct a coherent record out of the excess of their experience since they had left the village. Many impressions remained fragmentary, unrelated to any whole adjustment.

This they knew, though, and could not mistake it: they were lonely. In the midst of teeming cities, in the crowded tenements and the factories full of bustling men, they were lonely.

Their loneliness had more than one dimension.

It had the breadth of unfamiliarity. Strange people walked about them; strange sounds assailed their inattentive ears. Hard pavements cut them off from nature in all its accustomed manifestations. Look how far they could, at the end of no street was a familiar horizon. Hemmed in by the tall buildings, they were fenced off from the realm of growing things. They had lost the world they knew of beasts and birds, of blades of grass, of sprays of idle flowers. They had acquired instead surroundings of a most outlandish aspect. That unfamiliarity was one aspect of their loneliness.

Loneliness had also the painful depth of isolation. The man who once had been surrounded with individual beings was here cast adrift in a life empty of all but impersonal things. In the Old Country, this house in this village, these fields by these trees, had had a character and identity of their own. They had testified to the peasant's *I*, had fixed his place in the visible universe. The church, the shrine, the graveyard and the generations that inhabited it had also had their personality, had also testified to the peasant's *I*, and had fixed his place in a larger invisible universe.

In the new country, all these were gone; that was hard enough. Harder still was the fact that nothing replaced them. In America, the peasant was a transient without meaningful connections in time and space. He lived now with inanimate objects, cut off from his surroundings. His dwelling and his place of work had no relationship to him as a man. The scores of established routines that went with a life of the soil had disappeared and with them the sense of being one of a company. Therefore the peasant felt isolated and isolation added to his loneliness.

Strangeness and isolation oppressed even those who returned to the soil. They too were lonely. Everywhere, great wastes of empty land dissevered the single farm from the rest of the world. Wrapped up in the unfamiliar landscapes of prairie distance or forest solitude, the peasants found nowhere an equivalent of the village, nowhere the basis for reestablishing the solidarity of the old communal life. Therefore they were each alone, in city and in country, for that of which they had been a part was no longer about them.

The shattering loneliness disrupted the communion of persons and places and events. This was difficult enough for those who found agriculture their calling; the change of scene upset the traditional calendar, falsified the traditional signs of nature that paced the year's activities. But that destroyed communion was more difficult still in the urban places. In the cities, the seasons lost entirely their relevance. For the worker, winter and spring were very much alike; whether he worked and how he worked had nothing to do, as it had at home, with the passing cycle of the year.

If the outward aspects were the same — the falling snow or warm summer wind — that only made more poignant the sense of lost significance. And they never were long the same; tinged with soot, the virgin snow at once acquired the pavement's gray, or the dull wind dragged the smell of city heat through confining streets. So it was with the noteworthy days. Formal observances persisted for a time; the villagers longingly went through the motions, celebrated saints' days, mourned at the time of memories. But snatched out of context these occasions had not the old flavor. Self-conscious under the gaze of strangers, the peasants could no longer find the old meanings. For all peasants, and particularly for those dominated by the mechanical monotony of factory or construction labor, their loneliness entailed also the desolating loss of the precious sense of solidarity. Without that, was there any purpose left to life.

Was it not true, did not your whole experience teach you the futility of striving? *What needs must be no man can flee!* How helpless were humans before the forces arrayed against them! Of what value were calculations? In the Old Country, at least, you could take care, do what was necessary in the proper way at the proper time, follow experience and use the knowledge of generations. Even so, your very emigration is evidence of the slight value of all precautions. Search back over your lifetime. Think: have you reason to believe that wiser decisions on your part could have stayed the famines, put off the displacements? And how much deeper is your helplessness now than then; now you cannot even recognize the proper ways.

Every element of the immigrants' experience since the day they had left home added to this awareness of their utter helplessness. All the incidents of the journey were bound up with chance. What was the road to follow, what the ship to board, what port to make? These were serious questions. But who knew which were the right answers? Whether they survived the hazards of the voyage, and in what condition, these too were decisions beyond the control of the men who participated in it. The capricious world of the crossing pointed its own conclusion as to the role of chance in the larger universe into which the immigrants plunged.

It was the same with their lives after landing. To find a job or not, to hold it or to be fired, in these matters laborers' wills were of slight importance. Inscrutable, distant persons determined matters on the basis of remote, unknown conditions. The most fortunate of immigrants, the farmers, knew well what little power they had to influence the state of the climate, the yield of the earth, or the fluctuations of the market, all the elements that determined their lot. Success or failure, incomprehensible in terms of peasant values, seemed altogether fortuitous. Time and again, the analogy occurred to them: man was helpless like the driven cog in a great machine.

Loneliness, separation from the community of the village, and despair at the insignificance of their own human abilities, these were the elements that, in America, colored the peasants' view of their world. From the depths of a dark pessimism, they looked up at a frustrating universe ruled by haphazard, capricious forces. Without the capacity to control or influence these forces men could but rarely gratify their hopes or wills. Their most passionate desires were doomed to failure; their lives were those of the feeble little birds which hawks attack, which lose strength from want of food, and which, at last surrendering to the savage blasts of the careless elements, flutter unnoticed to the waiting earth.

Sadness was the tone of life, and death and disaster no strangers. Outsiders would not understand the familiarity with death who had not daily met it in the close quarters of the steerage; nor would they comprehend the riotous Paddy funerals who had no insight of the release death brought. The end of life was an end to hopeless striving, to ceaseless pain, and to the endless succession of disappointments. There was a leaden grief for the ones who went; yet the tomb was only the final parting in a long series of separations that had started back at the village crossroads.

In this world man can only be resigned. Illness takes a child away; from the shaft they bring a father's crippled body; sudden fire eats up a block of flimsy shanties, leaves half of each family living. There is no energy for prolonged mourning. Things are as they are and must remain so. Resist not but submit to fortune and seek safety by holding on.

In this world the notion of improvement is delusive. The best hope is that matters grow not worse. Therefore it is desirable to stand against change, to keep things as they are; the risks involved in change are incomparably more formidable than those involved in stability. There is not now less poverty, less misery, less torture, less pain than formerly. Indeed, today's evils, by their nearness, are far more oppressive than yesterday's which, after all, were somehow survived. Yesterday, by its distance, acquires a happy glow. The peasants look back (they remember they lived through yesterday; who knows if they will live through today?) and their fancy rejoices in the better days that have passed, when they were on the land and the land was fertile, and they were young and strong, and virtues were fresh. And it was better yet in their fathers' days, who were wiser and stronger than they. And it was best of all in the golden past of their distant progenitors who were every one a king and did great deeds. Alas, those days are gone, that they believed existed, and now there is only the bitter present.

In this world then, as in the Old Country, the safest way was to look back to tradition as a guide. Lacking confidence in the individual's capacity for independent inquiry, the peasants preferred to rely upon the tested knowledge of the past. It was difficult of course to apply village experience to life in America, to stretch the ancient aphorisms so they would fit new conditions. Yet that strain led not to a rejection of tradition but rather to an eager quest for a reliable interpreter. Significantly, the peasants sought to acknowledge an authority that would make that interpretation for them.

Their view of the American world led these immigrants to conservatism, and to the acceptance of tradition and authority. Those traits in turn shaped the immigrants' view of society, encouraged them to retain the peasants' regard for status and the divisions of rank. In these matters too striving was futile; it was wiser to keep each to his own station in the social order, to respect the rights of others and to exact the obligations due. For most of these people that course involved the acceptance of an inferior position. But was that not altogether realistic? The wind always blew in the face of the poor; and it was in the nature of society that some should have an abundance of possessions and others only the air they breathed.

The whole configuration of the peasant's ideas in the United States strengthened the place in his life of the established religion he brought with him. It was not only an institutional reluctance to change that held him to his faith, but also the greater need that faith satisfied in the New World.

Emigration had broken the ties with nature. The old stories still evoked emotional responses in their hearers; and the housewives still uttered imprecations and blessings and magic words to guard against the evil eye. But it was hard to believe that the whole world of spirits and demons had abandoned their familiar homes and come also across the Atlantic. It was hard too to continue to think in terms of the natural cycle of growth, of birth, death, and regeneration, away from the setting in which it was every day illustrated in peasant life.

Instead these immigrants found their Christianity ever more meaningful. Here they discovered the significance of their suffering. It was true, what the priest said, that evil was everywhere present in the world; they had themselves experienced the evidence of it. It was true they were imperfect and full of sin, not worthy of a better lot. What they tried bore no results. What they touched turned to dust.

Still all this toil and trouble was not without purpose. What seemed on the surface like the rule of chance in the world was not really so, but part of a plan. The whole of it was not yet revealed, man could not see the end, only the start, because this was not an earthly plan. Rather it extended far beyond this immediate existence and would reach its culmination in an altogether different life that came after the release of death.

Fixing his vision on that life eternal which would follow this, the peasant perceived that caprice in mundane things was an element in an ordered design. If injustice now seemed to triumph, then it was only that retribution should come after. Did the evil flourish, then would they be punished. Were the good oppressed and humiliated, it was to make their rewards the richer. This he knew was the mystery and the reason for his being in the universe.

As he participated in that other mystery of the divine sacrifice that assured him salvation, all the scattered elements of his existence became whole. Let him but have faith enough in the God Who had gone to the cross, for him; Who had come over the water, with him; and he would be repaid for the loss of his home, for the miseries of the way, and for the harshness of his present life. Not indeed in this world, but in an everlasting future. For the lonely and isolated, for the meek and humble, for the strangers, there was hope of a sort, and consolation.

The migration to America had destroyed the context of the peasants' natural religion. Yet the resigned passivity with which they once had faced the endless round of births, deaths, and regenerations had lived on into the New World. The circumstances of their coming, alone and among foreigners, had perpetuated that sense of helplessness, had driven into the texture of their Christianity an otherworldly fatalism.

Never would they understand how this had happened or even that it had happened. They were never capable of contrasting their own situation with that of those other uprooted ones who remained in the Old World. Not all who left the village had gone to America; and the ideological development of those whose remove was to some other place in their own country took a distinctive turn of its own.

In England, for instance, the peasants displaced by the eighteenth-century revolutions in agriculture had drifted often into the growing industrial cities where they encountered circumstances as trying as those that met the transatlantic immigrants. In England too the migrants became an exploited proletariat; and their intellectual adjustment, in some respects, was analogous to that of the peasants in the United States. In England too could be seen the pessimistic reflections of a miserable life, the conservatism that grew out of resistance to inexorable changes, and the continued willingness to accept authority and to recognize status.

But there was also a significant difference. The peasants who came to America brought with them their established churches to be re-established in new communities in the New World. They transferred their faith intact and rarely were tempted to deviate from it; their foreignness alone sufficed to keep them out of the native American denominations. The peasants who migrated within England, however, did not bring their own churches with them. In London and in the rising manufacturing towns there were some churches of the established religion, of course. But they were not peasant churches; were the poor newcomers to crowd in among the pews of the well-dressed city folk, they would hardly feel at home. Those who did not remain entirely unchurched were more likely to resort to the humble chapels of the dissenters, where all benches were alike. They would be less strangers there than in the elegant edifices of the urban parishes.

A like development occurred in parts of Germany where a number of pietistic sects in the disturbed areas of the southwest weaned away some of the peasants at the end of the eighteenth century and early in the nineteenth. In Scandinavia there were similar inroads, by Methodists in Sweden, by Haugeans in Norway.

His situation made the dissenter a protester. Standing outside the established church he had to account for his difference. Incapable of justifying his affiliation by the universality of his group, he could only justify it by its particularity. This was a small group, but a select one, a group into which members were not born but into which they came. These were chosen people, people who bore a mission that demanded they be different.

Redemption for the dissenter was not the simple reward of faith; it was the product of achievement of a mission. Not resignation but a striving toward improvement was the way; and life on earth was not merely an entry into the afterlife but an opportunity by which man could demonstrate what he could make of himself. This world was therefore a place of intrinsic significance and humans had power by their wills to control their fates within it.

These people had not found their adjustment to the disruption of the old village life complicated by the transfer to a New World, a transfer so frightening that those involved in it could not venture to think outside the terms of their peasant heritage.

Sometimes the dissenting peasants, already displaced, made a second move; or more often their children did. Their American experience would then be not like that of the peasants who had come directly, but more like that of other dissenters who had never been peasants. Among the artisans and traders gathered up in the general stream of migration were several groups that had never been members of an established church, never shared fully the village views.

In that sense, the extreme of dissent, because they were altogether outside the Christian community, were the Jews. Although they had lived in close contact with the peasants for hundreds of years, they had remained apart, strangers in the society. Although the contact between the village and the Jewry was always close, often intimate, the separateness of the two persisted. Among the Jews too the role of dissenter in the midst of a solidary community evoked the consciousness that they were a chosen people, that they had a unique destiny and mission, and that the world was a field in which they could profitably labor toward improvement.

The difference that already marked the dissenters off from the peasants in advance of emigration was deepened by the experience of settlement in the United States. The dissenters had always occupied an abnormal place in peasant society; they had been the outsiders who did not belong. In America they found their position the only normal one; here, there was no established church, no solidary community; everyone to some degree was an outsider. Since the dissenters had often larger resources of capital and skill than the peasants and were more fortunate in their economic adjustment, the impact of immigration was often stimulating. They could come to identify America with their New Canaan and interpret their mission in terms of an American success.

Yet even these people were immigrants and bore with the peasant the marks of their migration. No matter how fortunate their lot, they had lost an old home and had suffered the pains of fitting themselves to a new environment. There was no danger any immigrants would grow complacent about their settlement or forget their strangeness. They had only, any of them, to think of what ideas were held by Americans longer in the land to know what a cleavage there yet was between the old and new comers. Confronted with the prevalent notions of the inevitability of progress, of the essential goodness of man and his capacity to rule his own life, of the optimistic desirability of change, peasants and dissenters alike felt a chill distrust, a determination to resist, a threat to their own ideas.

That determination was expressed in their criticism of the deficiencies of life in the United States. To the immigrants America seemed unstable; it lacked the orderly elements of existence. Without security of status or the recognition of rank, no man, no family, had a proper place in the social order. Only money talked, for Americans measured all things in terms of gold and invariably preferred the superficial and immediate to the permanent and substantial.

These reactions reflected the urge to strengthen old values and to reaffirm old ideals. Precisely because migration had subjected those to attack, it was necessary aggressively to defend them, to tolerate no change because any change might have the most threatening consequences. In that sense all immigrants were conservatives, dissenters and peasants alike. All would seek to set their ideas within a fortification of religious and cultural institutions that would keep them sound against the strange New World.

FIVE

Religion as a Way of Life

A MAN HOLDS DEAR what little is left. When much is lost, there is no risking the remainder.

As his stable place in a whole universe slipped away from under him, the peasant come to America grasped convulsively at the familiar supports, pulled along with him the traditional bulwarks of his security. He did not learn until later that, wrenched out of context, these would no longer bear the weight of his needs.

Even in the Old World, these men's thoughts had led ineluctably to God. In the New, they were as certain to do so. The very process of adjusting immigrant ideas to the conditions of the United States made religion paramount as a way of life. When the natural world, the former context of the peasant ideas, faded behind the transatlantic horizon, the newcomers found themselves stripped to those religious institutions they could bring along with them. Well, the trolls and fairies will stay behind, but church and priest at very least will come.

The more thorough the separation from the other aspects of the old life, the greater was the hold of the religion that alone survived the transfer. Struggling against heavy odds to save something of the old ways, the immigrants directed into their faith the whole weight of their longing to be connected with the past.

As peasants at home, awed by the hazardous nature of the universe and by their own helplessness, these people had fled to religion as a refuge from the anguish of the world. Their view of their own lives had generated a body of conceptions and of practices that intimately expressed their inmost emotions. It was not only that they held certain theological doctrines; but their beliefs were most closely enwrapped in the day-to-day events of their existence. The specific acts of being religious were the regular incidents of the village year. Their coming needed no forethought, indeed no consciousness. Their regularity was an aspect of the total order of the village. That was a feature of their attractiveness.

The peasants found also attractive the outward aspects of their religious institutions. The very formality of structure and organization had a meaning of consequence to them. They were all communicants of established churches, whether Roman Catholic, Lutheran, Anglican, or Orthodox. In some lands, where the monarch professed the same faith, to be "established" meant that the Church and State were closely united. That was true in Italy, Germany, Scandinavia, England, and Russia. But that link was not the essential element in establishment which also existed in countries such as Poland and Ireland, where Catholic peasants lived under non-Catholic rulers.

Recognition by the government and special treatment in law were only the surface indications of a deeper significance. To the peasants, establishment meant that their religion held a fixed, well-defined place in their society, that it was identified with the village, that it took in all those who belonged, all those who were not outcasts. Establishment in that sense gave these people a reassuring conviction that they belonged, were parts of a whole, insiders not outsiders.

The other attributes of establishment were appropriate

also. About these churches was no confusing cloud of uncertainty. Their claim to men's allegiance rested on a solid basis of authority. It was not an individual choice that was involved in the process of belonging, but conformity. So, everyone else did. So it had been done year before year, generation before generation, as far back as the peasant could reckon . . . ever. The very rights and privileges of the Church, its lands and possessions, were evidence of its legitimacy and longevity. It was unthinkable not to be a member; it demanded a considerable feat of the imagination to conceive of what it would mean to be excluded, to draw down the censure of the entire community, to be barred from every social occasion.

There was no need to argue about these matters, to weigh alternatives, to consider. The Church gave no reasons for being; it was. Its communicants were within it not because they had rationally accepted its doctrines; they had faith because they were in it. Explanation in terms of reasonable propositions was superfluous; the Church was accepted as a mystery, which called for no explanation. These peasants felt the attractiveness of the demand on their faith as of the demand on their obedience to authority. Such, their own ideas had led them to believe, were the sources of certainty.

Village religion was, as a matter of course, conservative. Peasants and priests alike resisted change. They valued in the Church its placid conviction of eternal and universal sameness, of continuity through the ages, of catholicity through Christendom. The very practices that stirred them now reached back to the earliest times. Here and in precisely this manner, generations of untold ancestors had worshiped. Dimly over the gap of years, fathers and sons engaged in a common communion, assured by the permanence of forms.

The peasants were certain of the fixity of their church in space as well as in time. This priest who ministered to them in this parish was not an isolated individual but one who had an established place in a great hierarchical structure that extended through society. Above the priest was a sequence of other dignitaries rising to loftier and loftier eminence to the one supereminent above all, pope or patriarch, king or emperor. When the retinue of the bishop pranced through the village, when that personage himeslf appeared attired in all the magnificence of his vestiture, when his distant countenance framed in the miter of his majesty looked down on the assembled community, then the people humbly in his presence were elevated through the dignity of his own imposing power. He had ordained the priest, stood guarantor of the efficacy of the parish rites, brought the village into communion with the whole world of true believers, made the peasant certain there was order in the Church and security of place for each soul within it.

Yet the grandeur of religion did not leave it aloof from its communicants. Splendid though it was in appearance, extensive and powerful in its compass, it was still close to the life of each man. The hierarchy that reached up to the most exalted also reached down to the most humble.

The Church was familiar to the peasants' day-to-day existence. Its outward forms and ceremonies were established in the round of the year. By long usage, each festival had a seasonal connotation through which, in the same celebration, were commingled the meanings of the distant Christian event and of the proximate changes in the immediate world of nature. All the acts of worship were embedded in a setting of which the landscape, the weather, and the sight of the heavens all were aspects. Each holiday thus had substance and individuality, a whole and entire character of its own. Its coming filled the whole place and the whole day, spread out from the church through the road where the procession passed to the blessed field around, extended on from the early service at the altar to the feast and the accompanying jubilation. Each occasion was thus local to the particular village, the possession of each participant, a part of his way of life.

This the peasants had in mind when they hoped, most eagerly, to re-establish their religion in the New World.

It was not only the attractiveness of such elements of form that moved the immigrants to reconstruct their churches in America; it was also the substance embraced in those forms. These people were anxious that religion do and mean in the United States all that it had back there before the Atlantic crossing. At home, worship had brought to the worshiper a pleasure that was aesthetic in nature. If in the new land he had the occasion, which he had rarely had in the old, to talk about the quality of that satisfaction, the peasant put the words of his description around specific impressions of the service — the stately manners, the inspiring liturgy, the magnificent furnishing. But such descriptions he knew were inadequate; for beyond the beauty that adhered to these things in their own right was a beauty of essence that grew out of their relationship to his own experience as a human being. Lacking the habit of introspection, the peasant could not set words to that satisfaction. He could only feel the lack of it.

How comforting were the ceremonial movements of the priest and how stirring his sermon — not at all a bickering argument but a be-gestured incantation! Here was not so much an effort to persuade man to be good as a reminder that he was bad, in effect magically to cleanse him. Indeed, magical qualities inhered in all the acts of worship. Touching on sin and the remission of sin, on evil and the warding-off of evil, these practices made sense in terms of peasant ideas.

In the rite before his eyes, the man could see that the world in which he lived was not whole, did not of itself justify itself. No. This was merely a dreary vestibule through which the Christian entered the life eternal that lay beyond the door of death. Long and narrow was the passage and bitter dark. With utmost striving was the crossing made, and little joy was in it. But there was a goal, and there would be an arrival. The bells that tolled at the culmination of each service would toll also at each soul's release, when the hard journey, over, would lead to its own compensation for the troubles of the way.

The promise of life to come, and the meaning of the life of the present, was consolation. At that expected future, retribution, rewarded good and punished evil, would make whole the order of mundane things, explain the lapses of justice, the incongruity of achievements, the neglect of merit in the existence of the peasant. To the congregation, devoutly silent under the plaster images, the monotonous chant affirmed over and over that the perspective of eternity would correct all the disturbing distortions in the perspective of today.

Faith brought the affirmation that man, though the creature of chance that appearances made him to be, was also actor in the great drama that had begun with the miracle of creation and would end in the miracle of redemption. For him, God had come to earth, had suffered, and had sacrificed Himself to save all humanity. That sacrifice, repeated at every mass, was the visible assurance of meaning in the universe.

The same sacrifice transfigured the communicants who shared the mystery. Wafers and wine, blood and flesh, united them in the togetherness of their common experience. Not only they within the village, but through the village to the uncounted numbers elsewhere, to their own ancestors in the churchyard who had also once shared, still shared. In the salving rite of Communion, there mingled with the satisfaction of the act itself the sentiments of village loyalty, the emotions of family love, and the awareness of fulfillment of the ideal of solidarity.

If the peasants made a way of life of the establishment of their religion, so those who were not peasants made a way of life of their dissent.

The dissenting churches made no claims to universality,

could imbue their members with no general sense of belonging, indeed left them with the consciousness of being outsiders. But, as outsiders, the Jews or Quakers or Baptists had to cherish the differences which were the marks of their election. Such sects could not take their membership for granted; they had to stress a continuing process of conversion and dedication, whether that be intellectually or emotionally arrived at. Out of the desire to protect their distinctive differences from obliteration in societies so much oriented around the peasant and out of the need to lend dignity to the process of conversion, these groups had also achieved an order of holidays, a formality of services, and a rigid mode of observances that, together, constituted a way of life.

Religion for these people was not as much tied to a locality as for the peasants. The appearance of things played not so prominent a role in the dissenting as in the established churches. Chapel and synagogue by their nature were not so likely to make a visual appeal, and rite was not so conspicuous in their practices. The congregations were more likely to be attached to the evidences of their own participation in worship as individuals — how they sang this psalm or offered up this prayer. For these evidences reminded them of their own consciousness of community as a group; and though they were a community of noncommunicant outsiders, still that consciousness was precious to them, worthy of preservation wherever they were.

Become immigrants and arrived in America, peasants and dissenters therefore alike struggled to reconstruct their churches. In the manner of doing, there were differences among the various groups. But the problem of all was the same: how to transplant a way of religious life to a new environment.

The immigrants began with the determination that their emigration would not destroy the ties that bound them to the church. For years they kept alive a connection with the Old

Country parish. Letters from the other side brought news of the place and the people; letters from this side brought gifts to embellish the building, and, sometimes, requests for counsel from the priest.

But the immigrants thought it more important still to bring their churches to the United States, to reconstitute in their new homes the old forms of worship. At heavy cost and despite imposing obstacles, they endeavored to do so. Often when a phase of the struggle was over — say, a new edifice dedicated — they would look back with relief and surprise at the height of the difficulties surmounted.

The conditions of emigration and the hardships of the crossing were immediate sources of confusion. On the way, in the ships, the terrible disorder made troublesome any ritual observance. The prolonged lapse of unsettled time obscured the calendar; on the move, no day was individual from any other. Without the ministrations of a priest, without the sustenance of a whole community, the worshiper was limited to his own humble resources of prayer. It would take an effort to regain the richness of experience he had once enjoyed.

The end of the journey was the start of new tribulations. In the United States the immigrants encountered a most discouraging situation. All the conditions of religious life in America were different from those in the Old World. As the newcomers struggled to adjust themselves, they discovered a maze of barriers that separated them from the desired objective, transplantation of the old churches.

It was difficult, for instance, to understand the diversity of religious affiliations. In Europe the established church was universal; only a few outsiders dissented. Here a vast variety of sects divided the population, and did so according to no meaningful pattern of social, economic, or sectional status. In outward aspect, in occupations, in respectability, one could not distinguish the members of one denomination from another. All these people furthermore associated with each other on terms of complete equality. There seemed no reason therefore why a man should not change his church as freely as his hat. Indeed, to the immigrants it seemed the Americans were perilously near to doing so all the time.

Every religion therefore was in open competition for adherents with every other. There was no establishment in the United States; no church was connected with the State or favored by the laws. What was more, no sect had so secure or commanding a position in any other way that it could compel members to come to it or penalize those who did not. In all the great cities, throughout the West, and in many parts of the South, the churches were almost all equally new and stood on approximately the same footing. Even rural New England, where the Congregationalists had at first held an exceptional position, after 1850 approached the general condition.

The absence of an authoritative national, or even a regional or local, church was unfamiliar and disturbing. The privacy of beliefs, the freedom to enter what denomination he wished — or none at all — placed before the immigrant the necessity of giving answers to questions that had never been asked of him before. Without the aid of priests, for it was in the nature of the movement that laymen came in advance of the clergy, these humble people had to make the most difficult of decisions. That they insisted on re-creating the old churches testifies to the strength of the old ties.

Such decisions involved not principles alone, but all sorts of concrete, practical considerations. With the most devout will in the world, a church would not appear unless there were funds for an edifice and a staff for its service.

The problem of finances was sufficiently oppressive. At home the peasants had never to consider the means of paying the expenses. The Church supported itself by grants either from the State or from the income of its own lands; the communicants contributed only the fees for particular services and these were fixed by the force of age-old custom. All such revenues disappeared with immigration. New ones to replace them were the minimal cost of reconstituting the churches in America.

Then the immigrants discovered that costs could not be minimal in the New World which compelled them to take on many additional charges not known in the Old. Here the pious had to create afresh, and at once, what in Europe had always been at hand, the product of centuries of growth. Everywhere the newcomers went they purchased buildings or, where they were able, erected new ones. They accumulated all the furnishings and the appurtenances necessary for the service and for all that raised what funds their own efforts brought them.

They could count on little help. The Roman Catholics occasionally benefited from the assistance of philanthropic monarchs like King Ludwig of Bavaria, or from the donations of missionary organizations, the Austrian Leopoldine Verein and the French Society for the Propagation of the Faith, or most of all, from the services of the international orders. But such aid, valuable as it was, was trifling against the enormity of the need. By and large, the money that built the churches and other religious institutions was assembled from the earnings of humble laborers who painfully accumulated what they scarcely could spare and devotedly gave what they could.

The magnitude of the task was multiplied by the circumstance that it was executed without the support of the kind of authority that had familiarly operated on the peasants at home. There was, to begin with at least, only a skeletal hierarchy and no corps of clerics to supply leadership. Under the American voluntary system, the churches had no sanctions. They counted for support on the good will and loyalty of their communicants. A bishop could not simply command and expect to be obeyed; his orders evoked a response only to the degree that he catered to the wishes of his flock. Law in the United States increased the uncertainty by defining the congregation as the church incorporate, and naming the laymen rather than the priest as owners of its property. Yet there were limits to the powers of a majority of the membership, for a minority was always free to secede and drift off in its own direction. If the immigrants held together and achieved as much as they did, it was because the longing that moved them sprang from a common stem in their life before emigration.

The transition from establishment to voluntarism was more difficult for peasants than for dissenters. The latter had known, at home, how it was to support a church through their own efforts. In America indeed their situation improved, for the neutrality of the state was better than its hostility. Here all sects were in the same position.

Paradoxically that very equality of situation threatened the survival of the dissenting groups. The sense of election grew weaker in the absence of persecution by a dominating church. Unless constantly reminded of the particularity and uniqueness of their own form of dissent, individuals might be tempted to drift off into other analogous denominations.

Dissenters and peasants both, therefore, saw a danger in the pervasive latitudinarianism of religion in the United States. Too many Americans were ready to believe that salvation could come through any faith or none, that ethical behavior and a good life rather than adherence to a specific creed would earn a share in the heavenly kingdom.

There was a double menace to this delusion. To begin with, it put to nought the sacrifices of establishing the immigrant religions. If all roads led to salvation, why trouble with great difficulty and enormous expense to hack out one's own. Why not follow the well-established easy paths others had already marked? Experience shouted the denial. In the missions, in the chapels, where the strangers came to pray, there the voices were of aliens and the ways were not the same. There were not the satisfactions that a full religion brought. No salvation could be there.

There was also a more subtle threat in latitudinarianism. The American ideas might penetrate the immigrant churches themselves, undermine the old ideas. That would deprive the newcomers, in particular the peasants, of their promised reward. For these people salvation was the compensation for faith and suffering, not for good behavior. They would not have the shift in emphasis.

The problem was, the whole effort, no matter how earnest, was out of context. You can build a church, but you cannot re-create the site, wipe out the surrounding city, restore the village background. You can reassemble the communicants; but can you re-create the communion, wipe out the effects of the crossing, and restore the old piety? A new environment has disorganized the old order. Determined men long for reorganization, struggle to effect it.

Invariably the way seemed to be the complete transfer of the old religious system to the New World. It was not simply the Gospel and priest the immigrants would bring with them, but holidays and processions, ancient costumes and traditional rites, the whole life of religion at home. All these they wished to replant in the unreceptive soil of America. The only way to be sure of survival was to insist on the rigid preservation of the whole.

The process of replanting was arduous, left each of the newer religions a painful history writ not so much in the blood of martyrs as in the sweat of loyal laborers.

Oldest, and ultimately largest, of these churches in the United States was the Roman Catholic Church. By the end of the eighteenth century, American Catholics had outlived the prejudices earlier directed against them. They then constituted a community that was small in size but well-established and secure in social position. Composed primarily of the native-born, the Church counted among its communicants some of the wealthiest merchants and planters in the country. The only consequential immigrant group at first were the

French, who wielded an influence disproportionate to their numbers because the community was served largely by French clergymen displaced by the revolution in France. Yet these had no significant difficulties with the native Catholics for they shared a common point of view; indeed, American priests were generally trained in French seminaries, and it had earlier seemed possible that a subject of Louis XVI would become the first American bishop.

In the course of the nineteenth century, however, immigration added to the Catholic population a mass of new communicants that quickly overshadowed the original body. Coming from parts of Europe historically distant and separate from each other, from the western coast of Ireland to the eastern slopes of the Carpathians, the newcomers brought with them different and decided notions as to what was the proper form of the Church, wished each to perpetuate the unique qualities of the religious life they had practiced at home. The outcome was a long period of internal dissension.

First to arrive in large numbers were the Irish. In the 1790's there were already disputes in some parishes as to what nationality the priest should be. On scores of petty details the Irish found themselves at odds with the old established Catholics, native and French. And in a few places grievances mounted up until they broke out into open conflicts that called forth the intercession of the civil authorities.

Through the first three decades of the nineteenth century the situation of the Roman Catholic Church remained in balance. The native Catholics had the advantages of respectability and wealth; they added to their strength by occasional conversions from among Protestants and by recruiting the children of immigrants. But they could still hardly hold their own. With few facilities for training priests, there was always a shortage of American clergymen; and some bishops, to their eventual regret, were willing to gamble on the dubious qualifications of stray clerics who wandered up from the West

Indies or across from the continent and did much damage before their past records caught up with them.

The Irish on the other hand had behind them the potent resources of an immigration that mounted steadily in volume, and that brought to the New World not only an ever-larger flock of communicants, but also their pastors, made available from the Old Country. Already in the 1830's Irish names were prominent in the priesthood, although not yet among the bishops.

Soon thereafter, the full impact of the great migration transformed American Catholicism. Church membership became overwhelmingly Irish in composition, and Irish-Americans assumed some of the most distinguished places in the hierarchy in the United States. By the middle of the nineteenth century Catholicism in this country showed a pronounced Hibernian cast.

The scattered parishes still predominantly native American or French fought in vain to retain their autonomy and distinctiveness. The battle was fought out over the effort of the laity to retain a determining voice in the management of church property and thus indirectly of religious affairs. The practice of some of the earliest Catholics had followed that of the Protestant denominations and had vested control in Boards of Trustees. Stubbornly these boards resisted the demand they relinquish authority, so stubbornly as to precipitate a series of schisms from Boston to New Orleans, so stubbornly that the Church of St. Louis in Buffalo was placed under an interdict in 1851 and its trustees excommunicated three years later.

But the bishops won. They were bound to win, for they had the devoted support of the mass of their Irish communicants to whom the issue was simply that of whose churches these were to be. With the rights of the laymen the immigrants had little concern; the peasants at home had never presumed to interfere with the management of the priests' property, and were only concerned with their rights as worshipers. Those they thought would be less well guarded by the strange trustees than by bishops and priests of their own kind. By the time the Third Plenary Council in 1884 ruled decisively on the question, it was already settled as a practical matter.

Yet the clerics who gathered for that impressive assembly in Baltimore already knew that the contest for control of the Church had not come to an end, had only taken a new turn. Shortly, the Irish immigrants would face an assault from two groups of coreligionists eager to purge Catholicism of its foreign influences, restore its American aspect. Again the weight of numbers would tell.

Discontent had developed first among native Catholics, particularly among converts like Isaac Hecker and Orestes Brownson, who had only a slight understanding of the peasant faith. Interested above all in proselytizing among Americans, such men regarded the Irish character of the Church as a positive impediment and claimed that Catholicism could only be attractive to native Protestants in the United States if it adapted itself to local conditions. This point of view also gained some adherents among the second generation, among the children of the immigrants who had never lived the life of religion in the Old World, who were impatient of their fathers' ways, and who valued the approval of the American society within which they had grown up.

These were all faithful Catholics, unwilling to deviate in the least from the Church's dogmas. Yet inevitably Americanization involved kinds of compromises. There was a wish to minimize the points of contention with other Americans: perhaps the parochial and the public school could be reconciled; perhaps a formula could be found to make room within Catholic social doctrines for American democracy and liberalism; perhaps the Church could itself participate in or encourage the movements for human amelioration that so absorbed people in the United States. The obstacle was the dull, inert conservatism of the immigrants, their blind adherence to tradition and obedience to the hierarchy. Because of them the Church was *run by a close corporation of discredited foreigners, and what a success they made of it in their own countries!*

Within the hierarchy were some supporters of such views, notably Archbishop Gibbons of Baltimore, Archbishop Ireland of St. Paul, and Bishop Spaulding of Peoria. Their most striking achievement was the creation of Catholic University of America, at Washington, an institution that was to be free of the control of the bishop of any specific diocese, that was not to be bound to any particular teaching order, and that was to provide the scholarly leadership for the new developments in American Catholicism.

Within the hierarchy were also the bitter opponents of the American idea, among them Archbishop Corrigan of New York and Bishop McQuaid of Rochester. Unrelenting in their hostility, they fought every innovation, and saw their resistance crowned with success in 1899 when the Pope, for reasons of his own, condemned what he called the doctrines of Americanism in the Bull *Testem Benevolentia*. Whether the supreme pontiff acted with an eye to American conditions or not the effect of his action was to assure the victory of the conservative wing and with it the continued dominance of the Irish in the Church.

Very likely, that victory would in any case have come; for at that very time the Americans were being driven to close ranks with the Irish against a greater threat to them both. Immigration from Germany, from Italy, and from eastern Europe was bringing to the New World newer groups of Catholics, groups which each insisted on recognition. The desire of so many different people to see re-created the precise forms of their old churches seemed, for a while, a menace to the whole Catholic order in the United States.

The earliest German Catholics had established themselves with relative ease. Arriving at the same time as the Irish, they settled either on farms or in sections of the cities where they could create German parishes. There were in fact a few German bishops. But the Germans who came later in the century found a more complicated situation. Settling in cities where the Irish were already dominant they had trouble setting up churches of their own, often found the bishops unsympathetic or hostile. That was the burden of the complaint thirty-two German priests addressed to the Pope in 1884. That was the tenor of the argument set forth in a tearful pamphlet two years later by Father P. M. Abbelen, Vicar-General of the Diocese of Milwaukee.

The Italians judged their situation more calamitous still. Arriving toward the end of the century, they moved into residential districts that in most cities had formerly been occupied by the Irish. With the intense desire of all peasants, the Italians longed to reconstruct their old village churches. They were Catholics, but the Catholic churches they found in the neighborhoods they occupied were Irish and not Italian — as different from what was familiar to the new-comers as the chapels of the Episcopalians or Methodists. They were not content, and sought to recapture the old authenticity. The result was a struggle, parish by parish, between the old Catholics and the new, a struggle that involved the nationality of the priest, the language to be used, the saints' days to be observed, and even the name of the church.

In this contest, the attitude of the bishops was critical. And there was the greatest grievance of all, for by the 1890's the hierarchy was almost entirely of Irish descent. Do what they could on a local basis, the scattered Germans and Italians were still not strong enough to dispute the control of the diocese. Since power was lodged almost entirely in the hands of the bishops, the fight seemed lost before it was properly begun. Large sectors of the immigrant population were discontented, and there seemed a real possibility that the Church would witness a substantial dropping off in its membership.

Concern with these problems was widespread; but a solution was painfully hard to come at. The most radical proposal was advanced in 1890 in the Lucerne Memorial, a document drawn up under the influence of Peter Paul Cahensly. Cahensly, a German interested in the fate of his coreligionists in America, suggested that the diocese in the United States be based not on geography but on nationality. Instead of following the traditional territorial divisions, the Irish, Germans, and Italians were each to have their own parishes which would then fall into separate Irish, German, and Italian hierarchies. Thus the shock of migration would be eased for Catholics and the dangers of loss of faith minimized. Against this scheme the Irish and American bishops united to secure a condemnation from the Vatican which saw in it an implicit denial of the fundamental catholicity of the Church.

But to reject the proposal was not to solve the problem which rather grew more complicated with the arrival of newer groups of immigrants. The Poles, Lithuanians, Hungarians, and Syrians found themselves minorities within minorities and were therefore more dissatisfied, more open to the temptation of falling away from the Church. Not only were many becoming apathetic and unaffiliated, but such grievances stimulated the proselytizing activities of the Protestant denominations; by 1918 there were some twenty-five thousand Italian converts alone in New York City.

Most distressing of all were the internal dissensions, the breaches of discipline, and the schisms that divided the Church. Always these began with local issues and sometimes were confined within the parish. Thus the Italians of the North End of Boston, dissatisfied with the Franciscans in charge of St. Leonard's, who were partial to the Irish, seceded in 1884 and, on their own, formed the San Marco Society. It took years of controversy before the Archbishop was induced to recognize their church.

But sometimes the divisions became permanent and spread rapidly beyond the localities in which they were initiated. So

in the 1890's three independent and spontaneous controversies between Polish parishes and their Irish bishops in
Scranton, Buffalo, and Chicago cut loose from the Church a
substantial body of communicants who ultimately united
under a hierarchy of their own in the Polish National Catholic Church in America. Similar movements created an independent Lithuanian and, for a time, an independent Italian
church.

Apart from the heady business of complaining and organizing, there was, though, no satisfaction here. All these efforts
at preservation only led to change, and in the change the
village church was in any case lost. Generally with time there
came a succession of compromises that accepted the Cahens-
lyite conception of the national parish in practice and enabled each group of immigrants to find a way of worship of
its own choosing.

Only sometimes no compromise is possible. Someone must
accept the heartache of a radical decision. In 1890, the Right
Reverend John Ireland receives the Archpriest Alexei Tovt,
pastor within the diocese of a Catholic church in Minneapolis. The Archbishop is shocked because the priest does not
kneel, disturbed because the priest is not celibate. There is no
violation of doctrine here; the Archbishop knows that Father
Tovt is a Uniat, that Uniat Catholics have a dispensation to
follow the Greek rites, and that their clergy are free to marry.
Yet, knowing all this, the head of the diocese still cannot
refrain from upbraiding the seeming breach of decorum.
Now Father Tovt is offended; the Archbishop's effrontery
seems an invasion of the traditional privileges of his Carpatho-
Ruthenian congregation. He and his flock secede and accept
the Orthodox faith. In the next half-century, several hundred
thousand Uniats follow that lead. In a Pennsylvania mining
town, how can an Irishman grow accustomed to meeting the
wife and children of a Catholic priest? How long can the
Ruthenians accept the slights of misunderstanding, bow to

the imputation that their ancient practices are not worthy of preservation?

The centralization, the discipline, and the order of the Catholic Church, its long experience in reconciling national differences, and its international tradition, all were inadequate to contain the peasants' urge to reconstitute their religious life in America exactly as it had been at home in the village.

In the other immigrant churches, where the degree of control was not so high, resettlement in America was even more disruptive. Every local variation struggled for expression through years of bitter confusion.

Immigrants from several regions of Europe brought Lutheranism to the New World. Yet despite an essential uniformity in dogma, they established not one but several Lutheran churches.

The German who came to the United States in the nineteenth century found Lutheran churches already in existence in many parts of the country. These hardly satisfied the newcomer, however. Although they had been founded in the previous century by other Germans, they had lost contact with Europe and been Americanized, tainted with laxity of observance and with latitudinarianism. The growth of the denomination through the addition of immigrants was accompanied by a thoroughgoing reformation. Through the work of the Missouri Synod, organized by C. F. W. Walther, there was a determined effort to return to the purity of practice frittered away by its predecessors.

Nevertheless, succeeding groups insisted upon their own churches and their own synods. Not, indeed, that the established churches in Europe were much concerned; the Church of Sweden, for instance, advised its members coming to the United States simply to join the Episcopal Church. But the Swedish immigrants could neither accept that advice, nor move into the German establishments. Everywhere they created churches and bound them into a synod of their own. And later comers did the same; the Norwegians, the Danes, the Icelanders, the Finns, and the Volga Germans suffered through like experiences. They arrived, and were unhappy with the varieties of Lutheranism they discovered in the United States, for those seemed to have been diluted by contact with Americanism. Invariably a full religious life seemed to demand the creation of still newer churches closer to the familiar Old World models.

So also it was with the various Eastern churches. The period of immigration was not over before there were five major Orthodox establishments: the Greek, Hellenic, Russian, Serbian, and Antiochean; and several of these were in turn divided by schisms. Divisions, the origins of which were lost in obscure European causes, were here perpetuated through the devotion of the immigrants and their desire to keep alive the traditional forms of worship as embodiments of a way of life.

Dissenters encountered comparable difficulties of adjustment when it came to setting up their churches in the United States. These people had never been established and were therefore not disestablished by migration. They were acquainted with the notion of conversion and tended to stress the ethics of behavior as well as the ceremonial of forms. An individual who slipped into some American approximation of his own sect therefore faced not so painful a wrench out of his earlier religious experience. Nevertheless, the ties to old ways proved binding for dissenters too. They struggled stubbornly to maintain their identity as religious groups and to reconstruct the old faiths in the New World. Little bands of Welsh Methodists or Scottish Presbyterians or Italian Waldensians devoutly held on, and often sought in their settlement in America new justification for the sense of mission they bore.

The extreme dissenters, the Jews, followed a pattern of

development much like that of the immigrants who transplanted established religions. In the case of this group, the lack of a hierarchy and of any discipline outside the congregation encouraged very rapid splintering. Any ten Jews were free to form a synagogue and to worship in what way they willed. As soon as the numbers were large enough, the multiplication of congregations began. Already in the 1850's differentiations had appeared among the English, the Germans, the Poles, and the Bohemians. And when the volume of immigration increased toward the end of the nineteenth century, the divisions became more minute. The men of a single province or of a single town assembled to find God in their old ways.

As for the Catholics and the Lutherans, the New World for the Jews was a threat to the old ways. In a land where there was no establishment, they were no longer exceptional outsiders. Where all people were equally at home, these were no longer in exile. The Americanism of Judaism was the Reform Movement, which gathered force at midcentury and reached its ultimate expression in the two decades after 1880, at the same time as the analogous trend in Catholicism. The emphasis on adjustment to conditions in the United States involved a sacrifice of parts of the traditional ritual, conformity to some of the modes of the Protestant sects, and an extreme view of religion as primarily a system of ethical precepts.

Like other newcomers, the Jewish immigrants found such changes unsatisfactory. Persistently they held to their Orthodoxy. The marble temples that arose in the better neighborhoods, the dignified sermons, and the quiet services attracted them not at all. In ruder buildings, hastily converted from stores or homes or abandoned churches, they sought the consoling flavor of familiar worship.

The dissenters too, then, were engaged in the quest for a religious way of life in the New World that would be the same as in the Old. This was the common immigrant experience. In the American environment, so new and so dangerous, these people felt more need than ever for the support of their faith. Yet the same environment, in its very strangeness and looseness and freedom, made it difficult to preserve what could be taken for granted at home.

With great hardship and against impressive physical and financial difficulties, the immigrants achieved some degree of success. Out of the scrimped earnings of poor laborers rose monumental edifices capable of serving thousands of communicants.

From time to time, though, they must have reflected, they who came there to seek ease of spirit, that this was still not the Old Country church, that what they had recaptured was more the form, and that out of context, and not so much the way of life. Outside, the crowded street pulsed through the city, disregarding what was within. Here they would never reestablish the old relationship that, back there, had given religion so large a role in their society. Could they then push down the frustrating sense of loss, the fear of emptiness in forms? A possession of infinite value had disappeared in the course of the migration — the inner meaning of their own existence in the universe.

Yet there was no alternative but to continue as before to hold on to what was left, the form; to resist where possible any change in that. Their religious life accordingly grew rigid; they became far more conservative than those of their fellows who had remained in Europe. *I know this much, that I am a Catholic, and I perform the duties of a Catholic as far as I can. I am not devout, for I have no time to pray because every Sunday I must work and — I confess it to you alone — I work even on Easter from 7 until 12. But I will remain a Catholic until I die. . . .* Yield not on the jot or tittle lest the whole writ change — as it must.

This they had learned, however, in the course of their coming and settlement, that adjustment to the circumstances of life in the United States brought them not nearer to but more distant from other Americans. The very process of getting established revealed to each group the differences that divided it from every other. The immigrants thus caught a glimpse of the apartness, the separateness implicit in Americanization. And it would be not long before they saw the full extent of it.

SIX

The Ghettos

THE PLACE WAS important too. Settlement in America had snipped the continuity of the immigrants' work and ideas, of their religious life. It would also impose a new relationship to the world of space about them. In the Old Country setting, the physical scene had been integral with the existence of the men in it. Changes would have explosive repercussions.

In the United States, the newcomers pushed their roots into many different soils. Along the city's unyielding asphalt streets, beside the rutted roads of mill or mining towns, amidst the exciting prairie acres, they established the homes of the New World. But wherever the immigrants went, there was one common experience they shared: nowhere could they transplant the European village. Whatever the variations among environments in America, none was familiar. The pressure of that strangeness exerted a deep influence upon the character of resettlement, upon the usual forms of behavior, and upon the modes of communal action that emerged as the immigrants became Americans.

The old conditions of living could not survive in the new conditions of space. Ways long taken for granted in the village adjusted slowly and painfully to density of population in the cities, to disorder in the towns, and to distance on the farms. That adjustment was the means of creating the new communities within which these people would live.

Although the great mass of immigrants spent out their days in the great cities, there was always an unorganized quality to settlement in such places that left a permanent impress upon every fresh arrival. Chance was so large an element in the course of migration, it left little room for planning. The place of landing was less often the outcome of an intention held at the outset of the journey than of blind drift along the routes of trade or of a sudden halt due to the accidents of the voyage. Consequently the earliest concentrations of the foreign-born were in the chain of Atlantic seaports: Boston, Philadelphia, Baltimore, New Orleans, and most of all New York, the unrivaled mart of Europe's commerce with America. For the same reasons, later concentrations appeared at the inland termini, the points of exchange between rail and river or lake traffic — Cleveland, Chicago, Cincinnati, Pittsburgh, and St. Louis.

In all such places the newcomers pitched themselves in the midst of communities that were already growing rapidly and that were therefore already crowded. Between 1840 and 1870, for instance, the population of New York City mounted by fully 50 per cent every ten years; for every two people at the start of a decade, there were three at its end. (In all, the 312,000 residents of 1840 had become 3,437,000 in 1900.) Chicago's rise was even more precipitate; the 4000 inhabitants there in 1840 numbered 1,700,000 in 1900. Every ten-year interval saw two people struggling for the space formerly occupied by one.

These largest cities were representative of the rest. The natural increase through the excess of births over deaths, with the additional increase through the shift of native-born population from rural to urban areas, and with the further increase through overseas immigration, all contributed to the enormous growth of American municipalities. To house all the new city dwellers was a problem of staggering proportions. Facilities simply did not keep pace with the demand.

To house the immigrants was more difficult still. For these people had not the mobility to choose where they should live or the means to choose how. Existing on the tenuous income supplied by unskilled labor, they could not buy homes; nor could they lay out much in payment of rent. Their first thought in finding accommodations was that the cost be as little as possible. The result was they got as little as possible.

The willingness to accept a minimum of comfort and convenience did not, however, mean that such quarters would always be available. Under the first impact of immigration, the unprepared cities had not ready the housing immigrants could afford. The newcomers were driven to accept hand-me-downs, vacated places that could be converted to their service at a profit.

The immigrants find their first homes in quarters the old occupants no longer desire. As business grows, the commercial center of each city begins to blight the neighboring residential districts. The well-to-do are no longer willing to live in close proximity to the bustle of warehouses and offices; yet that same proximity sets a high value on real estate. To spend money on the repair or upkeep of houses in such areas is only wasteful; for they will soon be torn down to make way for commercial buildings. The simplest, most profitable use is to divide the old mansions into tiny lodgings. The rent on each unit will be low; but the aggregate of those sums will, without substantial investment or risk, return larger dividends than any other present use of the property.

Such accommodations have additional attractions for the immigrants. They are close to the familiar region of the docks and they are within walking distance of the places where labor is hired; precious carfare will be saved by living here. In every American city some such district of first settlement receives the newcomers.

Not that much is done to welcome them. The carpenters hammer shut connecting doors and build rude partitions up across the halls; middle-class homes thus become laborers' — only not one to a family, but shared among many. What's more, behind the original structures are grassy yards where children once had run about at play. There is to be no room for games now. Sheds and shanties, hurriedly thrown up, provide living space; and if a stable is there, so much the better: that too can be turned to account. In 1850 already in New York some seven thousand households are finding shelter in such rear buildings. By this time too ingenuity has uncovered still other resources: fifteen hundred cellars also do service as homes.

If these conversions are effected without much regard for the convenience of the ultimate occupants, they nevertheless have substantial advantages. The carpenter aims to do the job as expeditiously as possible; he has not the time to contrive the most thorough use of space; and waste square feet leave luxurious corners. There are limits to the potentialities for crowding in such quarters.

There were no such limits when enterprising contractors set to work devising edifices more suitable for the reception of these residents. As the population continued to grow, and the demand with it, perspicacious owners of real estate saw profit in the demolition of the old houses and the construction, between narrow alleys, of compact barracks that made complete use of every inch of earth.

Where once had been Mayor Delavall's orchard, Cherry Street in New York ran its few blocks to the East River shipyards. At Number 36, in 1853, stood Gotham Court, one of the better barrack buildings. Five stories in height, it stretched back one hundred and fifty feet from the street, between two tight alleys (one nine, the other seven feet wide). Onto the more spacious alley opened twelve doors through each of which passed the ten families that lived within, two to each floor in identical two-room apartments. (one room, 9 × 14; one bedroom, 9 × 6). Here without interior plumbing or heat were the homes of five hundred people. Ten years later, there were some improvements: for the service of the community, a row of privies in the basement, flushed occasionally by Croton water. But by then there were more than eight hundred dwellers in the structure, which indeed continued in use till the very end of the century.

That these conditions were not then reckoned outlandish was shown in the model workmen's home put up by philanthropic New Yorkers at Elizabeth and Mott Street. Each suite in this six-story structure had three rooms; but the rooms were smaller (4 × 11, 8 × 7, and 8 × 7). There were gas lights in the halls; but the water closets were in sheds in the alleys. And well over half the rooms had no windows at all.

At the middle of the nineteenth century, these developments were still chaotic, dependent upon the fancy of the individual builder. But the pressure of rising demand and the pattern of property holding gradually shaped a common form for the tenement house. The older barracks still left waste space in alleys, halls, and stair wells; and they did not conform to the uniform city real-estate plot, twenty or twenty-five feet wide and one hundred feet deep. As the cost of land went up, builders were increasingly constrained to confine themselves to those rectangular blocks while pushing their edifices upward and eliminating the interstitial alleys.

Ultimately, the dumbbell tenement lined street after street, a most efficient structure that consumed almost the entire area of the real-estate plot. Attached to its neighbors on either side, it left vacant only a strip, perhaps ten feet deep, in the rear. On a floor space of approximately twenty by ninety feet, it was possible, within this pattern, to get four four-room apartments.

The feat was accomplished by narrowing the building at its middle so that it took on the shape of a dumbbell. The indentation was only two-and-a-half feet wide and varied in length from five to fifty feet; but, added to the similar indentations of the adjoining houses, it created on each side an airshaft five feet wide. In each apartment three of the rooms could present their windows to the shaft, draw from it air and light as well; only one chamber in each suite need face upon the street or rear yard. The stairs, halls, and common water closets were cramped into the narrow center of the building so that almost the whole of its surface was available for living quarters.

These structures were at least six stories in height, sometimes eight. At the most moderate reckoning, twenty-four to thirty-two families could be housed on this tiny space, or more realistically, anywhere from one hundred and fifty to two hundred human beings. It was not a long block that held ten such tenements on either side of the street, not an unusual block that was home for some four thousand people.

There were drastic social consequences to living under these dense conditions. The immigrants had left villages which counted their populations in scores. In the Old World a man's whole circle of acquaintances had not taken in as many individuals as lived along a single street here. By a tortuous course of adjustments, the newcomers worked out new modes of living in response to their environment. But the cost of those adjustments was paid out of the human energies of the residents and through the physical deterioration of the districts in which they lived.

The tenement flourished most extensively in New York, the greatest point of immigrant concentration. But it was also known in Boston and in the other Atlantic ports. In the interior cities it was less common; there land values were not so rigid and commercial installations not such barriers to the centrifugal spread of population. From the barracklike buildings of the area of first settlement, the immigrants could move out to smaller units where at least the problems of density were less oppressive. Little two-story cottages that held six families were characteristic of places like Buffalo. Elsewhere were wooden three- or four-floor structures that contained a dozen households. Even single homes were to be found, dilapidated shanties or jerry-built boxes low in rent. Yet internally these accommodations were not superior to those of the tenement. In one form or another, the available housing gave the districts to which the immigrants went the character of slums.

Well, they were not ones to choose, who had lived in the thatched peasant huts of home. Nor was it unbearably offensive to reside in the least pleasant parts of the city, in Chicago over against the slaughterhouses, in Boston hemmed in by the docks and markets of the North End, in New York against the murky river traffic of the East Side. Such disadvantages they could survive. The hardship came in more subtle adjustments demanded of them.

Certainly the flats were small and overcrowded. In no room of the dumbbell tenement could you pace off more than eleven feet; and the reforming architects of 1900 still thought of chambers no larger than those of Gotham Court. In addition, the apartments shrank still further when shared by more than one family or when they sheltered lodgers, as did more than half those in New York at the end of the century. But that was not the worst of it.

Here is a woman. In the Old Country she had lived much of her life, done most of her work, outdoors. In America, the flat confines her. She divides up her domain by calico sheets hung on ropes, tries to make a place for her people and possessions. But there is no place and she has not room to turn about. It is true, everything is in poor repair, the rain comes through the ceilings, the wind blows dirt through the cracks in the wall. But she does not even know how to go about restoring order, establishing cleanliness. She breaks her back to exterminate the proliferating vermin. What does she get? A dozen lice behind the collar.

The very simplest tasks become complex and disorganizing. Every day there is a family to feed. Assume she knows how to shop, and can manage the unfamiliar coal stove or gas range. But what does one do with rubbish who has never known the meaning of waste? It is not really so important to walk down the long flight of narrow stairs each time there are some scraps to be disposed of. The windows offer an easier alternative. After all, the obnoxious wooden garbage boxes that adorn the littered fronts of the houses expose their contents unashamed through split sides and, rarely emptied, themselves become the nests of boldly foraging rodents.

The filthy streets are seldom cleaned; the municipality is not particularly solicitous of these, the poorest quarters of the city. The alleys are altogether passed by and the larger thoroughfares receive only occasionally the services of the scavenger. The inaccessible alleys and rear yards are never touched and, to be sure, are redolent of the fact. In the hot summer months the stench of rotting things will mark these places and the stained snow of winter will not conceal what lies beneath. Here and there an unwitting newcomer tries the disastrous experiment of keeping a goat, adds thereby to the distinctive flavor of his neighborhood.

It was the same in every other encounter with the new life. Conveniences not missed in the villages became sore necessities in the city; although often the immigrants did not know their lack till dear experience taught them. Of what value were sunlight and fresh air on the farm? But how measure their worth for those who lived in the three hundred and fifty thousand dark interior rooms of New York in 1900!

There was the rude matter of what Americans called sanitation. Some of the earliest buildings had had no privies at all; the residents had been expected to accommodate themselves elsewhere as best they could. Tenements from mid-century onward had generally water closets in the yards and alleys, no great comfort to the occupants of the fifth and sixth floors. The newest structures had two toilets to each floor; but these were open to the custom of all comers, charged to the care of none, and left to the neglect of all. If in winter the pipes froze in unheated hallways and the clogged contents overflowed, weeks would go by before some dilatory repairman set matters right. Months thereafter a telling odor hung along the narrow hallways.

What of it? The filth was inescapable. In these districts where the need was greatest, the sewerage systems were primitive and ineffectual. Open drains were long common; in Boston one such, for years, tumbled down the slope of Jacob's Ladder in the South Cove; and in Chicago the jocosely named Bubbly Creek wended its noisome way aboveground until well into the twentieth century.

With the water supply there had always been trouble at home too: poor wells, shallow, and inconveniently situated. The inconvenience here was not unexpected. Still it was a burden to carry full tubs and jugs from the taps in the alley up the steep stairs. Not till late was city water directly connected with the toilets; it was later still to reach the kitchen sink; and bathrooms had not yet put in an appearance in these quarters. Then, too, the consequences were more painful: city dirt was harder to scrub away, and there was no nearby creek. It could well be, as they came to say, that a man got a good bath only twice in his life: from midwife and undertaker.

All might yet be tolerable were not the confining dimensions of the flat so oppressive. The available space simply would not yield to all the demands made upon it. Where were the children to play if the fields were gone? Where were things to be stored or clothes to be hung? Beds or bedding consumed the bedroom; there was only one living room, and sink and stove left little free of that. The man in the evening, come home from work, found not a niche for rest; the tiny intervals of leisure were wasted for want of a place to spend them. Privacy now was more often sought for than in the Old Country where every person and every thing had its accustomed spot. Yet privacy now was difficult to achieve; there was no simple way of dividing space too small to share. Under pressure of the want, the constricted beings bowed to a sense of strain.

Disorganization affects particularly the life of the home. In these tiny rooms that now are all they call their home, many traditional activities wither and disappear. Not here will the friends be welcomed, festivals commemorated, children taught, and the family unite to share in the warmth of its security. Emptied of the meaning of these occurrences and often crowded with strange lodgers, home is just the feeding and sleeping place. All else moves to the outside.

The street becomes the great artery of life for the people of these districts. Sometimes, the boys and girls play in back in the narrow yards, looking up at the lines of drying clothes that spiderweb the sky above them. More often the crowded street itself is the more attractive playground. They run in games through the moving traffic, find fun in the appearance of some hopeful street musician, or regard with dejected envy the wares of the itinerant vendors of seasonal delicacies, the sweet shaved ice of summer, the steaming potatoes and chestnuts of fall and winter.

The adults too drift out, sit on the steps, flow over onto the sidewalks. The women bring their work outdoors, the men at evening hang about, now and then talk. They begin to be neighborly, learn to be sensitive to each other. That is the good of it.

There is also the bad. The street in its strangeness is the evidence of the old home's disintegration. Why, the very aspect is forbidding: the dear sun never shines brightly, the still air between the high buildings is so saturated with stench it would take a dragon to hold out. These are all signs of the harshness of the physical environment, of the difficulties of living in these quarters, of the disintegration here of old ways. Those children in earnest play at the corner — who controls them, to what discipline are they subject? They do not do the things that children ought. No one does the things he ought. The place prevents it.

Almost resignedly, the immigrants witnessed in themselves a deterioration. All relationships became less binding, all behavior more dependent on individual whim. The result was a marked personal decline and a noticeable wavering of standards.

Some of the reactions to the new conditions of living were immediate, direct, and overt. The low level of health and the high incidence of disease were certain products of overcrowding. Residents of the tenements did not need the spotted maps of later students to tell them where tuberculosis hit, a terror of an illness that spread from victim to victim in the stifling rooms. If the cholera came, or smallpox, or diphtheria — and all did in their time — it was impossible to limit their decimating course. Little else by now remained communal; but contagion and infection these people could not help but share with each other.

The mortality rate was an indication of their helplessness against disease. The immigrants were men and women in the prime of life, yet they died more rapidly than the generality of Americans. Everywhere their life expectancy was lower; and, as might be anticipated, it was particularly infants who suffered. In one Chicago precinct at the end of the nineteenth century, three babies of every five born died before they reached their first birthday.

That, they might say, was sad, but in the nature of things. No act of will, no deed of commission or omission could stay the coming of death. The grim reaper, an old familiar fellow, had simply emigrated with them. But other consequences of living in these quarters confronted the newcomers with a choice or at least with the appearance of a choice. Under the disorganizing pressure of the present environment, men found it difficult, on the basis of past habits, to determine what their own roles should be. They could question neither the validity of the old values nor the exigencies of the new necessities. Having inherited the conceptions of their proper roles, they had been projected into a situation where every element conspired to force them into deviations. They yielded at the points of least resistance; not every one of them, but many, at one point or another. And those who withstood the pressure did so at the expense of continuous, exhausting strain.

What if a man were to think then (as some did) and say to himself: *Why shall I forever beat my head against this un-yielding wall? There will be no end to my toil, and my labor gains me nothing. For what a life do I work. And did not the time in any case come of idleness, when not a crust was in the house and I must go cap in hand for help?* His whole being would at first have revolted at the indignity of the thought; in the peasant world the person who did not earn his own bread was not fully a man, lost thereby status and esteem in the eyes of the community. But what status had the laborer in America to lose, what esteem? Was it then such a reprehensible thing to get by without work?

They recalled as they thought of it that at home also there were some who had habitually lived at the expense of others. That had itself been not so terrible; and indeed the beggars had even a magical or religious quality. The humiliation had come from the circumstance that forced a man into alms seeking: from his improvidence, or lack of foresight, or dissolute character, or spendthrift habits. But in America, pauperism was not sought out; it came of itself to good and wicked alike. No blame could attach here to him who could not always earn a livelihood, who came to depend for his sustenance on the gifts of charity.

In what they had there was precious little to keep those weary of the effort from following the persuasive logic of this

line of thought. Almost without self-pity and altogether without reproach, they surrendered to the institutions that maintained the dependent, or they abandoned their families, or
they became not quite permanent clients of the relief agencies. If they were aged and infirm the choice was quicker
made; if they were victims of accident or illness, quicker still;
and if they were left widowed or fatherless, then the doubt
hardly existed.

Suppose a man found the surrender to pauperism no solution, was unwilling to throw up the burden of his own
maintenance; but thought about it and struggled with it.
Every morning he would wake to face it, see through the big
eyes of fear the oppressive problems of the day ahead. He
could look through the narrow airshaft out at the blank wall
of his own existence, regard despondently the symbols of a
hopeless future. Loaded down with unbearable obligations,
many sighed with him who admitted, *Were it not for my soul
for which I am anxious, lest I lose it in eternity, I should
have drowned myself.* Some, in that last extremity, found the
charge of their own souls too heavy a responsibility.

Others yielded in a different way. They closed their eyes;
and as the lids of delusion fell and blotted out the brass
ugliness of the bed's footboard, they perceived in the sudden
perceptions of madness visions of the utmost delight. The
darkening walls fell away, revealed an undefined brightness
through which they, yes they themselves, ran lightly and
effortless, wrapped up in the enjoyment of some unimaginable pleasure.

Or, as on any other morning, you might come down in the
chill pre-dawn, half awake on the stairs, counting the creak of
your own treads, and turn, in hope of something today, onto
the street that led to market or shop. Only there would be
something peculiar this now in the shape of the shadows as
you hurried from island to island around the flickering
pillars of light. As your thoughts wandered their habitual

way over yesterday's disappointments and the fears of tomorrow, you began to pick out the fall of following footsteps;
round a corner and still they came; again; till, trotting
heavily, you outdistanced them — that time. What if they
should lie in secret wait, however; and what if among the
jostling strangers who swept around you as you hastened onto
the avenue were those already on to you? Who would hear
your cry, or care? They eyed you with their hostile stares,
condemning, pressed in upon you in seeming random movements. When you stopped against the tall board fence to take
the dreadful blow, you knew at once that this was he, and
struck and struck, till they pinned you down; and that was
all, while the foreign tongues murmured on above you.

The woman too found relief; so many dangers worried her.
Today they would not survive, the man and the young ones
perilously outside. He would lose the job or not bring home
the pay. There would be not enough to eat and, sickening, no
money for the doctor. She could no longer swallow her
anxiety and rubbed the harder on the board, over and over,
for the gray spots kept reappearing as she endlessly washed
them out.

Psychopathic disorders and neuroses, they were all one to
the admitting officers who kept the count of the insane. On
their rolls the immigrants were disproportionately prominent.

There were other means of release, temporary of duration
and therefore more subject to control. It was thus possible,
for a time, to dissolve in alcohol the least soluble of problems.
After a day's effort to hammer happiness out of the unyielding American environment it was good, now and then, to go
not to the narrow realities of home but to the convivial places
where the glass played the main part. The setting could take a
variety of forms: basement shops, combination kitchen-and-
bars, little cafés, the Irish grocery of 1850, the German
Bierstube of 1870, the Italian speakeasy of 1900 to which

prohibition would later bring another clientele. But the end was the same, a temporary relaxation of tension. And the end was so clear that some could achieve it alone, in the fastness of their own rooms, with the solitary company of a bottle.

There were immigrants who came to America with the inclination to drunkenness already well established. In Ireland, whisky went farther than bread as a relief from hunger; in Norway, eighteen quarts of alcohol were consumed for every person in the country each year; and elsewhere through Europe the habit of imbibing was well known. There were other newcomers who learned to know the consolations of a dram in the course of the crossing. A bit of grog was the regular prescription for seasickness; if it effected no cure, it dulled the misery.

It was that relief a man needed as much as the eyes in his head. Sometimes he drank away without thought what he had bathed in sweat to earn; but he gained in return an interval free of recollection or anticipation. In the good company, as his burdens lightened, he discovered in himself altogether unexpected but exhilarating powers, acquired daring and self-confidence beyond any sober hope. Well, and sometimes it would lead to a brawl, and the falling clubs of policemen, and the cold awakening of a cell; or, if not that, simply to the next day's throbbing reckoning of costs: what things the money might have bought! But there was none to point the finger of blame; and temptation came again and again. Not a few succumbed in every group of immigrants, though more in some groups than in others.

There was still another way of entering immediately into a realm of hope that shone in bright contrast to the visible dreariness about them. In that realm the evil dame, Chance, was transfigured into a luminous goddess; no longer as in real life did she strike down the lowly, but elevated them. Chance, here, ceased to deal out disaster; instead, conjured up the most heartwarming dreams.

Sometimes the men gambled among themselves, drew cards or lots for little stakes. There was a finger game Italians played, and among eastern Europeans a liking for pinochle. But these were sociable as much as gambling occasions, and had unpleasant disadvantages. The sum of little fortunes around the table hardly made a total worth the winning. One man's gain was another's loss; the joy of one, another's sorrow. Chance had not free rein; skill was as well involved, and the strain of calculation. Most of all, there was not the solitude in which the mind could drift away from time and place and rock itself in the comfort of hope.

Much preferable was some form of the lottery: the stakes were small, the rewards enormous; one might win, but none lost much; and chance was absolute. Lottery took many guises from the informal picks and chances of bar and shop to the highly organized enterprises city-wide in extension. Beneath was the attractiveness of an identical dream.

He can sit with a card, one of scores, in a club or saloon, check the squares, wait the call. Over and over and over again the little cage spins and no one knows when the little cage stops and a little ball hops and the number comes forth for the fortunate man. There's no telling — who knows? This may be when. The word's on his lips; let but chance give the sign and he will rise, *keno, lotto, bingo;* and all will be his.

She buys the slip from a policy man, who may be the corner grocer, the mailman, or anyone who in a daily round encounters a constant circle of people. Her number costs what she can spare, a dime, a nickel, just a penny. She chooses by what signs chance may give, a dream, an omen, a sudden intuition; and all day carries hope in her apron.

Did they really think to win who could not afford to lose? Yes, in a way they did, although they knew what odds were against them. But *why not* they? They would grant you that thousands lost for one who won, but could they surrender that one hope too? His hand that holds the card is soft and white, a hand that signs checks and gestures commands, the hand of a man who will drive to the comfort of a decent home. Her slip rests in the pocket of a gown, a gown that rustles leisurely as she walks with shining children up the steps. Indeed they have so often spent the money, and had the pleasure of dreaming it, it hardly mattered that they lost. At the price they paid, such dreams were cheap enough.

It was significant of such deviations — pauperism, insanity, intemperance, gambling — that they represented a yielding to the disorganizing pressure of the environment. These men did not step out of their roles as sober, industrious, thrifty breadwinners as a means of defying society, as a pure act of will. They deviated out of compulsion.

Where willful defiance of law was involved, the immigrants drew back. The rate of crime among the foreign-born was lower than among natives. There were frequent arrests for drunkenness; but those involved neither will nor, generally, crimes. And occasional petty thefts represented mostly a lack of clarity about property distinctions that had not applied at home. The peasant had recognized certain kinds of taking that were not robbery, by one member of a family from another, for instance, or of raw materials not the product of human labor, such as wood or game. The attempt to do the same in the United States led to trouble.

But the crime willfully planned and executed for gain rarely involved the immigrant. The lawbreakers often congregated in the districts in which the newcomers lived and sometimes recruited the American-born children, but not the immigrants themselves.

It was not hard to know what was going on, for after 1870 certainly these quarters were plunged into a regime of violence from which no one could escape. Organized gangs in alliance with the police terrorized whole territories. It was in the North End in Boston or down near the East Side in New York that their enterprises could most conveniently be planted: dance halls, saloons, gambling places, houses of prostitution, out of sight of the respectable citizens. The guardians of the law were unconcerned, beyond the need of recouping the investments paid out for their jobs. Already by 1900 Al Adams, the New York policy king, had a widespread network; and increasingly crime was removed from the area of free enterprise.

The sharpers and thugs found in the poor their readiest victims. Sometimes the boys at the corner would beat up a passer-by not so much for the handful of change they shook out of his pockets, but simply because his looks offended them, or for no reason at all. There'd be no thought of complaints; no one would listen and he who bore tales to the authorities would find the gangsters swift and merciless in retaliation. Death was never far from the door, why hasten its visit? In the New World, the immigrants feared to have recourse to the traditional peasant crimes of revenge — arson and homicide. Here was too much risk, too great an exercise of the will.

The inability to use force was the crowning irony of the immigrants' disorganization; the fact that they were law-abiding was less the product of their own choice than of fear to make a choice. As in so many other ways, the constricting environment forced them into deviations from their proper roles. If only a small number actually plunged into pauperism, or insanity, or drunkenness, many more lived long on the verge. And more still lived under the tension of avoiding the plunge; you could tell it by their new habits, endless smoking and the intrusion of profane swearing into their conversation.

Without a doubt they wished also to escape from the physical environment itself. As the years went by they got to know that the city held also pleasant tree-shaded streets where yards and little gardens set the houses off from each other. To these green spaces the most daring hearts aspired.

After 1850, cheaper rapid-transit systems brought the suburbs closer to the heart of the city. On the street railway the trolley took the horse's place and was joined by subway and elevated lines. Through these channels, the laboring masses spilled out from the district of first settlement to the surrounding regions. Naturally, this was a selective process; those who had a modicum of well-being, who could afford the higher rents and transportation charges, moved most freely. The poorest were immobilized by their poverty.

Those who went gained by going, but not by any means all they hoped for. Somehow, what they touched turned to dross. The fine house they saw in their mind's vision across the bridge or over the ferry turned out in actuality to have been converted into narrow flats for several families. In the empty spaces, little cottages rose; and long rows of two- and three-story attached buildings shut off the sight of the trees. The trouble was, so many moved that these newer places began to repeat the experience of the area of first settlement.

Never mind, for a time at least it was better. There was room to keep a goat, a few chickens; the men could sit at ease in their own front rooms facing the friendly street, while the women visited through the sociable low windows. This was a home to which attachments could grow, a place where deviations were less likely to appear.

And if in time the pressure of mounting population brought here too the tenement, and the spreading slum engulfed this first refuge, then those who could launched upon a second remove. Then a third. Till at last the city was a patchwork of separated districts, the outlines of which were shaped by the transit facilities, by the quality of available housing, and by the prior occupancy of various groups of immigrants. Always in this winnowing process the poorest were left in the older sections; the ability to move outward went with prosperity. Unfortunately it was the outer regions that were the thinnest settled. Least capable of organizing their lives to the new environment, the great mass long clustered at the center.

On the farms, space was too ample, not too little. Emptiness, not overcrowding, was the disorganizing element; and for those whose habits of life were developed in the peasant village, the emptiness of the prairie farm was in its own way as troublesome as the crowding of the city slum.

Here they called them neighbors who lived two or three miles off. Here one could stand on the highest rise of land and see nowhere but in the one farmstead any sign of man's tenancy. Such distances were too great to permit easy adjustment by the newcomers.

The peculiar characteristics of the prairie where the distances were greatest tested the immigrants to the utmost. In the midst of the open places they came by wagon and confronted the problem of shelter. They would live in what they could themselves build, for there was no community to help them; and certainly nothing was ready, awaiting their arrival. If they were fortunate, they found a nearby wood where the stove could rest and they could camp while the men chopped the logs for the cabin.

The cabin, no doubt, had its defects as a residence. It was small, perhaps twelve by fourteen feet in all; and above and below and about was mud, for the floor was as they found it and the spaces in the roof and walls were chinked with clay to keep the weather out.

But the people who settled into such quarters had only to compare situations with those who found no wood nearby, to count their own blessings. The cost of bringing timber in was at first prohibitive. If there were none on the spot, home would be of another material. Some would burrow dugouts into the slopes, return unknowingly to the life of the caves. Many cut the sun-baked surface of the earth, piled the sod in a double wall with dirt between, and in these huts spent a long period of trial.

Often years went by before such farmers advanced to the dignity of a frame house, with separate plastered rooms. There were first a barn and all the appurtenances of agriculture to be acquired. Meanwhile they got on in narrow quarters, felt the wind of winter through the cracks, heard the sides settle in the spring thaw, saw surprised snakes or gophers penetrate the floor.

Under such circumstances, there was an additional depth to their helplessness. No trees shielded them against the blast of winds. They were parched in the dry heat and they perished in the merciless blizzards. Hail and drought came and the clouds of grasshoppers that ate up their crops. On a limited monotonous diet the immigrants sickened, from the sudden shifts in climate the ague got them, from the prevalence of dirt, the itch. No doctors were near and home remedies or self-prescribed cures from bottles put a sad but decisive end to their misery. Alone in these distances they could expect no help.

That was the worst of it. The isolation which all immigrants sensed to some degree, on the farm was absolute; and not only on the prairie but everywhere. In the older Midwestern states, where the newcomers were not the first to settle, they found homes built and clearings made at their arrival; and soil and climate were not so hostile. Still, even there, they were detached, cut off from the company of other men. Each family was thrown in upon itself; every day the same faces round the same table and never the sight of outsiders. To have no familiar of one's own age and sex was a hard deprivation.

They would think sometimes of the friendly village ways, of the common tasks lightened for being done in common; they would remember the cheering inn, and the road on which some reassuring known figure could always be seen. At such times, alone in the distance, helpless in their isolation, a vague and disturbing melancholia fell over them. It was easier for them when they added acres and when stocked barns and heavy wagonloads gave a sense of substance and achievement to their lives. Still, even then would come regrets for the disorganization wrought in their existence by the place. Insanity appeared among some; others sought solace in alcohol; and most continued to work, under strain, eager for relief.

They would probably have said that it was the mill town which made the least demand upon them. This was not so large as a single city ward and here space was not at a premium; yet neither was there here the complete isolation of the farm. The immigrants' round of activities here fell into a unit the size of which they could comprehend.

What pressure there was came from the situation of such communities. Often a single company or at most a single industry supplied the employment for all the residents. Any man who came to work in the mine or factory was altogether dependent upon the sole hirer. He was not free to choose among jobs or to argue long about terms; he could only acquiesce or leave. In that sense, it was a condition of his membership in this community that he cut himself off from the world outside the town.

Confined within the immediate locality, the laborers discovered that there was plenty of space, but not plenty of housing. Despite the low density of population, the available quarters were so restricted there was serious overcrowding. As the workers arrived they found at first only the farm or village buildings, quickly converted to their use. The single men were likely to live in makeshift boardinghouses; those with families in cut-up portions of the old houses. Shortly either the company or individual investors threw up additional facilities. Into the surrounding farm land, narrow alleys were pushed, lined with three-story frame tenements or with tiny two-room cottages. The company which controlled all was hardly interested in increasing the supply of housing to an unprofitable excess over demand; nor was it anxious to go to the expense of providing gas, water, and sewerage. The results matched those of the city slums.

Still, the open fields were not far off, and there was not the same total lack of space. The disorganizing effects of the environment were therefore probably less harsh, the deviations less pronounced. What strain there was, was the product of confinement in the town and of constricted housing.

To some degree, these factory town immigrants, like those who went to the cities and those who settled on farms, found the physical conditions of life in America hostile. Nowhere could they recapture the terms of village life; everywhere a difficult adjustment began with the disorganization of the individual, now grown uncertain as to his own proper role. Reorganization would involve first the creation of new means of social action within which the man alone could locate himself.

From the physical as from the religious experience with the New World, the immigrants had gained a deep consciousness of their separateness. It seemed sometimes as if there were only one street in the world, and only a single house on it, and nothing more — only walls and very few people, so that *I am in America and I do not even know whether it is America*. This street was apart as if a ghetto wall defined it. On other streets were other men, deeply different because they had not the burden of this adjustment to bear. This street and those did not run into each other; nor this farm into those. If the immigrants were to achieve the adjustment to their new environment, it had to be within the confines of the ghettos the environment created.

SEVEN

In Fellow Feeling

STRANGERS IN THE IMMEDIATE WORLD about them, the immigrants often recognized, in dismay, the loneliness of their condition. Their hesitant steps groped around the uncertain hazards of new places and exposed them ever to perilous risks. No one could enjoy the satisfaction of confidence in his own unaided powers.

In their loneliness and helplessness, the immigrants reached for some arm to lean upon. There came a time, they knew, when a man was like a stray dog, driven away by all folk, glad to be caressed by any kindly hand. At many steps in his life's journey he came to points beyond which he could not go on alone; unaided he was doomed. Then it was well if help could come from others like him.

Consequently, the newcomers took pains early to seek out those whom experience made their brothers; and to organize each others' support, they created a great variety of formal and informal institutions. Then, at last, they came to know how good it was that brothers should dwell together.

The peasants, in their coming, did not bring with them the social patterns of the Old World. These could not be imposed on the activities of the New. The energies expended in reconstructing the churches revealed the forbidding proportions of the task of transplantation; and the environment, in any case, was hostile to the preservation of village ways. What forms ultimately developed among immigrants were the products of American conditions.

The crowded tenement neighborhoods spontaneously generated associations. Here people could not help meeting one another, their lives were so much in the open, so much shared. The sounds of joy and sorrow traveling up the airshaft united all the residents of the house; the common situation that cut these men off from the rest of the city itself united them. Within the ghetto could grow understanding, then sympathy, and in time co-operation.

Each building acquired a kind of organization, as families learned each other's character, got to know who could be depended on for what, and as they worked together in the necessary care of common facilities. When a crisis came, of sudden childbirth, of illness, of fire, it was the concern of all. In the warm summer evenings while their elders sat on the steps below, the young people would go up to the relative spaciousness of the roof, sometimes sleep the night there on the pebbled tar. Or groups together would venture on trips away, picnics in the park, rides on the ferryboat, or walks across the bridge. It was hard to believe, but true, that so much pleasure should come of talk. She spoke, next door, of events in an unknown place, of the misfortunes of someone else's family in someone else's village; and her tale had emotional force, as if it put into another setting familiar incidents and, by supplying them with generality, gave them meaning. So, strangers became friends. No need to ask what antecedents; the ability to communicate with each other was bond enough.

Down by the corner was, invariably, a place where the men could meet, talk without the constraint of woman's presence. At first some accommodating grocer measured out the spirits in a back room to small groups of convivial acquaintances. But after 1850 more rigid licensing laws had the effect of discouraging such informal establishments. Instead the saloon acquired a certain pre-eminence. But this was not the gaudy uptown emporium with which the readers of temperance tracts were familiar — a front for gambling and vice. Rather, its doors swung open upon modest groups of workingmen who cautiously invested nickels for beer and dimes for whisky for the warmth of companionship. In some places, indeed, the gathering point was not a saloon but a coffeehouse, or, later, a candy store; the site was less important than the coming together.

Here for a time would also be the setting of such occasions as needed the community for celebration. They remembered what affairs had been those weddings in the old home; why a week had not been too long, nor the whole village too many. In this land they had not the space in the crowded flats to welcome the immediate families. But there was gaiety in the room behind the bar where, flushed with temporary happiness, they paced off the once-familiar steps — only an evening, yes, and an early rising for work tomorrow, but a joy nevertheless, one to be long anticipated and long remembered. After a while these parties acquire importance enough to justify their own, more appropriate, premises. A hall is fitted out for the purpose; and if too long a period elapses with no wedding to make it merry, then some enterprising group is sure to contrive the pretext for a dance.

In the tenement, on the corner, in the hall, in none of these neighborhood encounters is there any rigid organization. These are spontaneous expressions of the desire to be not alone, to find understanding through communication with others. Yet, without design, the gatherings acquire form. Usage determines the proper ways of behavior; certain rules of propriety are established; and intimate little rituals develop. Each individual is known to his fellows. He has a reputation and plays a role; and whether he is the butt of laughter or the subject of respect, he is a person of character. That has great value to those who, outside the group, are anonymous integers in an alien society.

To these associations which were their own, and not those of strangers, they turned in the moments of trouble. Now and again the hat went round and the tinkle of reluctant coins recalled the imminent peril of all. But then, disasters were so frequent and so terrible it was an elementary precaution that some among these people should band together to accumulate the funds with which they could give mutual aid to each other. With this added function, the group achieved a more formal structure. To administer its affairs, to safeguard its cash, to allocate its benefits, it needed the services of officers. When those appeared the mutual aid society had evolved.

Although life itself was full of problems, the first concern of these societies was death. The dread transition to the mystery of the world beyond had always been laden with meaningful implications. Since this was not merely an end to mortal flesh, but the beginning also of another existence, they had at home reckoned it of particular importance that a man be laid away in the sacred ground of the cemetery among his friends and relatives. For these awesome proceedings tradition prescribed the precise rites; the dread consequences of failure or omission no one could foretell. Although the actual task of interring the body was regarded with disgust and assigned to some degraded individual, nevertheless the whole village had participated in this last communal duty to its members.

Here the forms were in danger. The isolated man might be buried by strangers, improperly, in an unhallowed place, far from his kin, forever to lie in desolate loneliness. More than anything in life itself, the immigrants wished security in death; and the first task of the mutual aid society was to provide that assurance. The cost was high here for what was almost free back there, and only the common action of the society adequate to meet it. Funerals became events of great neighborhood ceremonial importance, and the undertaker no longer a pariah but a person of consequence.

Once the dead were taken care of, for whom eternity was the concern, then there was time to think of the living. As the groups grew stronger, as they acquired reserves and financial stability, they could expand their functions in a variety of directions. Suppose a man was hurt in the foundry; suppose it crushed his chest, or broke his arm, or tore his leg away, what then? As easily as a blind hen found grain, he got compensation from the company. Yet a wife and the children had to be fed and himself he needed care.

In the village, such assistance had been among the obligations of the family. It was vain to rely upon such flimsy support here, however. Few households had the resources to take care of their own when illness struck, or accident; fewer still to extend aid to relatives or neighbors. The wiser course was to unite in precautionary saving. Let each one contribute monthly or weekly a fixed sum which would accumulate as a whole and upon which each could draw when necessary under the terms of an agreed-on plan. In illness as in death, the mutual benefit society came increasingly to be the main reliance of all immigrants.

The associations themselves met with a various fortune. They thrived or foundered, depending partly upon the honesty, prudence, and skill of the officers and partly upon the welfare of the members. Some societies, hopefully inaugurated, quickly came to grief when a treasurer absconded or through ignorance confounded his accounts or through unwise investments lost the savings. Others closed their affairs when depression or even just seasonal slack stopped the flow of dues and, at the same time, stepped up the requests for benefits. Perhaps the largest number maintained the precarious balance of income and expenditure through the lifetime at least of their founders.

On the other hand, a few flourished beyond any initial expectation. The presence of a handful of successful members would attract new recruits through the hope of favors or the prestige of belonging. With so heavy a social premium on joining, such organizations felt free to charge what fees they liked; yet growing wealthy, they found few calls from within for assistance. They were likely then to turn their attention to the improvident many who still needed help.

No doubt it was true that no one could be forced to aid the needy. But men were not beasts to be left to perish from want. The associations with funds to spare took on the obligation of relieving the misery of more newly arrived immigrants; the longer-settled but poor they tided over with loans or outright gifts; and the victims of accident or of personal maladjustment they helped with advice and what charity they could.

In addition, some groups through benevolence were induced to construct and maintain the philanthropic institutions the new conditions of living made necessary. The traditional duties of supporting the infirm were too onerous to be borne here by individuals. It was well enough in the peasant hut to find a corner for the old man or woman, to share what food there was. Or, the parentless could slip without difficulty into an uncle's household. And what attention the ill received, they received at home. In the crowded immigrant quarters such cares were enough to disrupt the family's precarious stability. Yet the prospect of confinement in the refuge maintained by the state or municipal government was frightening. The grandparents shuddered at the thought of spending their last days among uncomprehending strangers; orphans sent to such an asylum would surely grow away from the group; and the sick often preferred the possibility of death within the safety of their own houses to the unknown risks of the alien hospital. The old obligation therefore became a new one, not to find space in the flat or time from work for the accommodation of those who needed care, but rather to establish and support their own hospital, orphanage, and home for the aged to perform the task.

As the successful societies took on additional charitable functions, they acquired a variety of forms. In the early intimate days of the life of each, constitutional questions were of very slight concern. The organization then operated after the manner of the old village council, by discussion in which the weight accorded any opinion depended upon the respect accorded the individual who held it. Some associations then advanced to the respectability of a constitution and bylaws, copied in each case from some neighboring body, but derived ultimately from a common ancestry, the American corporation, board of directors, president, treasurer, secretary. Still others assumed the structure of the fraternal secret society. After 1850 particularly, Knights and Orders of many sorts flourished in a bewildering Gothic variety.

The magnetic element at the core of all, however, was always the opportunity for sociability. With the occasional association dedicated to intellectual and physical self-improvement, these provided the means by which like men got to know each other. The balls and picnics had the additional virtue of raising money; but their true end was sociability. And the event that excited greatest enthusiasm was the parade, a procession which enabled the group to display before the whole world the evidence of its solidarity, which enabled the individual to demonstrate that he belonged, was a part of a whole.

Sometimes, in the half-light of a brisk spring late afternoon when the parade was over or on the way home at night in the heady good cheer after the ball, a man would think, as he came up the steps of his house, *What if all this did not exist that I could be part of it, what if I were then alone among the teeming thousands on this block, had none to talk with, none to know and be known by!* The thought alone would inspire him with determination to keep safe the community he was creating.

All around were threats to its integrity. Everywhere in the

United States were laws that prescribed a minimum schooling for the children. The State itself sponsored educational institutions into which youngsters were drawn without cost, there to be brought up by aliens, taught alien ways in an alien language, generally by teachers of an alien religion. From this sore spot might spread a hostile influence that could undermine the health of the whole immigrant community. You could sense that danger in the derisive name-calling of the schoolyard, in the unbending severity of the principal, in the bloody fights of the boys on the way.

The alternative was to devise voluntary schools that would serve to strengthen rather than to weaken the coherence of the group. To do so involved a difficult and discouraging task. There was no precedent in the European experience of the newcomers. None of the countries from which these people emigrated had had an educational system that reached down to the peasantry. What efforts had been made in that direction were entirely State-supported.

Yet with devotion and at the expense of considerable sacrifice the immigrants attempted to construct autonomous schools which would leave in their own hands the training of their young. They raised funds and paid out fees for the sake of saving the children. But the measure of their success was not impressive. Among the Germans, Poles, Italians, Jews, and most other groups only a handful of institutions survived in a limited number of places. The Irish Catholics were somewhat better rewarded for their troubles. The earliest Catholic colleges had been directed at training for the priesthood and the earliest convent schools had attracted only an upper-class clientele. But as Irish influence became weightier in the Church the number of elementary schools set up to provide for the children of immigrants increased rapidly. Even within this group, however, parochial schools served only a minority by the end of the period of immigration. The expense was too great to be shouldered fully at once; yet delay established the children within the influence of the public institutions.

Fortunately the school was only one of several means of education. The labor of several hundred parents together could not maintain a building and teachers; but in the nineteenth century, several hundred subscribers could support a newspaper. Shortly after its arrival every group of immigrants found a medium of expression in a press of its own, edited to satisfy its own needs, and published in its own language.

This was a substantial achievement. In Europe, the peasantry had had nothing to do with such journals, considering them an expensive luxury and a waste of time. What happened within the village everyone knew, and there was no purpose to gathering useless information about what happened outside it. *We have grown old and we cannot read nor write*, their own parents had said, *yet we live. So you too may live without knowledge.*

In the New World there was no life without some kinds of knowledge; and often only his own press could give the immigrant the explanations his troubled experience demanded. The happenings of the old village and its environs were still of concern to him; yet that concern would not be satisfied in the general American papers. Let him but consult the sheet his fellows put out, and he would find recounted the doings in his own parish. Printed extracts from letters set forth the state of the crops, detailed events ordinary and extraordinary, and supplied a chain of communication with the Old Country.

It was the same with news that originated on this side of the Atlantic. The immigrants were interested in knowing about themselves. The record of births, marriages, and deaths within the group, the story of the various churches and societies, and accounts of diverse noteworthy local occurrences found a place in these pages and nowhere else. To the extent that these people had begun to constitute communities, they wished to be in contact with each other. Their own newspapers supplied the means of establishing that contact.

These were also the instruments through which the immigrants learned to interpret the issues and events of the larger American society within which they were situated. In the columns of their journals they read or heard read reports of the important incidents of the day, rendered in a manner that made meaning. The editorials put matters in an understandable form; expressing the viewpoint of the group, they supplied it with guidance in the face of all the difficult questions it confronted.

Finally, the press was the main repository of immigrant literature. Hard-pressed editors were always willing to fill their pages with borrowed or volunteered contributions, and their readers found these the most attractive sections of the papers. The stories were sometimes *as in real life;* that is, they dealt with familiar situations and scenes. Or, they were peopled with folk heroes depicted in accepted legendary poses. But the underlying themes were constant and embodied the fundamental ideas of the group. Such narratives gripped the attention because they repeated in other terms the truths immigrants perceived in their own lives: so indeed was faith rewarded and deviation from the old ways punished; yes, this was the result of the ingratitude of children; thus, alas, did betrayal come at the hands of strangers.

The poetry in these columns flowed largely from the pens of the readers themselves. The peasants particularly seemed no sooner to learn to write than they burst into rhyme. Their efforts were brief generally and the dominant tone that of nostalgic reminiscence. The most popular subjects were descriptions of old village scenes and events, sentimental outpourings at departures and partings, and expressions of sorrow at untimely deaths. It was as if these people for whom writing of any kind was difficult reserved this form of expression for those incidents which affected them most deeply. Despite the crudity of composition they wrote into these lines a sense of high emotion and of deep personal significance. It was for that, as much as for anything else, that the great mass of immigrants laid out their pennies when they took a paper.

An earnest longing to hear said what they felt, was responsible for the high esteem in which these people held the theater. More even than the press, the stage was the vehicle of popular culture in the second half of the nineteenth century. Every city of any size had a number of halls dedicated to the purpose — converted rooms crammed with benches before a makeshift platform, cavernous playhouses with galleries rising in tier after tier of lowered prices, and grand glittering auditoria where overly coy cherubs wriggled along the surface of the proscenium arch. Here resident companies and touring artists put in an appearance accessible to all; ten cents brought admission to anyone willing to climb high enough.

In these settings each immigrant group developed a theatrical life of its own. In places where the numbers were large enough to keep a steady stream of patrons coming, a stock company could play the year round. Elsewhere, itinerant troupers indulged the community for a week or two at a time. And the very smallest groups satisfied themselves with the performances of amateurs. In one city or another the drama flourished among each concentration of immigrants, German, Italian, Yiddish, Irish, Greek, Polish, and many others.

This whole realm of pretending had been outside the experience of the immigrants before their arrival. The holiday mummery of the peasants, the antics of wandering acrobats, musicians, gypsies, or animal trainers, had had quite a different meaning. Those were spectacles that induced the onlooker to marvel at the unnatural. But the theater was real. There were men and women in the familiar garb of life whose movements had the appearance of actuality. Yet the show of action held the audience in a spell, moved them to brokenhearted weeping, or, sometimes, to fits of hysterical laughter.

It was true that the popular drama made few demands upon the literacy of those who watched from the balcony. Nor did it take great power of concentration to follow the active movements on the stage. Plots were direct and simple, uncomplicated by subtleties of character delineation; often the story unfolded on a continuous plane of excitement, with one climax hot on the heels of another. By its reactions it might have seemed that the audience judged the merit of an actor by his agility.

But there was a more substantial basis for the attractiveness of the theater. The resident companies played an enormous repertory since they offered a new bill weekly, or twice a week, or more often still. Even with the license to borrow freely from the classics it was difficult to put on so many productions and still make a pretense at originality. Some troupes had their own playwrights who cut and pasted the dramas together; in others the producer did the job. But in either case the task of composition was essentially one of manipulating a limited number of stock situations and stock characters according to conventional patterns. A good deal was left to the skill of the actors at improvisation; and these accordingly were the key figures in the production.

Under these circumstances the role of the actor with reference to his audience was more sensitive than that of a newspaper writer with reference to his readers. For the performer could feel the immediate response of his auditors and, unhampered by a rigid script, adjust his lines for the most effective play upon their emotions. The rapport across the footlights gave expression on the stage to the hopes and fears, the intimate ideas and beliefs, of the immigrants who came to watch.

In melodrama the themes were much like those in the literary columns of the press. Colored robes gave ancient kings of a golden past authority as they rendered justice;

ingratitude slammed the door as the faithless child left home; evil personified in the fraudulent stranger walked its guileful way. So, it really could happen; whether the specific setting was distant or near, the audience saw generalized here the critical elements of its own situation.

The theater was also a house of mirth. Sitting there, a man could find laughter enough to last him a long time. For days reminiscent chuckles would accompany thoughts of the antics on the stage.

What was so funny? Why should the misadventures of a shabbily dressed laborer stir an audience of laborers to up-roarious amusement? Here is a clumsy clown who cannot make his way across a room without tripping himself. He is thrust into the company of elegant people in situations in which he must cover himself with ridicule. Clever gentlemen deceive him. Innocently he is embroiled with the police who pursue him. He lacks control, is drunk, or shortsighted, or stupid. Sometimes he achieves a paradoxical triumph, some-times is beaten into the dust; victory and defeat are alike unearned. Is that funny?

Those who lean back on the hard seats exhausted with merriment find the scene familiar. They recognize every character. Is the name Mike? Then he carries a whisky bottle and a clay pipe as he jigs across the platform. Fritz waddles on, big-bellied, clutching the mug of beer. Ike pulls the black derby hard down over his ears. Tony is not without his shovel. The mouths open and the lurid distorted speech that spills forth, in whatever language, clinches their identity.

Why then, they who laugh are looking into a great eccen-tric mirror. They see themselves — but all out of shape, grotesque, unhuman. They hold their sides as the teetering homunculi, pummeled down, bounce merrily up again. *Our family name is Carey, so happy, light, and airy, we came from Tipperary so far across the sea.* So far across the sea, my boys, and now? *We've struck a job so handy.* So handy? That's dandy; you're dandies. *Yes, with the shovel we're the dandies.*

This is the language of irony. To those whom experience gives understanding the meaning is clear. All this buffoonery exaggerates but slightly the real features of this slapstick life of theirs. Does not the whole migration have a bitter, contradictory outcome as if in mockery of the promise and fitness of things? It is all true, the tripping and trapping, the falling and brawling, the beating and cheating. Too true for tragedy! Only laughter draws the sting of it.

It was the gift of the theater to pull aside the curtains that concealed from these people so much of their strange world. They did not learn much from watching these comedies and melodramas, only this — that by perceiving what was general in their own situation, they could identify themselves with others who shared that situation. Like the societies, the schools, and the press, the theater was a means through which the immigrants came to know each other.

The man who joined a mutual aid association, who took a newspaper or went to the theater, was adjusting thereby to the environment of the United States. These were not vestiges of any European forms, but steps in his Americanization.

Yet the same steps brought him ever deeper within a separate existence, loose within the total community in which he lived. The neighborhood and the clubs added up to a society with its own activities and its own media of communication, a society whole and coherent within the larger American society. Paradoxically, as the immigrant adapted himself to the life of the New World, he found himself more often and more completely operating inside the limits of these cultural and social enclaves.

The prevalence of highly developed group activities did not in itself make the position of the newcomers exceptional. This was the general pattern of association in the United States. Those many generations in the country as well as those recently arrived found the most important social concerns here considered the function of voluntary, autonomous combinations, free of the State and all on an equal footing. In this realm of spontaneous organization, the appearance of immigrant associations was taken as a matter of course; every aggregation of individuals acted so in America. This was the means by which all groups discovered the distinctive similarities within themselves, the distinctive differences that cut them off from the whole society.

Becoming an American meant therefore not the simple conformity to a previous pattern, but the adjustment to the needs of a new situation. In the process the immigrants became more rather than less conscious of their own peculiarities. As the immediate environment called forth the succession of fresh institutions and novel modes of behavior, the immigrants found themselves progressively separated as groups.

Yet it was no easy matter then to define the nature of such groupings. Much later, in deceptive retrospect, a man might tell his children, *Why, we were Poles and stayed that way* — or Italians, or Irish or Germans or Czechoslovaks. The memories were in error. These people had arrived in the New World with no such identification. The terms referred to national states not yet in existence or just come into being. The immigrants defined themselves rather by the place of their birth, the village, or else by the provincial region that shared dialect and custom; they were Masurians or Corkonians or Apulians or Bohemians or Bavarians. The parents back across the Atlantic, troubled by a son's too quick abandonment of the old ways, begged that he keep in himself *the feeling of a Poznaniak.* (They did not say Pole.)

To some extent, village and regional affiliations remained the core of associational activities in the United States. But though this basis of selection might be adequate enough to recruit the members of a club, it was inadequate to a full group life.

To the houses on this city street, for instance, would come all the folk who had known each other at home; but they would hardly fill the place. Into the tenements would also come strangers from other provinces; but not indiscriminately. One criterion at least culled apart those who could find room from those who could not. In the closeness of these quarters there was no getting on together without the ability to communicate with each other. In the neighborhood, in societies, through the press and the theater common language was the means of recognition.

In 1837 there was a falling-out among the men planting a new settlement in Illinois. One faction wished the name of the township to be Westphalia, another, Hannover, each after its own native land. The compromise was significant — Germantown; the language took them all in.

So, generally, immigrant groups named themselves by their language rather than by place of origin. The experience of the Germans was repeated by almost all later comers; even in the twentieth century, "Syrian" societies included not simply those born in Syria, but all Arabic-speaking peoples. Awareness of the identity of the group had come through the concrete activities of the New World; and in those activities the ability to understand one another was critical.

In a few cases, language was an untrustworthy standard. In some situations men would meet and speak the same words yet not comprehend each other; some fundamental barrier obtruded. Religion, transplanted from the old home, was the most important source of such differences. Proximity to a church was a meaningful consideration in the choice of a residence. Assurance of the proper ritual at burial often determined a man's selection of a mutual aid society. And religious ideas weighed heavily in the decision as to which paper to take. Therefore the Catholic Irish tended to draw away from the other English-speaking immigrants and the Jewish Germans away from the other Germans.

However, neither language nor religion cut a clear line of universal validity around the group. Some individuals succeeded indeed in maintaining affiliations with several kinds of societies in reflection of the diverse links of tongue and faith; so a Danish Jew in Chicago would be among the founders of both the Scandinavian and the Jewish hospitals. Large aggregations of people were long uncertain of their own identity. Thus the Carpatho-Ruthenians long confused themselves with the Slovaks until the latter began to affiliate with the Czechs, at which point many among the first-named began to draw closer to the Great Russians.

There were perplexing problems of identity even among English-speaking immigrants, communicants of churches which had native American counterparts. Some of these people undoubtedly lost themselves at once in the indigenous community; but most did not. The peasants particularly followed the course of development of other newcomers.

The difficulty in their case was to discover the grouping most expressive of their common similarities. Until the middle of the nineteenth century the Ulster and Dublin Protestants were likely to count themselves Irish while other Protestants accepted the general designation, British. After 1850 the non-Catholic Hibernians more generally fell into the British category, while by contrast the Scots and Welshmen more often asserted their own individuality, founded separate societies and newspapers, and struggled to preserve or revive distinctive language and custom.

The determining elements everywhere were not general, but local. In the great cities the enormous accumulations of population made room for the most diverse combinations. In these places associations were quickest to take form; there were enough people of every kind so that every social desire could be satisfied. In the farming areas, on the other hand, the paucity of residents constricted such activities; the church often was the only organization to which the scattered individuals were drawn, and religion became the focus of communal life. The great variety of conditions in the mill and mining towns set for each its own pattern; the richness of the organizational life fluctuated with the size of the various groups. Everywhere, the forms of associational action were shaped by local conditions because these activities everywhere appeared in response to the specific needs of strangers in an unfamiliar environment.

The men who acquired here new modes of fellowship to replace the old ones destroyed by emigration earned thereby some sense of security against complete isolation. But their efforts, no matter how strenuous, could not forestall changes. The whole of American society was changing. These little immigrant islands within it could not withstand the trend.

Everything in the neighborhood was so nice, they would later say, until the others came. The others brought outlandish ways and unintelligible speech, foreign dress and curious foods, were poor, worked hard, and paid higher rents for inferior quarters. Gradually the older comers saw the new arrivals filter into the district, occupy house after house that became vacant before their advance, until the whole configuration of the place was transformed.

So the tenement regions of the cities became the homes of group after group of immigrants. Through the dark halls and crowded rooms moved the Irish and the Germans, the Italians and the Poles, and all the other wandering peoples, each in turn to make a way of life there. But not permanently; each was in time displaced by its successor.

Movement away from the tenement areas did not immediately destroy the associational life that had proliferated there. Often there was a vigorous continuity. In New York City, for instance, the Germans moved in a straight line northward along the East Side of the island and the Irish did the same on the West Side. Old institutions were transplanted to new settings and, as the suburbs fell before the immigrant advance, they took on some of the aspects of the neighborhoods of first settlement. Still, each removal, in the mind of the individual, raised afresh the question of his affiliations, offered him the opportunity to re-examine the question of where he belonged. This mobility gave all organizations a transient quality, prevented any from becoming fixed, rigid, customary.

Under such circumstances the immigrant societies themselves were bound to change. They had been spontaneous in their organization, but once set up, drifted out of the control of the mass of members. With growth a select leadership appeared; it took skill beyond the capacity of the ordinary laborer to manage the affairs of an insurance association or to edit a newspaper or direct a theater. And the interests and points of view of the leadership were not always the same as those of its following.

The man who took command of the immigrant group sometimes sprang from within the ranks of the newcomers. He had laid hands on the money to open a grocery or to take on contracts and had added by shrewdness and effort to his original store. The fellows who had come off the ship with him still toiled away for their uncertain daily bread, but he was successful, had faced the American environment and had mastered it. At home perhaps he had been only a swineherd, his father a landless cottier without respectable status in the village. But family dignity counted for nothing here. He merited consideration who had acquired a secure existence and had shown thereby his capacity to deal with the New World. The prestige of social office confirmed the leadership of such individuals.

Yet this person who had elevated himself above the others in the group had also thereby imperceptibly separated himself from them. Sure, there was a feeling of personal importance, of self-exaltation at the rise. At the family table there was a lavish spread of food and at the meetings of the Order there could be the munificent gestures of hospitality and donations. The insecurities were of another quality.

The laborer after all dealt mostly with others like himself. But the immigrant become businessman was thrown in with all sorts of people, salesmen, government officials, bankers; and, as the old saying had it, *Who goes among crows must croak like them, who gets among goats must jump like them.* It was necessary to get along with strangers, to win the esteem of influential outsiders. He who rose must learn to wear American clothing, let his fingernails grow like a gentleman, cultivate conformity in language and name, and still not drift so far away as to lose the respect of his own group. Such were the burdens of leadership.

The weight was even heavier for those who aspired to direct an immigrant group without having originated within the group itself. Antedating the mass movement from Europe, and continuing through the nineteenth century along with it, was a much tinier migration of political refugees, displaced by the recurrent revolutions on the continent. Repercussions of the French Revolution brought some; from Ireland came exiles after the disturbances of 1798, 1803, and 1848; from Germany came those dissatisfied with Metternich's repressions in the 1820's and with the failure of 1848; from Poland came the unsuccessful rebels of 1830 and 1863; and from eastern Europe came handfuls of socialists unsafe at home after 1880. The Land of Liberty was the universal refuge for dissentients everywhere.

These people in the Old World had had nothing to do with the peasantry; and in the New continued to stand apart. They were disposed to be apathetic if not hostile to religion; they were radical rather than conservative in politics; and they were liberal rather than traditional in their attitudes toward social institutions. Such substantial differences brought them closer in point of view to the native Americans than to the mass of newcomers. Yet only a few entered so readily into the society they found in the United States as to make for themselves independent careers here.

The most were driven back to the immigrant communities, which welcomed the services they could perform. They were literate, indeed often well-educated. They could talk and write, make favorable impressions as representatives of the group. Often such men acquired positions of responsible leadership without yet being integrated into the organizations they led. Suspended between the American society to which they spoke and the immigrant society which supported them, they felt the unremitting pressure to reconcile the two.

The same compulsion was heaviest of all when it fell upon those whom the circumstances of nativity gave affiliations in both the greater and the lesser society. One came a young child and went some terms to the public schools. Another cried as a newborn infant in the stifling tenement room and played ball on the street among the passing draymen's teams. They entered manhood with the American ideals absorbed from school and street, not strangers but familiar to the life about them.

Yet often the opportunities lay among their fathers' folk. There name and religion were advantages not disadvantages. There the accents of the old language, the acquaintance with the ways of the old neighborhood, were assets not liabilities. No young man in business or politics could afford to overlook connections within the immigrant group. For their part, the older people saw an attractiveness in these their youth who bore so much the aspects of Americans. The foreign-born would not always follow their native sons, but were willing to have them lead.

It was significant that immigrant associational activity drew its direction from men who somehow stood apart, from men who had this in common, that they were concerned with using their positions to make an impression in the general society. With that end in view they could not be content with the local club as it had remained under the original founders; a radical transformation was indispensable.

Confederation of existing organizations was the simplest step. After 1850 there were determined efforts within each immigrant group to create one or more national unions that would draw together the scattered societies. After 1880 such efforts achieved a measure of success; Alliances, Leagues, Orders covered the country, and the earlier parochial associations sank to the status of mere branches. In discussion the arguments for combination were plausible enough: funds would be more secure, influence more pervasive. But the men who listened and hesitantly acquiesced knew better, though they knew not how to say it: not they would go to conventions, sit on committees, be consulted by important personages. No, and the intimate meanings of the old meetings would disappear. Still, they were feeble in debate and could not hold out.

Nor could they long resist appeals that awakened attachments to the place of their birth. In the Old World all the nationalist currents of the nineteenth century had passed them by; indeed these people did not even identify themselves in such terms. And certainly emigration involved a rejection of the Old Country. Only in America, as strangers, had they learned from the inevitable contrasts with others to be aware of their own distinctive character.

Their American offspring turned this group-consciousness into nationalism. The sons of the immigrants had no memory of Old Country places, no recollection of the village solidarity. By actual membership in the group and by participation in its activities, they knew they were Irish or German or Italian or Polish. But that affiliation had meaning for them only as a kind of patriotism; and they projected onto their fathers' native lands the kinds of loyalty that, in the United States, seemed proper to a fatherland. Fervently they enlisted in movements to create new states or to support the policies of existing ones. Therein they received the support of the nationalistic émigrés already involved in similar causes and also the approbation of other Americans swayed by the common sympathy of the nineteenth century for oppressed nationalities.

No other form of immigrant association received such universal approval from outside the group. Who would be so stubborn as to remain unconvinced, to abstain from an activity that involved, at once, the renewal of ties with the place of one's birth and the acclaim of the whole country? For almost a century the Irish in America were wrapped up in the struggle for the independence of the Emerald Isle, a struggle for a time so intense as to produce armed invasions of the nearest British territory in Canada. The attitude of German-Americans to the Empire in 1870, of Italian-Americans to the Kingdom, of central and eastern Europeans to the successor republics of 1918, and of the Jews to Zionism, partook of the same quality.

Still a third assault was launched upon the original integrity of immigrant society, this one less successful. The men of radical ideas exiled to the United States attempted to enlist the newcomers in organizations directed against the existing order. Partly the revolutionaries were betrayed by their own ideology: they would never get to realize that the most oppressed economic order was not necessarily the most likely to rebel. The immigrant was an exploited unskilled laborer; they persisted in the hope they might turn his vague discontent into specific radical directions. In any case, the radicals were agitators by profession. Chance had thrown them in with a class with which they were not familiar. They would try to make converts all the same.

Between 1850 and 1880 an exotic agglomeration of socialists, anarchists, and freethinkers labored to find support within the immigrant associations. Though, as intellectuals, they made their voices heard with more volume than their numbers justified, they were hardly in a position to boast of their achievements after thirty years of trying.

After 1880, the radicals were inclined to capitalize on the neglect of the immigrants by the American labor movement. Recognizing the solidarity of these groups, the socialists attempted to enlist the foreign-born through such special agencies as the United German Trades and the United Hebrew Trades. Similarly, after 1900, the I.W.W. set up separate nationality locals and recognized the particular languages of the immigrants in order to gain support among them. But the deep-rooted conservatism of these people proved an insuperable obstacle to such proselytizing. At most the radicals raised disruptive, confusing issues or split the leadership; they could not arouse the enthusiasm of the masses.

Indeed the immigrant who had been at home in his own mutual aid society was dismayed by all these efforts to turn his joining into something else. The national alliances took on the appearance of power and wealth. Nationalistic agitation whipped up a display of emotions. In the Turners, in the Sokols, in the Zouaves — intricate patriotic associations — men deployed in fixed, rigid lines. But the touch of intimate friendliness, the sense of dwelling with one's brothers, vanished. Disappointed, he often dropped out; secession after secession continually reproduced the neighborhood societies which, after all, gave him what he wanted.

Only time went on and even these were not the same.

The will is not to change. But change comes. New words and ways insidiously filter in. *Someone speaks and you can only look at him on the street there, miserable in your lack of English.* Now phrases will be remembered, become familiar, enter into usage, be confounded with the old language. Someday the trolley signs will have a meaning and you will be interpreter for someone greener still.

The old coat disintegrates. Its rugged homespun had come along; its solid virtues had taken the strain of the full way since the old tailor had put his labored stitches into it. The new is one of many, indistinguishable from the rest. Cheaper, it transforms the wearer; coming out the factory gate he is now also one of many, indistinguishable from the rest.

In New York a German mutual aid society debates the disposition of its funds. The Hildise Bund collects the periodic dues from its members but is concerned lest some sudden press for benefits or some mishap with investments leave it unprepared to pay. In 1868 the association enters into an arrangement by which a local insurance company underwrites the risk. That is the beginning of the business of industrial life insurance that makes the Metropolitan Life the largest in the world. Ultimately the company will bypass the society. Immigrant agents write policies for their countrymen; at lesser cost, with greater security, they perform the old mutual aid functions.

In many other ways, it was tempting to establish compromises with the economies of the wider American institutions. The ruinous expense of separate school systems among some groups was evaded by leaving to the public system the general secular subjects, adding to them outside instruction in religion and language. Disgruntled boys went off to afternoon or vacation *Svenska Skolan* or *Talmud Torah* to acquire in supplementary classes the learning their parents valued.

The parents themselves were sometimes tempted to follow along after their American children's manner. By this means the immigrant press was subtly undermined, though it continued yet to show the signs of growth. As long as the flow of newcomers continued, circulation figures soared. The sheets expanded, and weeklies turned into dailies.

Yet many an editor could see the signs of a change. The boys grew up and would not take the trouble to read in the foreign language. Instead they turned to newspapers in the more familiar English, newspapers being molded to their tastes by perspicacious men alive to the potentialities of this new public. Before the end of the nineteenth century the signs were unmistakable. From St. Louis, Joseph Pulitzer had brought to New York a rich experience as publisher of a German newspaper; the enormous expansion of the circulation of his *World* took its start from the attractiveness of the paper to the second generation of German-Americans. The contemporaneous activities of William Randolph Hearst stood in the same relationship to Irish-Americans.

These mass journals assimilated many characteristics of the immigrant press. They emphasized the sensational and dramatic at the expense of pure news; they devoted space to the doings of the local associations and of local personages; the serial story was at home in their pages; and they stood ready to advise their readers in the most intimate manner. Finally, they catered consistently to the nationalistic emotions of the organized immigrant movements. All this a mass circulation enabled them to do cheaply and lavishly. It was no wonder that even some in the first generation were inclined to lay down their pennies for these papers, simple in language, big with headlines, and fat with pictures.

On the stage where the demands of literacy were still less pressing, the process was already further advanced. From the start there had been a liberal exchange of plays and personalities between the immigrant and American theaters. The hard-pressed Yiddish dramatist who turned out a script a week did not hesitate to borrow plot or characters elsewhere successful; and an individual like Barney Williams had already given a broader currency to the Irish comic. All were absorbed onto the developing vaudeville stage. There the young people, and often their elders as well, could see in successive turns the laughable antics of the recognizably Irish, or German, or Jewish, or Italian; and these the more attractive because interspersed with the trickery of acrobats and magicians and flavored with the lilt of song and dance.

No doubt immigrant impresarios attempted to compete, just as immigrant editors made the effort to rival Hearst and Pulitzer in sensationalism — in both cases in vain. The mass medium that reached the greatest numbers commanded the greatest resources. Once the peak of new arrivals passed, immigrant press and stage alike began to weaken. And already the nickel shows where dim pictures flickered on a screen foreshadowed a medium more popular still that would complete the process.

There was a cost. The whole purpose of the new press and the new entertainment was to reach the widest audience; the means, to reach the most universal common denominator. Steadily the distinctive characteristics were rubbed down, the figures became generalized and blurred. Eternally Maggie continued the pursuit of Jiggs and the Inspector the Katzenjammer Kids; but not so much, and ever less, did these evoke the response of recognition as Irish or German. More often, upon the scene walked unidentifiable men of uncertain paternity, men of vague and colorless names who lived remote lives. Tears and laughter still might come but without the former meaning. Generalization had wiped out the awareness of their own particular situation the immigrants had once recognized in those pages, on that stage.

In the strange world of lonely men, the immigrants had reached out to each other, eager in the desire to have brothers with whom they could dwell. In the fluid and free life of America, they found the latitude to join with one another, to contrive institutions through which they could act, means of expression that would speak for them.

But the same fluidity and freedom ultimately undermined the societies, the press, and the theater, that at the start they encouraged. While the immigrants, through those institutions, were adjusting to the American environment, the

American environment was adjusting to their presence. An open society offered ample scope for mutual give-and-take.

Those who had themselves made the crossing, who recalled from their own experience the meaning in their lives of the first coming-together with friends, would struggle to preserve the old associations. But their sons were not likely to make the attempt. And they themselves would often taste the sadness of defeat.

EIGHT

Democracy and Power

ONE ORGANIZED ACTIVITY raised problems of altogether another order. Immigrants could associate in lodges and publish
newspapers to their hearts' content. These were voluntary
activities and had no effect upon any but their members. But
when groups formed after the same fashion entered politics,
the consequences were entirely different.

The difference sprang from the unique qualities of political action. The end of politics was the exercise of power
through the State — in which were embodied all the socially
recognized instruments of control and coercion. In this realm
was no room for the voluntary; control was one and indi-
visible. The Irish who built Carney Hospital in Boston did
not thereby limit the ability of the Jews to found Beth Israel,
or of the Yankees to support the Massachusetts General. But
an election had only one outcome and, once the contest was
over, left only victors and vanquished. Here the separateness
of the immigrants was an immediate challenge to all other
groups.

To many pursuits of the New World the immigrant was
strange upon arrival; to politics he was strangest of all. His

European experience had included no participation in government; every question related to these matters would be new to him.

In the Old World (except perhaps in France), the State had been completely external to the peasant's consciousness. In the business of ruling he did not act, was only acted upon. Nowhere but in France (not even in England until 1884) did he possess the privilege of taking part in the selection of administrators or in the determination of policy. Nowhere therefore did he seriously expect that the State might further his welfare or safeguard his rights.

Indeed, he knew well — and this experience did teach — that the government was the tool of those who governed; and those who governed — the gentry, nobility, or the Crown — acted from interests that were remote from, or hostile to, his own. Where parliaments existed they were the arenas in which middle-class city people debated with his own masters; he had not yet the notion that this might be the means of redressing his own grievances.

Quite the contrary! The peasant never learned to understand how power could emanate from that impersonal abstraction, the State. That Boards or Benches could do anything he refused to believe. Behind the bureaucrat's desk, beneath the judge's robe, he could see only a man. But these men played always the official with him, refused to respond as human beings; and that he could not comprehend. He preferred therefore, in need, to turn to the local nobility, who might be cajoled or appealed to, and who could be held to the personal standards of behavior that befitted their stations. Or, sometimes, he thought of the religious figure of the sanctified King as his distant protector who, if only he were told, would surely intercede for his devoted subjects. In Ireland and Poland, where the overlords were alien, the peasants had not even the consolation of that daydreaming.

Realistically, the villagers knew the State only in its role of harsh, unfriendly exploiter. Its taxes were worse than the landlords' dues; the latter at least were visibly expended in the manor house, the former went off to some remote incomprehensible purpose. The government exacted forced labor to build and mend roads the husbandman could have done without. Most oppressively of all, in many places, it conscripted the young men to serve in the remote world. At the most crucial point of their lives, when they were ready to marry and to create families, the army took them away, interfered with the whole order of inheritance and upset the stability of the village.

The State assumed its most horrifying guise when the perverse foolishness of its officers dragged it into war. The peasants dreaded the bloody disasters which no pen could describe, no mind embrace. Men were so fearful at the very thought of it that they wept; they knew that all would perish when it came. It was not glory the trumpets blew for them, but doom, in ravaged fields and flaming homes and men on horseback trampling over the supplicating bodies.

This was power; and it was not theirs. In the face of it nothing could be done. The tillers of the soil resented it as they resented everything that despoiled the fruits of their labor. But there was no escape. As with the weather or with any other unpredictable superior force, passive resignation was the only tolerable reaction. After all, it was the docile calf that thrived and lived to suck much milk. The gendarme encountered no resistance, only sullen, silent suspicion, or a grudging appeasement by gifts to keep trouble away.

The same grievances shaped the attitudes of the dissenting people. They were fully as remote from the State as the peasant and in addition suffered from discriminatory legislation if not from outright persecution.

And what was government that any immigrant should acquire a more favorable impression of it in the course of his journey? Government was a succession of malevolent obstacles in the way of getting to America. It foreshortened the earth, putting up high walls in the way of the free movement of people. In its name men found themselves betagged with strange papers, herded about like cattle. Its visible symbol was the outstretched, uniformed palm. Such, on arrival, was the newcomers' conception of power.

Perhaps they thought the New World would be different. If so, the first contacts disabused them of the idea. The immigration officials of the Land of Liberty were not unlike those anywhere else. Subsequent experiences also confirmed the old assumptions.

In pillared halls the laws are made, the briefs are read, the judgments rendered, in proper form, engrossed, signed, sealed. Of the majesty of the law, however, the immigrant has another view. Down by the corner the policeman twirls the symbol of his authority. Within the beat, he is government. But the limits of his power are well recognized. Shyly he averts his eyes as he passes this house or that. He cannot see where cards are dealt, where liquor flows beyond its hours, where ladies peep through curtained windows. With the shopkeeper, on the other hand, he is severe, and the incautious peddler often knows his wrath. Fortunately it is not hard to turn away that wrath; a soft answer and a generous purse deflate his zeal.

The wise laborers stay out of the way, make themselves unobtrusive. They expect no help, and count themselves lucky if only they can remain unnoticed. They know the dangers of entanglement with the law.

That time one unwittingly violated an ordinance . . . or, coming home, was drunk one night . . . or from dim description resembled the thief, and was picked up and brought to court . . . In the turmoil of the crowded room he felt already lost. Should he explain himself in his own halting English, or should he resort to the services of the notoriously inadequate interpreters? Perhaps in the bustling outer lobby some sticky individual with claims to being an attorney had attached himself, for what ulterior purpose the wretch, in his own mind already convicted, could well imagine. Meanwhile the magistrate stared gloomily at the long calendar before him and monotonously dealt out the repetitious decisions.

In all these matters bribery and the taking of bribes abounded and the mighty profited at the expense of the poor. But a man alone could not fight City Hall. It was best to be unobtrusive and resigned, to seek advice when it was needed from some trusted local acquaintance — the steamship agent whose window bore a notary's seal, or the saloonkeeper who, after all, had a government license framed beneath the spotted mirror. All this was entirely as it had been in the Old Country.

But there was one difference. Having settled and survived the five years, the newcomer was expected to become a citizen. Docile, he did what was expected of him. One day he took an oath, received a certificate, was naturalized.

You might say, *Well, what was one paper more? In his lifetime, many had been given him.* This one, carefully hidden in the bottom of the trunk, was unique. It made the foreigner an American, equal in rights with every other man. With this document, he was told, came a prompt accession to power. Now he was no longer a mere subject, but a person of consequence, one who shared in the selection of his rulers. How? By casting the vote. Why? Because, he was told, the United States was a democracy.

Now this was a conception the immigrants found it difficult to comprehend. The underlying assumption that in political relationships there was a fundamental equality among men did not square with their own deep-rooted ideas of status, with their own acceptance of differences of rank. Everyone knew that respect was due to the elders in a community, that a farm hand was not on a level with a farmer, an ignorant cottier with a husbandman of substance. Each individual had a place within which he ought to stay. To push oneself forward, to set oneself high, was a grievous sin. Otherwise there would be no order in the world. Search the memory of their experience as they would, these people could find nothing in their life in the Old World or the New that would confirm the democratic hypothesis that they themselves could participate meaningfully in the exercise of power.

Naturalization did not therefore immediately make voters. That would come only when their own American needs led the new citizens to the ballot box.

The first encounters with the practice of governing came in their local associational activities. In time each society acquired a constitution and bylaws, no doubt printed from stock forms the printer supplied and no doubt frequently honored in the breach. Still, here they elected officers, and conducted debates, and made rules. If these affairs had little effect upon the world outside, they nevertheless gave the members a taste of what politics involved.

In fact, some of the actions did begin to impinge upon the contests for control in the larger arena. The organizations with nationalistic ends could not fail to be drawn into American party politics. To the leaders agitating for independence for Ireland or Poland or Czechoslovakia it was clear that support from the United States Government would immensely forward their causes. There was some hope that such support might be enlisted. In the midcentury revolutions in Europe, this country had actively interceded on behalf of the rebels; and it continued to take an interest in the plight of minorities everywhere. Popular approval of the principle of self-determination and the traditional pride in the role of America as the Mother of Republics encouraged the immigrants to hope that some sort of official assistance might further their movements.

Generally, they were not clear as to what aid they had in mind. Despite occasional protests from the European powers affected, the United States permitted these groups to carry on with the utmost freedom; little republics in exile floated loans, printed money, even raised armies. The aspiring liberators wanted more. They wished the United States to conduct its foreign policy with some regard to their aspirations. Pressure from potential voters, they thought, might attain that objective. Such pressure would not be effective unless there were a coherent group voice to make heard its desires. As leaders in the immigrant community, graced with heroic reputations from old struggles, they were in a position to labor for such political solidarity.

With the rapid growth in the number of foreign-born voters, American politicians increasingly were conscious of the necessity of satisfying the interests of the naturalized citizens. In the party platforms appeared planks that espoused the immigrant causes: Irish independence, Italian nationalism, Zionism. Such commitments involved no severe strain upon their drafters' consciences; these statements were not only expedient, but they conformed with the general, widely accepted American sympathy for all oppressed peoples.

The response of the mass of immigrants was paradoxical. The talk about nationalism was stirring to the emotions and the endorsement of prominent statesmen was flattering to the pride. But the new citizens were not thereby moved into political action. Now and then an exceptional patriot like the Fenian Patrick Collins, in Massachusetts, or the Forty-Eighter Carl Schurz, in Missouri, achieved prominence as an officeholder. Generally, however, all these appeals were incapable of organizing a disciplined body of voters. In a decisive test in 1884, for instance, the combined energies of Patrick Ford, John Devoy, and the *Irish World* were incapable of moving the Irish-Americans of New York to vote for James G. Blaine for the presidency.

This apathy indeed was due to the difficulty of focusing nationalist enthusiasm upon politics. Since the main end of these movements was to influence foreign policy, they were mostly concerned with federal elections. But the doings in

Washington were of only remote interest to the immigrant; they involved characters he did not know and broke into his consciousness only at long four-year intervals. In addition, the nationalist organizations as such did not have the hold on the mass of newcomers that did the more spontaneous, local associations. It was the latter that would open the way to a fuller participation in politics. The cities would be pre-eminent in this respect, for there the life of the societies was most vigorous. In rural regions the political awareness of the foreign-born would be less frequently stirred.

As in other adjustments to the American environment, the second generation were the intermediaries. From the start, the children of the immigrants were more intimately implicated than their parents. The schools had acquainted them with the mechanisms of politics and had also imbued them with the conviction that government was susceptible to popular control and capable of serving popular interests.

Furthermore, many youngsters growing up in the confused decades after 1850 came to understand that the state might also be the means of their own personal advancement. As the sons of immigrants, without the inherited advantages of capital or family connections, not many roads to success were open to them. In politics, any office was available to him who could command the support of numbers; and in many places, the immigrants who had no other assets had at least the weight of numbers. The connection with a community of the foreign-born might be an impediment in other endeavors; in the quest for office it was a positive aid. The problem was to devise the means of utilizing that connection.

As a boy in Brooklyn, "Hughey" McLaughlin was already a leader among his cronies. Big and strong, handy with his fists in a fight, he commanded the respect of the lads who hung around the firehouse. One employment after another was not quite to his taste; but in the neighborhood he was well known, and favorably. In 1855 his opportunity came. Taken on at the Navy Yard, he was put in charge of a group of workers, a gang, with the title of Boss Laborer, soon shortened to Boss.

These were the essential elements. To hold his own position it was necessary that he retain the favor of the political authority that appointed him. He did so by the ability to deliver a certain number of votes. And he was able to deliver those votes because he controlled a fund of desirable jobs. In time, McLaughlin extended the scope of his operations from the Navy Yard to the whole municipality. The relationship between votes and jobs remained the same.

Throughout the country in the great cities, other bosses became the heads of other gangs. Some had assembled followings as foremen or contractors, others by growing up in a district where they exercised continuing leadership as a gang of boys grew up to be a gang of voters. Everywhere the connection between these allegiances and the opportunity to work was plain. In an economy that condemned the immigrants to unskilled labor a large percentage of the available jobs were directly or indirectly dependent upon political favor. Aqueducts and streets the city built for itself; trolley, gas, telegraph, and electric lines were laid by companies franchised by the city; and every structure, as it went up, was inspected by the city. One pair of hands was much like another when it held the shovel; the employers of unskilled labor were wise enough to treat indulgently the wishes of the municipal officials in whose power it was to let contracts or grant permits.

The job was at the center of the boss's attractiveness. But he was also able to call forth a more general sense of attachment. Often the feelings of group loyalty focused upon him. He was a member of many associations, made friends on every block. In the columns of their own newspapers his name appeared frequently. His achievements cast their reflected glory on the whole community and he in turn shared its sense of solidarity. In that respect he stood at an advantage over every competitor for the immigrants' leadership. He had sprung from among them and substantially remained one with them.

Furthermore, he spoke for them. After the Civil War as the national parties in election after election chewed over the same stale issues, a great dullness settled down over their campaigns. Few people cared to take the trouble to distinguish how the position of the Democrats differed from that of the Republicans on civil service reform or the tariff. Few even bothered to learn what those problems were about. These were remote and abstract questions that did not directly touch on their own lives. The immigrant might sometimes read an article on such a matter in his newspaper but was less likely to be persuaded by any intrinsic ideas on the subject than by the character of the persuader. If a trusted source said that when a Democrat is President misery comes, that if the Republicans win the factories will open, the new citizen was likely to accept the statement without cavil.

The local issues were the important ones. Whether there should be a new public bathhouse in Ward Twelve, whether the city should hire extra laborers, seemed questions of no moment to the party statesmen. To the residents of the tenement districts they were critical; and in these matters the ward boss saw eye to eye with them. *Jim gets things done!* They could see the evidence themselves, knew the difference it made in their own existence.

The boss took command of the group in political matters. The old-line nationalist leaders still commanded the respect of their fellow countrymen but could not compete with the boss for votes. That fact Bourke Cockran discovered, in New York, when he met the opposition of Croker of Tammany Hall. Patrick Collins learned the same lesson in Boston, and an identical moral was pointed in other cities throughout the country. The machine gave form to the immigrant vote.

The ambitious politician, however, could not get very far if his power rested only on the loyalty of a bloc of immigrant followers. The instability of settlement prevented the consolidation of control on that basis. Tammany could not be sure how long its dominance of the East Side wards would last, or Lomasney in Boston of the West End, when the original Irish residents moved out and their place was taken by Jews and Italians. The successful chieftains were those who expanded their roles beyond the little group within which they had grown to power.

Hugh McLaughlin had perceived this. In his White House Saloon or in his office on Willoughby Street, he had made himself available to all comers. On the corner in Boston where his boyhood gang had whiled away the time, Martin Lomasney built the Hendricks Club. By the century's end, behind the whitened windows of an empty store, in the back room of a saloon, upstairs above the dance hall — under a variety of designations there was in every ward a place where a man could go and see the boss, or see someone who would in turn see the boss.

I think that there's got to be in every ward a guy that any bloke can go to when he's in trouble and get help — not justice and the law, but help, no matter what he's done. The old man reminisces as the incidents of a long career come back. What requests had not been made of him! And often enough he'd stepped in without waiting to be asked. Time and again one of the boys would let him know: the poor fellow had allowed his payments to lapse and now the widow had not the burial money; or, the furniture was being put out in the street and them with no place to go and the wife ailing at that. Baskets at Christmas, picnics, boat rides on the river or lake, and a ready purse at the mention of any charitable collection — these were all within his realm of obligations.

But mostly he had intervened at the points at which his people encountered the difficulties of the law. Between the rigid, impersonal rulings of the statute and the human failings of those ignorant of its complexities he stood as mediator. The poor lad who had an extra glass and by some half-remembered encounter ended the night in jail, the shopkeeper whose stand edged beyond the legal limit onto the sidewalk, turned to him whose contact set matters straight. They had all sat there explaining their troubles, the liquor dealer and the peddler worried about licenses, the contractor and the real-estate owner involved in deals with the city. They had come to him because they knew he was *fair* with his *favors*.

Those vain fools up on the hill had laughed and then seethed with indignation when he had torn the legislature apart so that wretched Italian could vend his peanuts on the grounds. The fulminations against "peanut politics" had been all to the good. They had confirmed the popular impression that he championed the little men against the big, the humble against the proud. Hundreds who themselves never had the occasion to turn to him firmly believed in his accessibility. The image, his own and theirs, was that of the kindly overlord, the feudal noble translated from the manor to the ward — above the law and therefore capable, if properly approached, of doing better justice than the law.

There was a price, of course. An exception made for one lawbreaker could be made for another; if the frightened peddler could get off, so too could the swaggering tough. After all, the turkeys in the baskets, the bubbling kegs of beer at the end of the long picnic tables, all cost money. Whose money?

There were persons who would pay the bill. The thriving gambling industry of the 1870's stood on a tenuous relationship with the police. With expanded operations and greater capital investments, the operators of the keno, faro, and policy games could not tolerate a situation in which they were at the mercy of the extortions of every precinct lieutenant and his underlings. Nor would saloonkeepers willingly expose themselves to the assaults of temperance fanatics with their zealous insistence upon awkward closing hours or even upon total prohibition. An accommodating boss like Mike McDonald in Chicago provided protection in return for moderate occasional contributions from some two thousand gamblers in Chicago.

This source of support was not very secure, however. With time, the big promoters moved into the shadowland of legality and became less dependent upon protection. Some advanced to the ownership of bucket shops or indeed to the dignity of brokerage offices; others began to make book on horse racing and prize fighting, now legitimate enterprises. The older forms of speculation catered increasingly to the less profitable poor and were left to the attention of the petty promoter, from whom not much could be drawn in the way of assessments.

Some bosses and their wives were, at the same time, stricken with social aspirations. Having made their way in the world, they wanted the visible symbols of having done so. Mike McDonald had made Carter Harrison mayor. Why should not the one be as respectable as the other? Unfortunately there were limits to the enjoyment of success; when McDonald moved to a fine suburb and began to play the gentleman, he lost his following and was unseated by Bathhouse John Coughlin and Hinky Dink Mike Kenna, two ungentle characters still close to the source of the votes.

If it was unsafe to desert one's proper district, at least some leaders hoped to surround themselves with other forms of respectability. They preferred not to deal with gamblers and saloonkeepers, but with nice people. And by this time there were some nice people quite eager to deal with the wielders of political influence. The perspicacious boss could become the familiar of the banker and the traction magnate, be taken to lunch in a good club (though not made a member), and puff his chest in the company of the financially mighty. Within the grant of government in these years were all sorts of profitable franchises, for laying trolley tracks, for building subways and electric and water lines, for the disposing of garbage. The interests concerned with these privileges were willing to aid the co-operative politician, aid to such an extent that he would not any longer be dependent on his emoluments from faro or overhours beer. The New York Dutch had a word for it, *boedel*.

Boodle was honest graft. When they floated the gas company they set aside a block of shares for the good fellows. No cash down — their credit was good. When the franchise came through and the stock prices rose in the market, the shares could be sold, the original purchase price paid, and a tidy balance would be left for the deserving. Or even if the capitalists were forced to lay out a flat sum without these complexities, that didn't hurt anyone. Such practices were not too far from the ordinary practices of legitimate business to offend any but the most tender consciences. Occasional revelations by shocked reformers did not alienate the boss's constituency; they merely endowed him with the additional romantic aspects of a Robin Hood.

Rivalry, not moral disapproval, provoked the serious troubles. In many matters the municipality shared jurisdiction with the state; and in the halls of the legislature, the city machines ran head-on into collision with the politicians who had long operated on a statewide basis. These men had not the assistance of the formal organization of the machine, but they had earlier consolidated their positions through alliances of key officeholders. Generally they were native American, as was the bulk of their following; and they drew their support from the farming areas and from the small towns. In most parts of the country they had the advantage of an anachronistic distribution of power which favored the rural at the expense of the urban districts. Years of bitter struggle followed the appearance of the immigrant organizations, as the state party chieftains attempted to mobilize minority national blocs to undermine the authority of their metropolitan competitors. In New York and Massachusetts, for instance, the Republicans attempted to woo the Italians and Jews to break the hold of the Irish Democrats on the city vote.

In time, however, there was an accommodation. Spheres of influence were defined and divided. Live and let live. Perhaps the appearance on the scene after 1900 of a crew of miscellaneous reformers and liberal independents drove the various manipulators of power into a union of convenience. In any case, shortly after 1910 the old acerbity was dulled and an era of more peaceful relationships ensued.

It was not surprising that the boss should see in the stirring of reform interests a threat to his own position. But it was significant that the mass of immigrants should regard the efforts of the various progressives with marked disfavor. In part this disapproval was based on the peasant's inherited distrust of radicalism; but it was strengthened by a lack of understanding among the radicals that deprived them of all influence among the newcomers.

In the case of the Italians and other central Europeans, the revolutions of the mid-nineteenth century had added fear of the pillaging reds to the traditional suspicion of revolutionaries. All these old misgivings crossed the ocean to the New World. Conservative enough at home, the peasants had become more conservative still in the course of migration. They dreaded political change because that might loosen the whole social order, disrupt the family, pull God from His throne; the radicals themselves talked that way and confirmed the worst such suspicions. Naturally the influence of the churches on both sides of the Atlantic was thrown in the balance on the side of stability and confirmed the unwillingness of the immigrants to be involved in any insurgent movements.

At only one point, and that very early, had there been the

basis of a rapprochement of the newcomers with radicalism. In the 1840's and 1850's the émigré nationalist leaders were strongly tinged in their thinking by liberalism. But they had difficulty even then in controlling their following; and the outcome of the revolutions in Europe, together with the hostility of the clergy, forced them either to surrender their heterodox ideas or to sink themselves into obscurity.

As to the native reformers, those were always an outlandish breed to the immigrants. The insistence upon framing platforms which included such curious planks as women's rights, temperance, and Sabbatarianism cast upon them all the suspicion of eccentricity. Their religious tolerance and nonsectarianism seemed to reflect a lack of interest in religion; and already before the Civil War the battle lines were drawn over such issues as the public school system.

The division persisted down through the end of the century. The failure of socialists and anarchists to win an important position in the associational life of the immigrants prevented them also from using these groups for political ends. And with few exceptions — Henry George for a time was one — American radicals met the stubborn opposition of the foreign-born voters. The populists made no headway at all in districts where the newcomers were numerous, and William Jennings Bryan could not hold the loyalty of such traditionally Democratic groups as the Irish.

The crisis came toward the close of the century, and in the first decade after, with the gradual formulation at many hands of a newer progressivism. Among the men involved in these movements there was certainly no trace of the wild-eyed reformer of the 1840's. Whether they fell in the camp of Theodore Roosevelt or Robert LaFollette or any of the other figures who spoke for the trend, they were not at all inclined to tear apart and reconstruct the whole society. Yet their doctrines failed also to attract the immigrants.

To begin with, the movement lacked channels for communicating with the foreign-born citizens. There were among the progressives enough members of the second generation to have done so. But these, by the nature of the case, were the children of the immigrants who had broken with their parents' communities, who through education or personal advancement had moved away from the old beliefs and the old societies. They did not identify themselves with any group and therefore commanded the confidence of none.

On the other hand the reformers often found themselves in the position of attacking the recognized immigrant leaders. There was always the temptation to rely upon the tactics of exposure, to show up the corruption and venality of politicians; and there was often also an inclination to make clear the antecedents of those exposed. To blame the poor government of American cities on their immigrant residents was indeed calcualted to win the favor of the native-born. But it drove the foreign-born to defend the boss as one of their own. In fact the reformer acquired the reputation of an informer, one who tattled and spitefully revealed the peccadilloes of essentially good men.

This attitude the progressives could not understand. *The immigrant* (one among them complained) *lacks the faculty of abstraction. He thinks not of the welfare of the community but only of himself.* It never occurred to this critic that precious little thought was given by others to the welfare of the newcomers. If they did not consider their own interests, no one else would.

Certainly few among the reformers ever paused to consider what were the needs and interests of a new citizen or ever tried to imagine what such a one would have thought of their own confident remedies to the world's ills. The whole pack of innovations in the structure of government seemed to the foreign-born to be either mere tinkering or some subtle plot to steal control by undermining the familiar ways of political action. There was not likely to be much immigrant support for the initiative, referendum, and similar proposals.

The controversies over trusts and the regulation of business were also remote. Such issues excited the entrepreneur and the farmer; they had no immediate relevance to the life of the industrial worker. Debates about restraint of trade and railroad rates went on in a realm that did not directly concern him. He could only judge the attitudes of the reformers when they narrowed down to questions that had a direct bearing on his own mode of existence. And it was precisely on such questions that the reformers were farthest from him in point of view.

The problems of American municipalities had long troubled many men involved in the progressive movements. If innovations were slow to be introduced on a national scale, perhaps they could more easily be put into practice locally. Reform administrations had actually held office in some cities; and people could examine not only their professions but also their practices. Both alienated large numbers of immigrants.

There had been a mockery in the old boss's voice as he thought of the mistakes of his opponents: *I never saw a man in my life who made economy his watchword who was not always defeated before the people.* What did they promise, those fine folk who came gingerly into the district just before the election? They pledged themselves to lower taxes to voters who had no property to be taxed. They talked of balanced budgets and improved administration. Efficiency. System. Apply business methods to government.

As the score mounted up against them, they complained about corruption, ascribed their failure to the stuffed ballot box. Well, often enough the "floater" did come in to mark the paid-for crosses, and "repeaters" did move from precinct to precinct. But the reformers never understood it was they themselves had earned defeat, never realized that the most of the people they addressed did not want government to be a business. Efficiency too often expressed itself in an inhuman disregard for the individual; and system too often meant an unbending application of impersonal rules. A progressive administration often was one that laid off men to balance the budget. To the immigrants, the abstract principle was not worth the suffering it entailed. The boss knew that, as the reformers did not. Ultimately he was always the victor.

Yet among the new political currents that disturbed the closing years of the nineteenth century and the opening years of the twentieth there were some that also drew in the boss and through him a large part of his following. For many leaders it became increasingly difficult to operate on the old familiar personal level. There came a time in their careers when it was hard to apply the customary techniques. It was difficult to keep up with the new people who moved in; there were occasional lapses in recognition before the flow of hailing faces. With more applicants than places, each appointment made one friend and a half-dozen enemies. There was a strain, which grew heavier with the years, to the apportionment of favors.

Of course, there were no voluntary retirements. No one dropped the reins of power simply because the tug was too severe. The chief came as ever to the office and drove the best course he could. But often he wished there were some way to generalize the favors he dealt out. Or was it beyond the range of possibility that he should ever have for all his followers rewards, and never a denial?

The boss had not himself been forward in holding office. He had no wish for the prestige, knew well where the real power lay, and preferred to let someone else bear the responsibility. But the men who did become mayors and aldermen or governors and legislators shared his uneasiness about the burdens of control. In addition, some among them, without any thought of disputing his authority, nevertheless had vague ambitions that somehow they might make a name for themselves by helping those who had elected them.

A shrewd politician then could also observe the slow accumulation of potential voting strength around a new nucleus, the labor organization. The rising craft unions, mostly already affiliated with the American Federation of Labor, were rather unfriendly to the unskilled immigrant workers. Yet among their members were many of the second generation, linked through associational ties with the boss and his machine; and the advantages of an alliance came frequently to the minds of both political and labor leaders. The unions could hardly overlook the possibilities of such support in their struggle for recognition and position. In the building trades, municipal ordinances and inspection could be powerful weapons, properly controlled. Any striker knew the value of having the police on his side. In the bitter warfare with intransigent employers, labor, like capital, had sometimes summoned force to its aid. In a few cases, the hired racketeers had actually taken over, assumed the real leadership of the unions; and these men often, through their interest in gambling and other illegal enterprises, already had connections with the machine. In other cases, the emergence of city-wide councils or labor assemblies created agencies through which an understanding could be reached. This connection with labor, together with the will of the boss to generalize his favors and the aspirations of the office-holders, combined to direct immigrant political activity into new channels.

It came out differently at the hands of various men. For this was not the application to practice of an idea already understood, but the gradual working toward an idea from practices that circumstances dictated. Often corrupt alliances with the underworld and the familiar peanut politics mingled incongruously with the newer procedures; and often those who acted did not themselves understand the nature of their actions.

Back in 1892 John Peter Altgeld had become Governor of Illinois. Himself an immigrant, he had been put in office by the Irish and Germans, to whom he had pledged himself to protect the Catholic and Lutheran parochial schools. His connections led to Chicago, to the boss Mike McDonald, to the gambler Joe Martin, to the carpenter George Schilling of the old eight-hour-day association. Just after the turn of the century in San Francisco, Eugene Schmitz and Abe Ruef had come to power with the aid of the Union Labor Party. A little later in Eastern state legislatures the representatives of the city machines were making themselves heard with uncommon vigor — such men as Al Smith in New York or David I. Walsh in Massachusetts or Joe Tumulty in New Jersey.

There was not then even a program to the specific measures they sponsored. It may have been a law to force the companies to sell five-cent cakes of ice, or one to compel factory owners to install safety devices, or one to limit the hours of women. But there was not much certainty as to the theoretical grounds on which they rested. A few of the Catholics among these politicians had heard of the social encyclicals of Leo XIII; a few Germans knew of the developments in the Fatherland; a few Jews were thinking of an American equivalent for their tradition of charity. But the measures they furthered stemmed from more specific roots. These proposals were responses of men who, for a variety of motives, remembered their own antecedents. When the thoughts came back of the hot tenement room, of the pinned-up sleeve where the crushed arm had been, of the muffled sobs through the wall where the weary mother could not rest, then there welled up a painful recollection of the desperate needs that had once engulfed them. Yes, even as they leaned comfortably back, with their shining shoes on the oak desk, some chance glimpse through the window would bring to mind the urgency with which strangers, alone in a new and hostile world, had longed for security.

The machine that opened to the immigrants the prospect that the State might be the means through which the beginnings of security could come thereby assured itself of their loyalty. It also opened up the possibility of a very limited and very tentative collaboration with the reformers. The latter were still wrapped up in a kind of liberal thinking that refused to acknowledge that government could play a positive, directing role in society. Yet the progressives were also responsive to the appeal of humanitarian sentiments and, as they entered the second decade of the twentieth century, now and then they confronted measures that seemed undeniably good, however troubling they might be to laissez-faire assumptions. On workmen's compensation, factory and wage legislation there was room for an unrecognized accord between boss and "do-gooder."

The alliance had not yet become deliberate. A brief opportunity passed in the years when Woodrow Wilson became the spokesman of the reform impulse. As Governor and President he had received the credit for a number of enactments that seemed to help the laboring man; and his wartime nationalities policy had drawn the support of many immigrants by then interested in the fate of their old homelands. On the other hand, a number of influential groups came to hold him responsible for the "betrayal of Versailles" — the Irish, who saw in the League an instrument to secure the power of Great Britain; the Germans, dismayed by the vindictive terms of the Peace; and the Italians, disappointed at the boundary settlements.

As important perhaps was the fact that Wilson had never really broken through the limitations of the traditional reformer. In New Jersey he had disloyally quarreled with the machine that had elected him and had devoted much of his energy to tinkering with the forms of government. And as President he was sometimes insensitive to the particular desires of substantial groups in his following.

In any case, the era of Wilson led only to the era of normalcy. The reform tide ebbed. At the same time the likelihood of new legislation that might advance the security of the working people also receded, as the dominant political trend in the 1920's rejected any state interference in economic matters. In that decade the hold of the bosses on their following was stronger than ever.

Later, after the gates were closed and newcomers were no longer welcome, after a great collapse had shaken the confidence of other Americans, the surviving immigrants would find fresh hope that government might concern itself with their security. They would find this concern one of the various meanings of the New Deal; and their loyalty would not then be divided by the necessity of choosing between their own machines and reform. At that later time, the import of reform had changed so that it could swallow up their machines, bosses and all.

But that was later and it would be more often their sons that would see it than they. Many would never have the satisfaction of knowing what currency their humble aspirations would have. They had started with this simple notion, that government was power; they had learned that, from its being always used against them at home. Democracy had extended to them the opportunity to take hold of that power and the New World experience had begun to teach them how. Untutored and unskilled, they had often to depend upon men moved by selfish interests of their own. Only slowly the immigrants had made a start of understanding that the power of the State could serve their proper ends.

NINE

Generations

SOMETIMES AT NIGHT she'd wake and turn to feel if he were there. She'd reach the space across to where he lay, sense the reassuring bulk of him. She'd hug the thought. *All else has passed away with our passing from that place. But this will never change. By holy matrimony he has made me wife and mother to his family. That* (fiercely) *we can hold intact.*

In morning's light the certainty was gone. Through the day the fear came that this most intimate part of life would not remain the same. At the stove later she paused while the long spoon in her hand continued its mechanical stirring; she looked in bewilderment at the gathering table. Would the strangeness of the setting make strangers also of these her dear ones? Resolve came back, but confidence not altogether. It would be a desperate battle to hold firm in these relationships, outside the context that had nurtured them.

The difficulty was that formerly the family had not been a thing in itself, but an integral element of the village community. It had been fixed in a framework of numerous links and knots that held each individual within it in his place. As the functioning unit within the economy it was the means through which bread was produced and consumed. No one could live except as the member of a family.

As the medium for holding and transmitting land, its stability had been vital to social order. Every change in its structure affected the whole community. On the quality of a single marriage depended the welfare of all the brothers and sisters and less directly a widening circle of other persons. The connection with the soil had also been an element in extending these affiliations beyond the single household to a broad range of other kin tied together by inheritance, of blood and of possible claims to a common patrimony.

The family had therefore never been isolated. Its concerns were those of the entire village. While each home was expected to be the source of its own discipline, the community stood ready with sanctions of its own to make sure that children were obedient, that parents were good, and that relatives were helpful to each other. The network of mutual rights and obligations had thus the support of both an inner and an outer control.

Emigration took the family out of the village. The mere going was disruptive. The struggles of departure and resettlement subjected the household to a severe strain under most trying and most unusual conditions and at the same time deprived it of the counsel and assistance upon which it had traditionally depended. When so many new decisions were to be made, they had to be made alone. That alone distinguished the new family from the old.

In America also the economic unity of the common household enterprise disappeared. The minority who found their way to the farms or who, by their labors, maintained little businesses where wife and children could work along with the father, held on to the former ways. Vestiges of the old order also remained in the sweating homework system; as the father brought back the bundles that would be sewn into shirts or twisted into artificial flowers, the gathered group in the tenement room recaptured the sense of common effort familiar in recollection from the Other Side.

These were, however, but byways in the economy. In the characteristic immigrant employment, the individual was hired as an integer. He was one line in the ledger, one pair of hands on the floor, one pay envelope at the window, with no reference to who was there at home. Ultimately this pattern supplanted all others. Would they continue to take his bidding, to toil in the dim room with him, the one to pocket all, when they could go out to be their own wage earners? There was no point to it. Of what inheritance could he deprive them?

Properly speaking the family no longer had an income; there were only the combined incomes of its members. The larger unit was now a source of weakness rather than of strength. Those who could, broke away; it was madness for a man who was capable of supporting himself to maintain the ties of uncle or cousin when those ties would only draw off a share of his earnings. Those who remembered the old obligations, alas, were generally those more likely to consume than to produce — the aged, the weak, the ill. With these the circumstances, and with no outside force to assign the blame, the extensive family of the Old World disintegrated. *So it is now, a brother stabs his brother, a sister drowns her sister, for profit's sake.*

Steadily the relatives dropped away; the husband, wife, and children were left alone. Where need compelled additions to the income of this narrower household, it was better to take in boarders, tenants, on an impersonal, cash-down basis. The more compelling duties of the old extended family were treacherous here; it was safer by avoiding them to transform the relationship into one of mere occasional sociability.

The bonds to those left at home also disintegrated. There was a piece of land, and if he had not gone away it would have been his; but having gone away he ought not ask that it be sold and money sent to him in America. Endless quarreling followed. Or the old folks, staying, bitterly resented the departed son who should have been the staff on which they might lean in age. *You went to make money and you forgot that you left parents; may God and your own children care for you as you for us.*

Is it the loss of income they minded, or the sadness of being abandoned? *We cannot know whether we shall yet speak with you, embrace you, at least once before our death.* It does not matter. The demands are too heavy on both emotions and purse. The old ties gradually are loosened. The family steadily tapers down to the conjugal unit, a father, a mother, and their immediate offspring. The New World has separated them from all the others who would have been one with them in the Old.

Perhaps for that reason she wished so intensely to hold together what was left. From mistress in an extensive household she had become mother of a more intimate group; that hard core she would labor to keep intact.

The early experiences of the new family entity fed her hopes. That they were cut off from all else that was familiar led the members to value each other the more. With whom else could they discuss the memories of the past and the problems of the present? Depending upon each other because there was no one else upon whom they could depend, they drew steadily together.

The very process of migration had been shared. Mostly they had come together, together faced the open road and the close quarters of the steerage. In the long lapse of time between departure and arrival, they were deprived of the busying occupations of the farm, of the comradeship of neighbors, and had for company only one another. The occasion was one for deeper understanding; and long after the final settlement, recollections would come back of the joys and tribulations of the way, come back to unite those who had made the journey together.

The warmth of participation in the enterprise of crossing cheered even those later immigrants who divided for the critical steps, husband first to make a start, wife and children after. Such a separation created problems of its own, but it did not of itself lessen the attachment of the partners to it. Though the ocean lay between, they were joined by the gravity of the common effort.

That is why, as the years passed and they thought back to the first exploratory days in America, it seemed to them that the family had been strongest and purest before its exposure to the new life. As strangers they had known no one. Evening brought them always back together. Excited with discoveries or downcast with disappointments, they communicated to one another the freshness of each occurrence. They knew then they were one like the meager loaf from which they would begin each to slice the sustenance of all. It was a tenement room or a sod hut. But it was home; and those who came to it worn out with wandering acquired for home an enduring devotion.

Only soon, the conditions of their being in the United States would break in upon them. The narrow family would not remain alone together. Individually, its members in going out would make each their own adjustments to the society about them, and coming back would be less alike. Man and woman, boy and girl, they would find for themselves new roles and establish for themselves new relationships. It would happen more quickly in the cities than on the farms where a rural environment extended the family's isolation. But ultimately it would happen everywhere. The woman meditating by the stove would resist it. But already as they took their places her heart chilled to the fear of failure.

Across the long table they confronted each other, the two who were now central to all. It was as if daily they felt the need of a fresh view of the familiar features in the light of the new experiences. In the anxious regards were mingled two questions. Is this the same being united to me those many years ago and now still unchanged? How adequate will this union be to the present demands upon it?

Indeed these were no longer the man and woman joined in wedlock at that distant date; they had never then imagined that such questions might ever arise. Their marriage had not been the product of an individual passion, but a social arrangement under the oversight of the community. She had accepted the obligations of her situation, to be obedient and faithful, to further his health and comfort, to be a good and kindly wife, the crown of her husband's life. He had taken on the responsibilities of the efficient provider who would safeguard her from degrading work, keep want away, and mildly satisfy her will. The union upon which fortune smiled was one blessed with the dignified respect of the partners for their rights and duties.

The day they turned their backs upon the old home, the relationship began to change. At the very outset, the course of the crossing led to troubles. In the long suspended period between departure and arrival, neither he nor she had duties or could expect fixed dues. They were then thrown more together than ever before, but as never before found it difficult to judge one another. The intimacy of shared miseries brought them together, but, as it were, only to be the more conscious of each other's deficiencies. A sorry figure he made, lounging about from day to day with nothing to do; while her derelictions of housewifely obligations were served up in the stale biscuits of every meal.

If migration involved a temporary separation as, after 1880, it often did, the results were more disruptive still. He went away to the sound of the children's crying; and heard it echo through the months apart. In his unaccustomed singleness, he came to miss what before he had taken for granted, the warmth of the woman's presence. *As the fish thirst for water, so I long for you.*

It is hard to know what may happen across that far dividing distance. *Only I beg you write more often.* As the letters fail to appear, for she is not familiar to the pen, worries take their place, and suspicions. Resentful, he asks a friend in the village to inform him of her doings. Does she hold to the home? At the same time the fear will rise lest she be unable to manage. The stock of grain may be too small, the labor in the field too hard. Cautionary advice covers the pages he sends home.

She has the advantage of waiting in a known place in the company of the children. But her double role is burdensome; she cannot be as he was, head of the household. The boys are unruly and, though she gives them some of the broomstick, they are slow to obey. She hires a hand to help in the field, but he is negligent; he has not for her the fear as for a master. Often she thinks of her husband and what a life he must lead there among strangers, his work heavier than a stone, his strength being drained away into a foreign soil. *The day passes in labor but in the evening I long very much and at night I cannot sleep. We can be united in heart and thought but that satisfies me not. Take us or come back; let it be so or so; as it is I exist neither upon ice nor upon water.*

Sometimes the months stretch out and the separateness widens. He sets himself a goal: I will have a thousand rubles and then send for them. But the goal is never attained. Meanwhile he is hardened in his bachelor life and puts off indefinitely the day of reunion. Or she at home grows reluctant. The dread of the new place mounts up in her and feeds off the complaints in his letters. She wishes him back — enough of this America — and when the call comes, procrastinates.

Whatever division, long or short, appeared in the transplantation was not mended in the resettlement. On the farms, the man could resume his place as head of the household enterprise; but the millions who stayed in the cities found their positions drastically altered. She could not think that he was here satisfying his obligations toward the family. No longer the sole or even the main provider, he seemed to her wanting in the most critical duty of all. Why, there were times when she herself or the children earned more than he, times when he sat home idle while they went out to bring home his bread. When he was taken on, it was not at work she understood or could respect. Away at some menial task, she could not regard him as she had that husbandman who had once managed their tiny plot and had brought up her sons to follow in his steps.

Nor could he be satisfied as to her adequacy for the life of the New World. Deprived of the usual household chores of the garden, the needle, and the loom, she appeared often lethargic; the blood hardly ran in her veins. On the other hand management of the domestic economy under American conditions was frequently beyond her comprehension. When the results were unhappy — disorderly quarters, poor food — it was hard to draw the line between the effects of negligence and the effects of poverty and ignorance. The necessity that drove her to labor for others was the source of resentment, both because it reflected upon his own abilities and because it took her away from her proper job in the home.

Roles once thoroughly defined were now altogether confounded. The two got on under the continual strain of uncertainty as to their place in the family, as to their relationships to each other. And their experience, no longer one for the two, added constantly to that underlying uncertainty.

Sometimes it was he went out to the wide world, learned the language of the country, and grew sophisticated in the ways of the place, while she was confined to the flat and remained ignorant of the rudiments of English. *I at least know where there's an Eighth Street, and a One Hundred and Thirtieth Street with tin works, and an Eighty-fourth Street with a match factory. I know every block around the World Building and the place where the car line stops. But you know no more than if you had just landed.* Sometimes it was she, in service in some other's home, who earlier learned the ways — what food they ate and clothes they wore and how they sat of an evening in the polished sitting room. It was bitter hard to be the satisfying helpmate when one could hardly guess what wants the other had.

As the situation clarified, aspects at first hidden emerged with oppressive distinctness. In the Old World her status had been fixed by a variety of elements — whose daughter she was, what dowry she brought, into what family she married. Let her husband be unfortunate or unskillful or unthrifty, she had still a set place in the village. Here her fate was completely tied up in his success. What she was or had been mattered nothing, only what he could do. Well, it was galling to see what other, lesser women had, to watch their men push their way ahead. The utter dependence on his efforts put an acrimonious tone in her greetings as he came nightly home no better than before.

Nagging demands he could not meet confirmed his own inner doubts about himself. Was not the whole migration the story of his succession of failures? He had been unable to hold on to the land, to direct the family comfortably across the ocean or to establish it securely on this side. He felt respect ebb away and carried about a gnawing shame at his own lack of capacity. Most of all, he resented his loss of authority. Indeed he became accustomed to request, not to order, but knew it was not right it should be so; and he resented his wife's growing dominance over the household. It was a poor state of affairs when the cow showed the way to the ox.

In the secret night when her stirring waked him he did not move. Fatigue pinned him down. Yet sleep would not return. Instead an angry tension crept into his heart. Her body's presence intruded on his consciousness. Limbs rigid, he pushed the thought away; to this demand too he would not respond, by so much had he now lost his manhood.

Clenched eyelids would not keep the moonlight out. Not a beam came down the narrow airshaft; still his sight tingled to the streaks reflected from a distant meadow where they had walked amidst the long grasses, and had been young, eager for the enjoyment of each other to which marriage had opened the way. There had been no strain then; what the community had to that day forbidden, it now welcomed; and these two had been carried along by confidence in the rightness of their acts, by certainty they would each be gratified.

It was coming away that had first added wormwood to the taste. They had lost the benevolent oversight of the village which by its insistence on traditional propriety had answered every how and when. Now the deed required ever a decision; it raised ever some question; and it involved ever some clash of wills, his or hers. By leaving they had created doubts they knew not how to resolve.

He remembered the darkness of successive borrowed beds. In the enforced closeness of boardinghouses and shipboard he had stifled the groping desires. Years later, the confined warmth of many bodies would come back to assault his senses, would bring the painful recollection of urges never satisfied. And in this place that was their own it was rare that wish and opportunity coincided. In the cramped quarters they had been never alone and therefore never really together. Often there was the startling chill of interruption — the uneasy stirring of a child, the banging progress of a neighbor through the ill-lit hall. Always there was the uncertainty of when and how. Even the times when, flushed with the cheap certitude of liquor or with the passing exuberance of some new job, he had asserted his passion, there had followed inevitably an aftermath of regret and doubt. What had really been given and what received in these exchanges?

Perhaps he should not have expected more. He himself knew the dull indifference that came with being often tired. He knew too her deep fear of recurrent childbirth. Not that this was a subject of conversation between them; but it took no words to convey her dismay at each discovery of her condition. But the terms must be accepted, the price paid. Worse would follow the attempt to avoid it; often enough she had heard the stories of such a one, desperate at the approach of an eighth or ninth, who had sought the relief of self-abortion and had found only the painful death of blood poisoning. Vaguely also they suspected that there were ways of forestalling pregnancy. But the old wives' knowledge did not extend that far; in this matter the midwife was not helpful; and, as for doctors — why, if a woman had thought of them, she would have found it difficult even to frame the terms of her inquiry. The husband had once cautiously sounded out an apothecary, but got only a jocular response: *Better sleep out on the fire escape, Joe.* Besides it all smacked of the illicit and the shameful. The law frowned on it; the priest cautioned against it; and deep inner forebodings conjured up the visions of nature's reprisals for interference with her processes.

There was, therefore, not much joy to their desiring; the shadow of the reckoning was too close. There was no blame. Only, sometimes, as she nursed her discontent, the thought came to her that, if only he had managed better, all would be otherwise. And he, reading the accusations in her eyes, felt the pangs of a sudden guilt, the acknowledgment of his own inadequacies. At such times, a sullen anger entered the household, lingered unexpressed for days. The mornings when he went to work, he carried off a pained exasperation. Suspicions might come; the scandal of that other's wife, who with the boarder shamed her home, might cross his mind. The memory galled his wounds and, returned that night, edged his answers with acerbity. Peace then departed in an exchange of taunting words, then blows, and sad conciliation.

Some men surrendered. Confronted by intolerable burdens they deserted their families, lost themselves alone somewhere and put thus an end to this striving. Then the fatherless home, adrift, was not long from its foundering.

Mostly however they held together, the man and woman. Yes, partly it was the thought of the children that kept the family whole and partly it was the consciousness that in abandoning each other they would sever every last tie with their own past, diminish thereby their own human identity. Yes, often as they lay there, longing for escape to an undefined freedom, there was no move simply because the effort seemed too great, the means far out of reach.

But it was more than that that curbed the passing wish to flee. But it was more than that that drew them at last to each other. The old fixed order of respect between husband and wife had disappeared as the obligations on which it rested became irrelevant in the New World. Without the protective cover of well-defined roles they faced each other as individuals under the most trying conditions. That was difficult. But then as he looked upon this person who shared his bed and recalled the long way she had come, the sufferings she had borne, his heart went out to her. And then as she sensed the turning of his eyes upon her and thought of the little pleasure all his efforts brought, her heart went out to him.

It was not pity that sealed them in this attachment, but the brief glimmers of comprehension that they shared a life as they shared a bed. They were individuals, separate, two, and had been so since they left the village. But they had been two together. In those moments of recognition they knew they had been partners in a common experience and were now involved in a common situation. Only in each other could these beings find the complete understanding that would alone bring what they so desperately wanted, some reaffirmation of their own human dignity. For warmth they moved toward each other, for the warmth that came from the knowledge that here was consolation. Another knew and understood. That was a precious certainty, where all else was insecure.

About the children they can feel no certainty whatever.

This country is full of children. In the morning their clatter down the staircase fills the house. In the afternoon they occupy the streets. In the evening they pour back into the waiting flat which they quickly distend with the clamor of their ceaseless activity.

The immigrants were by no means strange to the idea of full families. The little ones had always made up a sizable part of the village population. But the spot had not been so taken up with their presence. They had had each their places, where they ought to be and where they ought not to be. They had had each their functions, what they ought to do and what they ought not to do. They had not been, therefore, so prominent in the sight of their elders.

Perhaps it was because, in these matters as in so much else, the Old World community had been very specific in its definitions of proper behavior. What a parent owed his offspring was clear. The child was to be fed, clothed, and housed decently as befitted the status and the resources of his father. The boys and girls were to be properly brought up, taught the skills necessary for their own adulthood and imbued with the beliefs necessary for continued membership in the community. It was their due at maturity to receive the land or dowry that would permit them to take the rank their ancestors had held; and one was not unduly to be favored at the expense of his brothers and sisters.

The obligations of the young were equally plain. They were to obey their elders and particularly him who stood at the head of the family, him whom they were to approach always in fear and with respect as the source of all authority. They were to assist, to the extent they were able, in the labors of the common enterprise; every age had its appropriate tasks. Even those fully grown but without households of their own were still to work for their parents. The unmarried had strictly speaking no property, no possessions of their own; if they went out to toil for strangers they were expected still to hand over their earnings to the father.

The neat balance of rights and duties was enforced by the village as a whole. Parents delinquent in the support or the discipline of their progeny, children remiss in compliance, could expect the swift censure of the organized opinion of their neighbors. There was no breaking the pattern of these relationships without a complete break with the community. But conversely, separation from the community by emigration would altogether disrupt the relationships of parents and children.

They might suppose it was the same as they strolled to worship on a holiday, Papa, Mama, and the boys and girls, covering the paved walk in a pair of uneven rows. They were wrong. Even then they knew the momentary solidarity would disintegrate before the day was over. They no longer cohered as a family and, as individuals, could scarcely say how they stood to one another.

The divisions created by differences of experience were too great. The older ones, sedately in the rear, had been eight or nine or in their teens in the year of the crossing. They had vivid memories of the Old Country, of the troubles that drove them off, and of the hardships of the journey. They spoke their mother's language and their unaccustomed English bore a heavy accent that united them with their past. Trained under the discipline of the household that had been, they were still ready to accept obligations. Necessity had long since heaped responsibilities upon them; no doubt they had been wage earners since soon after their arrival.

There was impatience in their scrutiny of the younger ones. Before them were two to be watched, scrabbling along without regard for appearances. These had been infants or little more when the migration came; their early childhood had passed under the unsettled conditions of the transition. They had never learned the proper ways at home, and a brief attendance at the public school had confused them so they knew not where they stood. They were clumsy in the speech of both the old land and the new; their names came from abroad but had already been corrupted into nicknames here. They were neither one thing nor the other.

At the head of the procession toddled the citizens. These more fortunate ones had been born into their environment. They had never known the Old World; they had not shared the experience of coming. They were Americans from the start, had lisped the words in English, and often received names appropriated from the older inhabitants.

It was at such times the parents were fullest of their responsibilities. As they led the way on these occasions they became gravely conscious of a disturbing uncertainty. What if the children should cease to follow, should take it into their heads to march off in some altogether strange direction! It was difficult enough to show them the right ways around the corners of the city blocks; it was infinitely more difficult to show them the right ways around the twisting curves of the new way of life.

As they consider the heaviness of their tasks, the mother and father grow somber. They remember the failures. Their minds go to that one who came to them as if on a visit, then sickened and went away. It occurs to them that they cannot possibly meet their obligations to the children. Not only that the food will hardly go around to nurture all, not only that the mended garments pass from one to another, but that by the act of migration, they, the parents, have destroyed the birthright of their sons and daughters. These boys who should be picking berries or hunting nuts, these girls who should be approaching mastery of the stove, have all been robbed and must endure the present, enter the future without their proper due. To each other, the parents acknowledge the guilt: *Yes, dear, and therefore let us sacrifice ourselves and live only for them. If there is any hope in this world, it is not for us but for them.*

It was easier to bend the neck in readiness than to be certain that the yoke would fit. With bewilderment the immigrants learned that to be willing to sacrifice was not enough, that their children must be also willing to accept the sacrifice; and of that there could be no confidence. The initial dissimilarities of experience widened with time as youngsters ventured out from the home and subjected themselves to influences foreign to their elders. The life of school and the life of street completed the separation between the generations.

If it did nothing else to the child, the school introduced into his life a rival source of authority. The day the little boy hesitantly made his way into the classroom, the image of the teacher began to compete with that of the father. The one like the other laid down a rigid code of behavior, demanded absolute obedience, and stood ready to punish infractions with swift severity. The day the youngster came back to criticize his home (*They say in school that . . .*) his parents knew they would have to struggle for his loyalty.

That was an additional reason why the immigrants labored to create educational institutions of their own; they hoped thereby to minimize the contest. But the parochial schools were expensive and spread very slowly; they accommodated at best only a small fraction of the children. The strong-minded and well-to-do could hold out against the pleas of their offspring who wished to go where everyone else went; mostly the newcomers were compelled by circumstances and by the law to depend on public instruction.

The building itself was familiar enough; this was one of the known landmarks of the neighborhood. The idea of attendance was also familiar; this had happened already to older brothers and friends. And as the lad entered the yard, even sight of the fellows playing or waiting in line had the appearance of familiarity; he recognized some from around his own block, the others were much like himself. The public school was universal, but each nevertheless reflected the quality of the homogeneous residential district within which it was situated. In effect it was Irish or Jewish or German or Polish; the first impression it made on the new scholar was that of the altogether familiar and the altogether expected.

The ringing bell broke the continuity of his life; as he

[218]

walked up the cast-iron staircase he left the narrow orbit of his home and moved into the limitless world. He stood in the stiff lines and sat motionless in the formal rows of seats. He learned silence and passivity who had never before felt restraints on his actions. He came to conform to rules: there were ways of rising and of sitting, ways to come dressed, ways to leave the room on certain occasions, and ways without words to signal the need. This order would now be his life.

Mostly the boys accede, and the girls too. At least the youngest do. There are truancies, some from their stubborn will, some from their shame at the poverty of clothing, some from necessity that keeps them home or sends them out to work. But mostly they give in and come. There is vaguely an understanding that the school will help them get on; and everyone else goes, so they go along. Besides they fear the law, want no trouble.

Only often, as they sat in the torpid classrooms, their attention wandered from the drone of recitations. Through the windows, gray filmed-over, they could see the bustle of purposeful men. By contrast, the school seemed empty of achievements, empty of the possibility of achievement. For what reason were they thus confined? What could they hope to gain from all this?

They did not ask those questions. They had long ago heard the trite answers. They came in order to grow up good and useful citizens. How would the school help them? By teaching them what was in these books.

Idly the boys fingered the battered volumes from which wisdom was to flow. There was no need to open them; the bold type of their pages was familiar enough from constant drilling.

THIS IS JACK. THIS IS JACK'S HOUSE. THIS IS JACK'S DADDY. JACK GOES SHOPPING. JACK GOES TO SCHOOL. ON THE WAY HE MEETS A COW. ON THE WAY HE MEETS A SHEEP. JACK COMES HOME. JACK FALLS ASLEEP.

And surely enough, across the top from page to page the

brightly colored pictures show it all. Blue-eyed and blond, Jack himself stares out over the nice white collar and the neatly buttoned jacket. Across the green lawn, from the porch of the pretty yellow house, a miraculously slim mother waves. By the side of a road that dips through the fields of corn, the animals wait, each in turn to extend its greeting. There it all is, real as life.

Except that it is all a lie. There is no Jack, no house, no brightly smiling "Mummy." In the whole room there is not a boy with such a name, with such an appearance. One can walk streets without end and there will be never a glimpse of the yellow clapboards, of the close-cropped grass. Who sleeps like Jack alone in the prim room by the window to be wakened by singing birds? *Good morning, Mr. Robin.* The whole book is false because nothing in it touches on the experience of its readers and no element in their experience creeps into its pages.

Falsity runs through all their books, which all were written to be used by other pupils in other schools; even the arithmetic sets its problems in terms of the rural countryside. Falsity runs through all their education. They learn the songs their mothers never sang. They mouth the words of precepts with no meaning: *A rolling stone gathers no moss. Make hay while the sun shines.* But what stone, what moss, what hay? The time that man appeared to speak from the platform and roused them, he shook them with his talk until they cheered the thin line at Bunker Hill, at Plymouth through the snow. *Our fathers' God, to Thee . . .* Then later they thought, *Whose fathers'?* Again a deception!

They themselves compounded the enormity of the untruth by the inability to give it the lie. From the desk the teacher looked down, a challenge they dared not meet. It was foolhardy of course to question her rightness. What an arsenal was at her command to destroy them! The steel-edged ruler across the knuckles was the least of her weapons. Casually she could twist the knife of ridicule in the soreness of their sensibilities; there was so much in their accent, appearance, and manners that was open to mockery. Without effort she could make them doubt themselves; the contrast of positions was too great. As she snapped shut the closet upon the symbols of her ladyhood within — the white gloves, the rolled-up umbrella, and the sedate hat — she indicated at once the superiority of her own status. There was visible evidence of her correctness in her speech and in her bearing, in her dress, and in the frequent intimations of the quality of her upbringing.

Perhaps a few were touched with sympathy at the condition of their charges. But what these offered was pity, nobler than contempt, but to the children no more acceptable. It was rare indeed to find the dedicated woman whose understanding of her students brought a touch of love into her work. After all, it was not of this they had dreamed in normal school when they had surrendered a part of their girlhood to acquire a profession, that they would devote the rest of their lives to the surveillance of a pack of unwashed ruffians. Mostly the teachers kept their distance, kept flickering the hope that a transfer might take them to a nicer district with nicer pupils from nicer homes. When that hope died, bitterness was born; and there was thereafter more savagery than love in their instruction. To admit the least question of the rightness of what they taught would undermine the whole structure of their self-esteem. So a boy should look and be, so a home, and so a parent. Many a woman, tired with all the years of it, looked out at her "scholars" tumbling into the street, and discovered a hidden crumb of satisfaction in the thought they were not so, nor the homes to which they'd go, nor the parents who'd greet them.

It took no uncommon sagacity to learn it was better not to question the teacher's world. The wise fellow kept his mouth shut and accepted it, he came to believe in a universe, divided as it were into two realms, one for school and one for home, and each with rules and modes of behavior of its own.

Acquiescence was no solution, however. Their lives could not be so divided. As the children of the immigrants grew up, they felt increasingly the compulsion to choose between the one way and the other. For some, the vision of the yellow house was peremptory. The kindness of a teacher, taken with the earnestness of the exceptional good student, may have opened the prospect of attaining it. Or the intense will of the ambitious youngster may have done so. Or the desperate dislike of a represssive home may have made this the only tolerable alternative. In any case, this way involved the complete identification with Jack, and that meant the total rejection of the origins and the background Jack could not have had.

Only a few, however, had the ability or the desire to make the radical break. The much greater number recognized the existence of the world they saw through school, were even willing to acknowledge its superiority, but they were not willing or, perhaps, not able to enter it themselves; their ties with their families were still binding. They developed perforce a kind of life of their own, an intermediary ground from which they could enter when necessary both the life of the school and the life of the home.

The setting generally was the street, where the young were free of oversight and masters of themselves. The boys and girls of an age who played together fell spontaneously into little coteries, for the very acts of play depended upon a sense of community and upon some degree of organization. There could be no games without rules and without subjection to the sanctions that enforced them. The interests of these groups changed as their members matured, from childhood to youth to adolescence to adulthood. But with notable persistence the members held together at least until marriage made them heads of families in their own rights or until they moved out of the neighborhood.

The structure of these organizations was simple, although they were endowed with a certain formality that mirrored the associational forms of the immigrant parents. There was a consciousness of belonging; you were in the gang and that set you off from outsiders. The sense of participation was tied to a specific place, a street or a district that was their own. Within the group each individual had a role which reflected his own capacities and qualities — the leader, the fighter, the buffoon, the clever one. And the whole was held together by a code of loyalty; they were in a common situation, understood one another and felt understood, and found strength in being together. In these matters the young folk followed the behavior and adopted the standards of their elders.

But the boys in the gang had also learned something from the school and from the world it represented. The teacher had told them, and the books, that the end was to get ahead, to make good, to strive so that success might come. They must not repeat the errors of their fathers who had not made good, had not gotten ahead. The consequences of failure were everywhere apparent about them.

They could see the point of such injunctions. Only the hoary aphorisms did not ring true. A penny saved was not in their lives a penny earned; or the best policy. They were not much in demand to fill posts as office boys, so that road to a vice presidency was closed to them; and the runaway carriage of the banker's daughter came rarely into their neighborhood. The atmosphere of the street, where so much of reality was in open view, was not congenial to the ideal of the self-made businessman.

The impulse toward success found expression in terms dictated by the nature of their own group life. In childhood they strove in the competitive play of the alley, games of pursuit and capture, of sides that struggled against each other for a goal. As the boys grew older and their gangs took form, there were fighting forays in the rivalry of block against block; or (and it was not much different), where space permitted, there were savage athletic contests for the winning's sake.

The growth of professionalism gave an enormous impetus

to this interest in sports which, after 1880, persisted on through adolescence to adulthood. On the baseball diamond, in the boxing ring, a lad could win fame and fortune. In these arenas, opportunity was free and only ability counted. The tone of one's name, the manners of speech and behavior, antecedents and affiliation were matters of no consequence. The pure capacity to succeed, with no other advantages, would bring the acclaim of the newspapers and wealth beyond the reach of these boys in any other way. The outstanding athletes who actually won such prizes were, of course, few in number. But each had his tremendous following of boys and young men who gained a kind of derivative satisfaction from his achievements and who sought within their own gangs to emulate his exploits. Increasingly the thoughts of the children were preoccupied with the events of the world of sport within which were played out the vivid dramas of American success and failure.

Down by the corner where the older fellows congregated another kind of game held out the excitement of winning and losing. Watching the parades at campaign time, the youngsters looked forward with anticipation to the age when they too might be old enough to carry a banner. Meanwhile on the outskirts of the crowd around the ladder, they heard the orators' stirring periods and yelled the slogans of their partisanship. Its members were not yet voters when the gang was pressed into service, performing the menial jobs that might nevertheless win it the boss's notice. Here too was the possibility of rewards and of public esteem; and here too they need not labor against the liability of their own background.

The pursuit of success might take still another form. On the same corner, or on another much like it, the same boys or others much like them waited to turn the fight within them to riches. The violence of their childish play would grow up into racketeering; there were opportunities in plenty for such efforts.

For some the chance came through politics itself; perhaps

they gained a proper "in" through roughing-up intransigent voters near the polls. For others the knock came in connection with gambling, or boxing, or labor organization, or in illicit liquor dealing. In whatever form, the ability to amass force in the gang, the willingness to defy rules the binding quality of which they did not recognize, and the burning desire by whatever means to elevate themselves above their origins, led such young men into organized criminality.

There were still other ways of rising, of course — the church, the stage, and the professions, for instance. But sports, politics, and the rackets had a larger importance even for the passive mass of the young who never ventured to be more than followers, who married and reconciled themselves to a stolid family life without the hope for success. For in these three endeavors were the closest approximations to the American standards of achievement open to persons like themselves. In no other way could the children of newcomers readily earn the appreciation of the whole society.

In the face of this whole development the immigrants were helpless. They had neither the will nor the ability to turn their offspring into other directions. The nominal authority of the fathers was only halfheartedly used; they were cruelly torn by the conflicting wishes that their sons be like themselves and yet lead better lives than they. Sensing that the school and street would tear the next generation away, the parents knew not how to counteract those forces without injuring their own flesh and blood.

If there was a serious one favored by the teachers who came home to sneer at the family ways, it was clear enough that when he could he would break away, change names, and drop all old connections. Could or should the father therefore stand in the way of his becoming a doctor?

That the brothers ran about all day with a crowd of wild ones was also disquieting. The worried parents could see no sense in the athletics, the infantile antics of grown men playing at ball. The immigrants had a deep fear of the consequences of the use of force in the rackets and an uneasy distrust of politics. But they could not deny that these were the ways to success, that these were the means of gaining the approval of the American onlookers. Even the older folk indeed derived a kind of satisfaction from the fame of men who bore names like their own, as if John L. Sullivan or Honus Wagner or Benny Leonard, somehow, testified to their own acceptance by American society. How could they then hold the youngsters to the traditional ideals of status and propriety?

In truth, the children were more in this world than they the parents. Often it was necessary for the fathers to turn for enlightenment to their sons. *We also keep a paper, but you have read more and studied in school.* The young wore their nativity like a badge that marked their superiority over their immigrant elders. It was this superiority that gave the second generation its role as mediator between the culture of the home and the culture of the wider society in the United States.

Accepting that role, the immigrants nevertheless resented it. It reversed the proper order of things. They could remember how they themselves had feared and respected the father; and they were embittered by their own failure to evoke the same fear and respect from their children. Beyond the loose behavior at the table and in the streets, these parents sensed the tones of ridicule. In their eyes the young Americans were undisciplined and ungrateful, good only at throwing stones and snow at strangers. When the boys and girls were small, it was still possible to curb their rebelliousness; the swift punishment of the strap held them temporarily in line. But as age increased their power, they were not so amenable to authority. As they grew in knowledge and in craftiness, as their earnings rose above those of the head of the family, they ceased to bow to restraints and would no longer be ordered about.

Adolescence was therefore a time of acute crisis, and particularly for the girls. As infants they had played with their brothers, but already at seven or eight they were excluded from the society of the gang and thereafter had little to do with boys. In girlhood they stayed close to their mothers since the home was to be their place. But even they could not be shut off from the world outside. They went to school or to work, observed the American familiarity of association between men and women, and soon enough revolted against the old restrictions. They learned to dress like others, with petticoats dragging behind to shut out the air and with their waists laced up in corsets so tightly the blood could not flow; and they lost their health — or so it seemed to their elders.

The worry was that they could not be guided by the safe rules of the Old World. They knew too much, boys as well as girls. Coming down Ann Street, they could not help but notice the "jilt shops" open for the dubious satisfaction of the sailors. Sometimes they could earn pennies distributing the cards of the brothels that flourished in their neighborhoods; and it was often years before they got to understand that a hotel could be other than a house of assignation. Why, even at home, through the thin walls, through the open windows, across the narrow courts, came the revealing sights and sounds. It was all familiar enough by the time they were of an age to conduct their own exploratory operations.

Well, such a girl or boy was open to error, by betrayal or by the longing for a withheld joy. Having spent the day in the closeness of the factory, having come back to the dank room where there was no room, it was release they sought and the assertion of themselves as individuals. Everywhere crowds hemmed them in so they had never the feeling of being one, uniquely one and not one of many. And so it might happen once when the sense of inner powers would no longer tolerate constriction, and the still night offered unaccustomed privacy, and there was a yearning for identity — to be a being, to desire and be desired.

Or, it might not happen; and then only the empty wish remained, returning evening after empty evening as the moody hours went by before sleep came.

Here was the ultimate barrier between the generations: they would never understand each other's conception of marriage. Sure, the parents tried to explain the nature of this most crucial step, that this was a means of extending on in time the continuity of the family, that it involved the sacrifice of personality toward some larger end: *From a maiden you will become a married woman, from a free being a slave of your husband and fortune.* The children would not listen. For them, marriage was an act of liberation by which they cast off the family ties and expressed themselves as persons through the power to love.

Nor could the children make their parents understand the longing for individuality. To enter upon such a relationship without consultation with one's elders, to make such decisions on the basis of chance impressions, to undertake this partnership with a stranger of unknown antecedents, was a madness of the reason. To many a saddened father and mother it seemed that their sons and daughters had moved gross passion to the center of marriage and had thereby obscured the true end of the family, perpetuation of the succession of generations.

Often enough, then, the old couple were left alone. Looking back across the years, they realized they had been incapable of controlling the course of events. Out of the village context and without the support of the community, the family as they had known it had been doomed. Though they clung to the vestige of home and urged their children to hold together, they would never recapture the essential solidarity.

Perhaps sometimes it occurred to them how much of these tribulations they would have avoided if only they had been able to find that farm and there to work united together. They need not have grieved over it. Certainly the immigrants in agriculture did not need to guard their boys and girls against the influences of the street; and there, where the father was still effective head of the household, his authority was not readily questioned. But the parents could no more keep America away in the country than in the city. As the young matured and discovered wills of their own in school and in more frequent worldly contacts, they too were rebellious and refused to be bound.

Indeed, the impact of separation, when it came, was more decisive on the farm. Lacking as rich an associational life as was possible in the urban places, the second generation had not so full a function as mediators between the cultures. The sparseness of settlement, moreover, was more likely to encourage marriage with strangers that cut the children completely off from their parents. Only here and there was an occasional township, closely knit, homogeneous, stubbornly resisting all changes in a declared antagonism to America. There the family might survive a generation in its traditional form because there the family could call on the support of communal sanctions analogous to those of the Old World. Nowhere else could it survive with its roots pulled out of the village soil.

Perhaps they never took the time to make a balance sheet of their lives, those two old ones left alone, never stopped to reckon up how much they had gained and how much lost by coming. But certainly they must occasionally have faced the wry irony of their relationships with their offspring. What hope the early seasons of their years had held was hope of efforts for their children's sake. What dreams they had had were dreams of the family transplanted, that generation after generation would bear witness to the achievement of migration.

In the end, all was tinged with vanity, with success as cruel as failure. Whatever lot their sons had drawn in this new contentious world, the family's oneness would not survive it. It was a sad satisfaction to watch the young advance, knowing that every step forward was a step away from home.

TEN

The Shock of Alienation

LETTERS BRING THE low voices across the sea. The unfamiliar pens grope for the proper words. When you ask somebody to write for you, you must go and treat him. Therefore you try yourself. In the store are printed forms. Sometimes they will do to transmit information. But you wish through this lifeless paper to do more than send news. With painful effort and at the sacrifice of precious time, you express the solidarity you still feel with those who stayed behind. The sheet is then the symbol of the ties that continue to bind.

Ceremonial salutations, *to my dearest* . . . to every him and her who filled the days of the old life and whom I will never see again. By this letter I kiss you. To the aged parents who bred and nurtured, who took trouble over, shed tears for me and now have none to comfort them; to the brother who shared my tasks and bed; to my comrades of the fields; to all the kin who joined in festivals; to the whole visible communion, the oneness, of the village that I have forfeited by emigration; to each I send my greetings. And with my greetings go wishes that you may have the sweet years of life, of health and happiness, alas elusive there and here.

They are wanderers to the wide world and often yearn

toward the far direction whence they have come. Why even the birds who fly away from their native places still hasten to go back. Can ever a man feel really happy condemned to live away from where he was born? Though by leaving he has cut himself off and knows he never will return, yet he hopes, by reaching backward, still to belong in the homeland.

It is to that end that the husband and wife and older children gather to assist in the composition; it is to that end that they assemble to read the reply. Little enough occurs to them that is worth recording, certainly not the monotonous struggle of getting settled. Instead their lines go to reminiscence, to the freshening of memories, to the commemoration of anniversaries. Later, when the art spreads and photographs are available at low cost, these are exchanged with great frequency.

Other acts of solidarity also absorbed the attention of the immigrants. Vivid recollections of the suffering they had left behind spurred them on in the effort to set aside from their own inadequate earnings enough to aid the ones who had not come. By 1860 the Irish alone were sending back four or five million dollars a year; a half-century later, the total remitted by all groups was well over one hundred and forty million for a twelve-month period. Often, in addition, some unusual disaster evoked a special sympathetic response — the church burned down, or famine appeared, or war. Such contributions recognized the continued connectedness with the old place. In time, that was further strengthened by involvement in nationalistic movements which established a political interest in the affairs of the Old Country, an interest the peasants had not had while they were there.

As the passing years widened the distance, the land the immigrants had left acquired charm and beauty. Present problems blurred those they had left unsolved behind; and in the haze of memory it seemed to these people they had formerly been free of present dissatisfactions. It was as if the

Old World became a great mirror into which they looked to see right all that was wrong with the New. The landscape was prettier, the neighbors more friendly, and religion more efficacious; in the frequent crises when they reached the limits of their capacities, the wistful reflection came: *This would not have happened there.*

The real contacts were, however, disappointing. The requests — that back there a mass be said, or a wise one consulted, or a religious medal be sent over — those were gestures full of hope. But the responses were inadequate; like all else they shrank in the crossing. The immigrants wrote, but the replies, when they came, were dull, even trite in their mechanical phrases, or so it seemed to those who somehow expected these messages to evoke the emotions that had gone into their own painfully composed letters. Too often the eagerly attended envelopes proved to be only empty husks, the inner contents valueless. After the long wait before the postman came, the sheets of garbled writing were inevitably below expectations. There was a trying sameness to the complaints of hard times, to the repetitious petty quarrels; and before long there was impatience with the directness with which the formal greeting led into the everlasting requests for aid.

This last was a sore point with the immigrants. The friends and relatives who had stayed behind could not get it out of their heads that in America the streets were paved with gold. *Send me for a coat . . . There is a piece of land here and if only you would send, we could buy it . . . Our daughter could be married, but we have not enough for a dowry . . . We are ashamed, everyone else gets . . . much more frequently than we.* Implicit in these solicitations was the judgment that the going-away had been a desertion, that unfulfilled obligations still remained, and that the village could claim assistance as a right from its departed members.

From the United States it seemed there was no comprehension, back there, of the difficulties of settlement. It was exasperating by sacrifices to scrape together the remittances and to receive in return a catalogue of new needs, as if there were not needs enough in the New World too. The immigrants never shook off the sense of obligation to help; but they did come to regard their Old Countrymen as the kind of people who depended on help. The trouble with the Europeans was, they could not stand on their own feet.

The cousin green off the boat earned the same negative appraisal. Though he be a product of the homeland, yet here he cut a pitiable figure; awkward manners, rude clothes, and a thoroughgoing ineptitude in the new situation were his most prominent characteristics. The older settler found the welcome almost frozen on his lips in the face of such backwardness.

In every real contact the grandeur of the village faded; it did not match the immigrants' vision of it and it did not stand up in a comparison with America. When the picture came, the assembled family looked at it beneath the light. This was indeed the church, but it had not been remembered so; and the depressing contrast took some of the joy out of remembering.

The photograph did not lie. There it was, a low building set against the dusty road, weather-beaten and making a candid display of its ill-repair. But the recollections did not lie either. As if it had been yesterday that they passed through those doors, they could recall the sense of spaciousness and elevation that sight of the structure had always aroused.

Both impressions were true, but irreconcilable. The mental image and the paper representation did not jibe because the one had been formed out of the standards and values of the Old Country, while the other was viewed in the light of the standards and values of the New. And it was the same with every other retrospective contact. Eagerly the immigrants continued to look back across the Atlantic in search of the satisfactions of fellowship. But the search was not rewarded. Having become Americans, they were no longer villagers. Though they might willingly assume the former obligations and recognize the former responsibilities, they could not recapture the former points of view or hold to the former judgments. They had seen too much, experienced too much to be again members of the community. It was a vain mission on which they continued to dispatch the letters; these people, once separated, would never belong again.

Their home now was a country in which they had not been born. Their place in society they had established for themselves through the hardships of crossing and settlement. The process had changed them, had altered the most intimate aspects of their lives. Every effort to cling to inherited ways of acting and thinking had led into a subtle adjustment by which those ways were given a new American form. No longer Europeans, could the immigrants then say that they belonged in America? The answer depended upon the conceptions held by other citizens of the United States of the character of the nation and of the role of the newcomers within it.

In the early nineteenth century, those already established on this side of the ocean regarded immigration as a positive good. When travel by sea became safe after the general peace of 1815 and the first fresh arrivals trickled in, there was a general disposition to welcome the movement. The favorable attitude persisted even when the tide mounted to the flood levels of the 1840's and 1850's. The man off the boat was then accepted without question or condition.

The approval of unlimited additions to the original population came easily to Americans who were conscious of the youth of their country. Standing at the edge of an immense continent, they were moved by the challenge of empty land almost endless in its extension. Here was room enough, and more, for all who would bend their energies to its exploitation. The shortage was of labor and not of acres; every pair of extra hands increased the value of the abundant resources and widened opportunities for everyone.

The youth of the nation also justified the indiscriminate admission of whatever foreigners came to these shores. There was high faith in the destiny of the Republic, assurance that its future history would justify the Revolution and the separation from Great Britain. The society and the culture that would emerge in this territory would surpass those of the Old World because they would not slavishly imitate the outmoded forms and the anachronistic traditions that constricted men in Europe. The United States would move in new directions of its own because its people were a new people.

There was consequently a vigorous insistence that this country was not simply an English colony become independent. It was a nation unique in its origins, produced by the mixture of many different types out of which had come an altogether fresh amalgam, the American. The ebullient citizens who believed and argued that their language, their literature, their art, and their polity were distinctive and original also believed and argued that their population had not been derived from a single source but had rather acquired its peculiar characteristics from the blending of a variety of strains.

There was confidence that the process would continue. The national type had not been fixed by its given antecedents; it was emerging from the experience of life on a new continent. Since the quality of men was determined not by the conditions surrounding their birth, but by the environment within which they passed their lives, it was pointless to select among them. All would come with minds and spirits fresh for new impressions; and being in America would make Americans of them. Therefore it was best to admit freely everyone who wished to make a home here. The United States would then be a great smelting pot, great enough so that there was room for all who voluntarily entered; and the nation that would ultimately be cast from that crucible would be all the richer for the diversity of the elements that went into the molten mixture.

The legislation of most of the nineteenth century reflected this receptive attitude. The United States made no effort actively to induce anyone to immigrate, but neither did it put any bars in the way of their coming. Occasional laws in the four decades after 1819 set up shipping regulations in the hope of improving the conditions of the passage. In practice, the provisions that specified the minimum quantities of food and the maximum number of passengers each vessel could carry were easily evaded. Yet the intent of those statutes was to protect the travelers and to remove harsh conditions that might discourage the newcomers.

Nor were state laws any more restrictive in design. The seaports, troubled by the burdens of poor relief, secured the enactment of measures to safeguard their treasuries against such charges. Sometimes the form was a bond to guarantee that the immigrant would not become at once dependent upon public support; sometimes it was a small tax applied to defray the costs of charity. In either case there was no desire to limit entry into the country; and none of these steps had any discernible effect upon the volume of admissions.

Once landed, the newcomer found himself equal in condition to the natives. Within a short period he could be naturalized and acquire all the privileges of a citizen. In some places, indeed, he could vote before the oath in court so transformed his status. In the eyes of society, even earlier than in the eyes of the law, he was an American.

It was not necessary that the immigrants should read deeply in the writings of political and social theorists to understand this conception of America. The idea was fully and clearly expressed in practice. The sense of being welcome gave people who had elsewhere been counted superfluous the assurance that their struggles to build a new life would be regarded with sympathy by their new neighbors. On such a foundation they could proceed to settle down in their own ways, make their own adjustments to the new conditions.

Significantly, the newcomers were not compelled to conform to existing patterns of action or to accept existing standards. They felt free to criticize many aspects of the life they discovered in the New World, the excessive concern with material goods and the inadequate attention to religion, the pushiness and restlessness of the people, the transitory quality of family relationships. The boldness of such judgments testified to the voluntary nature of immigrant adjustment. The strangers did not swallow America in one gulp; through their own associations and their own exertions they discovered how to live in the new place and still be themselves.

Until the 1880's the diverse groups in the United States got in each other's way only on very unusual occasions; generally rapid expansion made room for the unrestrained activity of all. Indeed the newcomers themselves did not then become issues; nor was there then any inclination to question the desirability of continuing the traditional open policy. But the second generation was an unstable element in the situation; as it grew in prominence, it created troublesome problems precisely because it had not a fixed place in the society. Standing between the culture of its parents and the culture of the older America, it bared the inadequacies of the assumption that the fusion of the multitude of strains in the melting pot would come about as a matter of course. The moments of revelation, though still rare, were profoundly shocking.

The discovery came most commonly in matters related to employment. However the native wage earner may have judged the effects of the immigrants upon the economy in general, he knew that these people did not directly compete with him for his job. But the children of the immigrants were Americans who were not content with the places that went to foreigners. On the labor market the offspring of the newcomers jostled the sons of well-established families. There was still no lack of space in a productive system that grew at an ever-accelerating pace. But the ambitious youngster every now and then hit upon the advertisement, No IRISH NEED APPLY! The hurt would affect him, but also his father. It would disclose to these immigrants, and to many who came later, the limits of their belonging to America.

In politics also there were occasions on which the activities of the new citizens met the hostility of the old. If the consequences then were more striking, it was because there was less room for competition in the contest for political control. There were times when groups of men, unable to attain their own ends through government and unable to understand their own failure, sought to settle the blame on the foreign-born in their midst. In the 1850's, for instance, agitation of the slavery question and of a host of reform proposals put an intolerable strain upon the existing party structure. Years of compromise had produced no durable solution; instead they had given rise to grave forebodings of the calamitous Civil War that impended.

At the point of crisis, the stranger who stood in the way of attainment of some particular objective became the butt of attack. Abolitionists and reformers who found the conservative Irish arrayed against them at the polls, proslavery politicians who made much of the radicalism of some of the German leaders, and temperance advocates who regarded an alien hankering after alcohol as the main obstruction on the way to universal abstinence — such people were the backbone of the Know-Nothing Party that leaped to sudden prominence in the election of 1854. The oddly assorted elements that entered this political coalition had little in common; it took them only two years to come to know each other better, and once they did the party fell apart. Nothing positive had drawn such men together; they were attracted to each other rather by the fears that troubled them all. Incapable for the moment of confronting the real divisions within their society, many Americans achieved a temporary unity by cohering against the outsider in their midst.

The Know-Nothing movement disappeared as rapidly as it had appeared. In that respect it traced a course later followed by similar movements that flashed across the political horizon — the A.P.A. of the 1890's and the anti-German agitation of the First World War. These brief lapses in relationships that were generally peaceful had no enduring effects upon legislation or upon the attitudes of the mass of the native-born.

But even very brief glimpses of the hatred that might be generated against them disturbed the immigrants. The memory of charges violently made lingered long after the charges themselves were no longer a threat. They left behind a persistent uneasiness. The foreign-born could not forget that their rights as citizens had once been challenged. Could they help but wonder how fully they belonged in the United States? Occasional street fights among the boys that pitted group against group, from time to time more serious riots in which the unruly elements in the town attacked the aliens, and the more frequent slurs from press and platform kept alive that doubt.

Yet until the 1880's confidence outweighed the doubt. So long as those native to the country retained the faith that America would continue to grow from the addition of variety to its culture, the newcomers retained the hope, despite the difficulties of settlement and the discouragement of sporadic acts of hostility, that there would be here a home for the homeless of Europe.

As the nineteenth century moved into its last quarter, a note of petulance crept into the comments of some Americans who thought about this aspect of the development of their culture. It was a long time now that the melting pot had been simmering, but the end product seemed no closer than before. The experience of life in the United States had not broken down the separateness of the elements mixed into it; each seemed to retain its own identity. Almost a half-century after the great immigration of Irish and Germans, these people had not become indistinguishable from other Americans; they were still recognizably Irish and German. Yet even then, newer waves of newcomers were beating against the Atlantic shore. Was there any prospect that all these multitudes would ever be assimilated, would ever be Americanized?

A generation earlier such questions would not have been asked. Americans of the first half of the century had assumed that any man who subjected himself to the American environment was being Americanized. Since the New World was ultimately to be occupied by a New Man, no mere derivative of any extant stock, but different from and superior to all, there had been no fixed standards of national character against which to measure the behavior of newcomers. The nationality of the new Republic had been supposed fluid, only just evolving; there had been room for infinite variation because diversity rather than uniformity had been normal.

The expression of doubts that some parts of the population might not become fully American implied the existence of a settled criterion of what was American. There had been a time when the society had recognized no distinction among citizens but that between the native and the foreign-born, and that distinction had carried no imputation of superiority or inferiority. Now there were attempts to distinguish among the natives between those who really belonged and those who did not, to separate out those who were born in the United States but whose immigrant parentage cut them off from the truly indigenous folk.

It was difficult to draw the line, however. The census differentiated after 1880 between natives and native-born of foreign parents. But that was an inadequate line of division; it provided no means of social recognition and offered no basis on which the *true Americans* could draw together, identify themselves as such.

Through these years there was a half-conscious quest among some Americans for a term that would describe those whose ancestors were in the United States before the great migrations. Where the New Englanders were, they called themselves Yankees, a word that often came to mean non-Irish or non-Canadian. But Yankee was simply a local designation and did not take in the whole of the old stock. In any case, there was no satisfaction to such a title. Its holders were one group among many, without any distinctive claim to Americanism, cut off from other desirable peoples prominent in the country's past. Only the discovery of common antecedents could eliminate the separations among the really American.

But to find a common denominator, it was necessary to go back a long way. Actually no single discovery was completely satisfactory. Some writers, in time, referred to the civilization of the United States as Anglo-Saxon. By projecting its origins back to early Britain, they implied that their own culture was always English in derivation, and made foreigners of the descendants of Irishmen and Germans, to say nothing of the later arrivals. Other men preferred a variant and achieved the same exclusion by referring to themselves as "the English-speaking people," a title which assumed there was a unity and uniqueness to the clan which settled the home island, the Dominions, and the United States. Still others relied upon a somewhat broader appellation. They talked of themselves as Teutonic and argued that what was distinctively American originated in the forests of Germany; in this view, only the folk whose ancestors had experienced the freedom of tribal self-government and the liberation of the Protestant Reformation were fully American.

These terms had absolutely no historical justification. They nevertheless achieved a wide currency in the thinking of the last decades of the nineteenth century. Whatever particular phrase might serve the purpose of a particular author or speaker, all expressed the conviction that some hereditary element had given form to American culture. The conclusion was inescapable: to be Americanized, the immigrants must conform to the American way of life completely defined in advance of their landing.

There were two counts to the indictment that the immigrants were not so conforming. They were, first, accused of their poverty. Many benevolent citizens, distressed by the miserable conditions in the districts inhabited by the laboring people, were reluctant to believe that such social flaws were indigenous to the New World. It was tempting, rather, to ascribe them to the defects of the newcomers, to improvidence, slovenliness, and ignorance rather than to inability to earn a living wage.

Indeed to those whose homes were uptown the ghettos were altogether alien territory associated with filth and vice and crime. It did not seem possible that men could lead a decent existence in such quarters. The good vicar on a philanthropic tour was shocked by the moral dangers of the dark unlighted hallway. His mind rushed to the defense of the respectable young girl: *Whatever her wishes may be, she can do nothing — shame prevents her from crying out.* The intention of the reformer was to improve housing, but the summation nevertheless was, *You cannot make an American citizen out of a slum.*

The newcomers were also accused of congregating together in their own groups and of an unwillingness to mix with outsiders. The foreign-born flocked to the great cities and stubbornly refused to spread out as farmers over the countryside; that alone was offensive to a society which still retained an ideal of rusticity. But even the Germans in Wisconsin and the Scandinavians in Minnesota held aloofly to themselves. Everywhere, the strangers persisted in their strangeness and willfully stood apart from American life. A prominent educator sounded the warning: *Our task is to break up their settlements, to assimilate and amalgamate these people and to implant in them the Anglo-Saxon conception of righteousness, law, and order.*

It was no simple matter to meet this challenge. The older residents were quick to criticize the separateness of the immigrant but hesitant when he made a move to narrow the distance. The householders of Fifth Avenue or Beacon Street or Nob Hill could readily perceive the evils of the slums but they were not inclined to welcome as a neighbor the former denizen of the East Side or the North End or the Latin Quarter who had acquired the means to get away. Among Protestants there was much concern over the growth of Catholic, Jewish, and Orthodox religious organizations, but there was no eagerness at all to provoke a mass conversion that might crowd the earlier churches with a host of poor foreigners. When the population of its neighborhood changed, the parish was less likely to try to attract the newcomers than to close or sell its building and move to some other section.

Indeed there was a fundamental ambiguity to the thinking of those who talked about "assimilation" in these years. They had arrived at their own view that American culture was fixed, formed from its origins, by shutting out the great mass of immigrants who were not English or at least not Teutonic. Now it was expected that those excluded people would alter themselves to earn their portion in Americanism. That process could only come about by increasing the contacts between the older and the newer inhabitants, by sharing jobs, churches, residences. Yet in practice, the man who thought himself an Anglo-Saxon found proximity to the other folk just come to the United States uncomfortable and distasteful and, in his own life, sought to increase rather than to lessen the gap between his position and theirs.

There was an escape from the horns of this unpleasant dilemma. It was tempting to resolve the difficulty by arguing that the differences between Americans on the one hand and Italians or Jews or Poles on the other were so deep as to admit of no conciliation. If these other stocks were cut off by their own innate nature, by the qualities of their heredity, then the original breed was justified both in asserting the fixity of its own character and in holding off from contact with the aliens.

Those who wished to support that position drew upon a sizable fund of racialist ideas that seeped deep into the thinking of many Americans toward the end of the nineteenth century. From a variety of sources there had been accumulated a body of doctrine that proclaimed the division of humanity into distinct, biologically separate races.

In the bitter years of controversy that were the prelude to the Civil War, there were Southerners who had felt the urgency of a similar justification. The abolitionists had raised the issue of the moral rightness of slavery, had pronounced it sinful to hold a fellow man in bondage. Sensitive to the criticism but bound in practice to his property, the plantation owner was attracted by the notion that the blacks were not his fellow men. Perhaps, as George Fitzhugh told him, the Negroes were not really human at all, but another order of beings, condemned by their natures to a servile status.

During the tragic reconstruction that followed the peace the argument acquired additional gravity. The formal, legal marks of subordination were gone; it was the more important to hold the colored people in submission by other means. Furthermore the section was now under the control of a national authority, dominated by Northern men; the vanquished faced the task of convincing the victors of the essential propriety of the losing cause.

For years after the end of the war, Southerners directed a stream of discussion across the Mason-Dixon line. Through their writing and talking ran an unvarying theme — the Negro was inherently inferior, did not need or deserve, could not use or be trusted with, the rights of humans. It did not matter how many auditors or readers were persuaded, the very agitation of the question familiarized Americans with the conception of race.

Eastward from the Pacific Coast came a similar gospel, also the product of local exigencies. Out of the dislocating effects of depression in 1873 and of the petering-out of the mining economy, there had developed in California a violently anti-Chinese movement. Those who regarded the Oriental as the source of all the state's difficulties were not content with what discriminatory measures the legislature could enact. They wished no less than the total exclusion of the Chinese.

Satisfaction of that demand could come only from the Federal Congress; and to get Congress to act, it was necessary to persuade representatives from every section of the reality of the menace. The attack upon the little brown rice-eaters, congenitally filthy and immoral, had the same consequences as the Southern charges against the Negro; it made current the notion of ineradicable race differences.

A third problem brought the prestige of many influential names to the support of the idea. The War with Spain had given the United States substantial new overseas possessions, government of which posed troublesome problems. In the traditional pattern of American expansion, additional lands were treated as territories, held in a transitional stage until the time when they would become states. But their residents were citizens, endowed with all the rights of residents of the older part of the Union.

Substantial bodies of opinion opposed the extension of such treatment to the newly acquired islands. The proponents of navalism and of an aggressive imperialism, businessmen interested in the possibilities of profitable investments, and Protestant clergymen attracted by the possibility of converting large numbers of Catholics and heathen preferred to have the conquered areas colonies rather than territories, preferred to have the inhabitants subjects rather than citizens protected by the Constitution. To persuade the nation that such a departure from past policy was appropriate, the imperialists argued that the conquered peoples were incapable of self-government; their own racial inferiority justified a position of permanent subordination.

By 1900, the debates over the Negro, the Chinese, and the Filipino had familiarized Americans with the conception of permanent biological differences among humans. References to the "realities of race" by then had taken on a commonplace, almost casual quality. Early that year, for instance, a distinguished senator, well known for his progressive temperament and scholarly attainments, spoke exultantly of the opportunities in the Philippines and in China's limitless markets. *We will not renounce our part in the mission of our race, trustee of the civilization of the world. God has not been preparing the English-Speaking and Teutonic People for one thousand years for nothing. He has made us the master organizers to establish system where chaos reigns. He has marked the American People as the chosen nation to finally lead in the regeneration of the world.*

These ideas were unsystematic; as yet they were only the unconnected defenses of specific positions. But there were not lacking men to give these rude conceptions a formal structure, to work them up into a scientific creed.

Sociology toward the end of the century, in the United States, was only just emerging as a discipline of independent stature. The certitude with which its practitioners delivered their generalizations covered its fundamental immaturity of outlook. The American social scientists approached their subject through the analysis of specific disorders: criminality, intemperance, poverty, and disease. Everywhere they looked they found immigrants somehow involved in these problems. In explaining such faults in the social order, the scholar had a choice of alternatives: these were the pathological manifestations of some blemish, either in the nature of the newcomers or in the nature of the whole society. It was tempting to accept the explanation that put the blame on the outsiders.

[247]

From the writings of the Europeans Gobineau, Drumont, and Chamberlain, the sociologists had accepted the dictum that social characteristics depended upon racial differences. A succession of books now demonstrated that flaws in the biological constitution of various groups of immigrants were responsible for every evil that beset the country — for pauperism, for the low birth rate of natives, for economic depressions, for class divisions, for prostitution and homosexuality, and for the appearance of city slums.

Furthermore, the social scientists of this period were not content with academic analysis. They were convinced their conclusions must be capable of practical application and often became involved in the reform movements which, by planning, hoped to set right the evils of the times. The sociologist eager to ameliorate the lot of his fellow men by altering the conditions of their lives found the newcomers intractable, slow to change, obstacles in the road to progress. Since few among these thinkers were disposed to accept the possibility they might themselves be in error, they could only conclude the foreigners were incapable of improvement. From opposite ends of the country, two college presidents united in the judgment that the immigrants were *beaten men from beaten races, biologically incapable of rising, either now or through their descendants, above the mentality of a twelve-year-old child.*

The only apparent solution was in eugenics, the control of the composition of the population through selection of proper stocks based on proper heredity. A famous social scientist expressed it as his considered opinion that *race differences are established in the very blood. Races may change their religions, their form of government, and their languages, but underneath they may continue the PHYSICAL, MENTAL, and MORAL CAPACITIES and INCAPACITIES which determine the REAL CHARACTER of their RELIGION, GOVERNMENT, and LITERATURE.* Surface conformity would only conceal the insidious subtle characteristics that divided the native from the foreign-born. The fear of everything alien instilled by the First World War brought to fullest flower the seeds of racist thinking. Three enormously popular books by an anthropologist, a eugenist, and a historian revealed to hundreds of thousands of horrified Nordics how their great race had been contaminated by contact with lesser breeds, dwarfed in stature, twisted in mentality, and ruthless in the pursuit of their own self-interest.

These ideas passed commonly in the language of the time. No doubt many Americans who spoke in the bitter terms of race used the words in a figurative sense or in some other way qualified their acceptance of the harsh doctrine. After all, they still recognized the validity of the American tradition of equal and open opportunities, of the Christian tradition of the brotherhood of man. Yet, if they were sometimes troubled by the contradiction, nevertheless enough of them believed fully the racist conceptions so that five million could become members of the Ku Klux Klan in the early 1920's.

Well, a man who was sixty then had seen much that was new in his lifetime; and though he had not moved from the town of his birth, still his whole world had wandered away and left him, in a sense, a stranger in his native place. He too knew the pain of unfamiliarity, the moments of contrast between what was and what had been. Often he turned the corner of some critical event and confronted the effects of an industrial economy, of an urban society, of unsettled institutions, and of disorderly personal relationships. And, as he fought the fear of the unknown future, he too yearned for the security of belonging, for the assurance that change had not singled out him alone but had come to the whole community as a meaningful progression out of the past.

It was fretfully hard, through the instability of things, to recognize the signs of kinship. In anxious dread of isolation the people scanned each other in the vain quest for some portentous mark that would tell them who belonged together. Frustrated, some created a sense of community, drew an inner group around themselves by setting the others aside as outsiders. The excluded became the evidence of the insiders' belonging. It was not only, or not so much, because they hated the Catholic or Jew that the silent men marched in hoods, but because by distinguishing themselves from the foreigner they could at last discover their common identity, feel themselves part of a meaningful body.

The activities of the Klan were an immediate threat to the immigrants and were resisted as such. But there was also a wider import to the movement. This was evidence, at last become visible, that the newcomers were among the excluded. The judgment at which the proponents of assimilation had only hinted, about which the racist thinkers had written obliquely, the Klan brought to the open. The hurt came from the fact that the mouthings of the Kleagle were not eccentricities, but only extreme statements of beliefs long on the margin of acceptance by many Americans. To the foreign-born this was demonstration of what they already suspected, that they would remain as alienated from the New World as they had become from the Old.

Much earlier the pressure of their separateness had begun to disturb the immigrants. As soon as the conception of Americanization had acquired the connotation of conformity with existing patterns, the whole way of group life of the newcomers was questioned. Their adjustment had depended upon their ability as individuals in a free society to adapt themselves to their environment through what forms they chose. The demand by their critics that the adjustment take a predetermined course seemed to question their right, as they were, to a place in American society.

Not that these people concerned themselves with theories of nationalism, but in practice the hostility of the "natives" provoked unsettling doubts about the propriety of the most innocent actions. The peasant who had become a Polish

Falcon or a Son of Italy, in his own view, was acting as an American; this was not a step he could have taken at home. To subscribe to a newspaper was the act of a citizen of the New World, not of the Old, even if the journal was one of the thousand published by 1920 in languages other than English. When the immigrants heard their societies and their press described as un-American they could only conclude that they had somehow become involved in an existence that belonged neither in the old land nor in the new.

Yet the road of conformity was also barred to them. There were matters in which they wished to be like others, undistinguished from anyone else, but they never hit upon the means of becoming so. There was no pride in the surname, which in Europe had been little used, and many a new arrival was willing enough to make a change, suitable to the new country. But August Björkegren was not much better off when he called himself Burke, nor the Blumberg who became Kelly. The Lithuanians and Slovenes who moved into the Pennsylvania mining fields often endowed themselves with nomenclature of the older settlers, of the Irish and Italians there before them. In truth, these people found it difficult to know what were the "American" forms they were expected to take on.

What they did know was that they had not succeeded, that they had not established themselves to the extent that they could expect to be treated as if they belonged where they were.

If he was an alien, and poor, and in many ways helpless, still he was human, and it rankled when his dignity as a person was disregarded. He felt an undertone of acrimony in every contact with an official. Men in uniform always found him unworthy of respect; the bullying police made capital of his fear of the law; the postmen made sport of the foreign writing on his letters; the streetcar conductors laughed at his groping requests for directions. Always he was patronized as an object of charity, or almost so.

His particular enemies were the officials charged with his special oversight. When misfortune drove him to seek assistance or when government regulations brought them to inspect his home, he encountered the social workers, made ruthless in the disregard of his sentiments by the certainty of their own benevolent intensions. Confident of their personal and social superiority and armed with the ideology of the sociologists who had trained them, the emissaries of the public and private agencies were bent on improving the immigrant to a point at which he would no longer recognize himself.

The man who had dealings with the social workers was often sullen and uncooperative; he disliked the necessity of becoming a case, of revealing his dependence to strangers. He was also suspicious, feared there would be no understanding of his own way of life or of his problems; and he was resentful, because the powerful outsiders were judging him by superficial standards of their own. The starched young gentleman from the settlement house took stock from the middle of the kitchen. Were there framed pictures on the walls? Was there a piano, books? He made a note for the report: *This family is not yet Americanized; they are still eating Italian food.*

The services are valuable, but taking them is degrading. It is a fine thing to learn the language of the country; but one must be treated as a child to do so. *We keep saying all the time, This is a desk, this is a door. I know it is a desk and a door. What for keep saying it all the time? My teacher is a very nice young lady, very young. She does not understand what I want to talk about or know about.*

The most anguished conflicts come from the refusal of the immigrants to see the logic of their poverty. In the office it seems reasonable enough: people incapable of supporting themselves would be better off with someone to take care of them. It is more efficient to institutionalize the destitute than to allow them, with the aid of charity, to mismanage their homes. But the ignorant poor insist on clinging to their families, threaten suicide at the mention of the Society's refuge, or even of the hospital. What help the woman gets, she is still not satisfied. Back comes the ungrateful letter. *I don't ask you to put me in a poorhouse where I have to cry for my children. I don't ask you to put them in a home and eat somebody else's bread. I can't live here without them. I am so sick for them. I could live at home and spare good eats for them. What good did you give me to send me to the poorhouse? You only want people to live like you but I will not listen to you no more.*

A few dedicated social workers, mostly women, learned to understand the values in the immigrants' own lives. In some states, as the second generation became prominent in politics, government agencies came to co-operate with and protect the newcomers. But these were rare exceptions. They scarcely softened the rule experience everywhere taught the foreign-born, that they were expected to do what they could not do — to live like others.

For the children it was not so difficult. They at least were natives and could learn how to conform; to them the settlement house was not always a threat, but sometimes an opportunity. Indeed they could adopt entire the assumption that national character was long since fixed, only seek for their own group a special place within it. Some justified their Americanism by discovery of a colonial past; within the educated second generation there began a tortuous quest for eighteenth-century antecedents that might give them a portion in American civilization in its narrower connotation. Others sought to gain a sense of participation by separating themselves from later or lower elements in the population; they became involved in agitation against the Orientals, the Negroes, and the newest immigrants, as if thus to draw closer to the truly native. Either course implied a rejection of their parents who had themselves once been green off the boat and could boast of no New World antecedents.

The old folk knew then they would not come to belong, not through their own experience nor through their offspring. The only adjustment they had been able to make to life in the United States had been one that involved the separateness of their group, one that increased their awareness of the differences between themselves and the rest of the society. In that adjustment they had always suffered from the consciousness they were strangers. The demand that they assimilate, that they surrender their separateness, condemned them always to be outsiders. In practice, the free structure of American life permitted them with few restraints to go their own way, but under the shadow of a consciousness that they would never belong. They had thus completed their alienation from the culture to which they had come, as from that which they had left.

ELEVEN

Restriction

IT WAS NOT OFTEN that his newspaper devoted its columns to the debates in the nation's Capitol. Generally the matters that concerned the legislators in Washington did not concern the immigrant.

But after 1900 he himself became the subject of deliberations in Congress. Investigating committees examined him, laws controlled him. He had to be interested, to follow with attention the fate of measures that would directly influence his own future.

He rarely stopped to wonder why he had acquired such prominence in the minds of the country's rulers. He knew he was an outsider and took it as a matter of course that those who belonged should wish to regulate him. He expected that governments should act capriciously and without regard to his interests. Therefore he was not surprised. In any case, in the unloading ships that daily brought the new thousands to Ellis Island were the continuing proofs that the traditional policy of free and open immigration still had vitality. There might be trouble with trachoma or with the likelihood of his becoming a public charge, but one way or another he could still bring his cousin over.

For almost two decades into the twentieth century, there-fore, the debate over immigration did not seriously alter the condition of the immigrants. The racist theorists delivered their judgments, to their own satisfaction demonstrated the inferiority of the newcomers. But the practical consequences emerged only when their theories acquired the force of law; and as yet there was no reversal in the line of legislation that encouraged immigration.

It seemed still the settled policy of government to keep the newcomers moving to the United States. In the nineteenth century, statutes had been enacted not to constrict, but to facilitate the flow. The state restrictions on the entrance of paupers and insane persons within their borders had aimed only to limit the permanently dependent who would be, from the moment of landing, burdens upon public charity. There had been no desire to inhibit the admission of normal people.

A federal act in 1882 had replaced the chaotic and contra-dictory state measures which the courts had frowned upon as unconstitutional. The new law did not go beyond its prede-cessors; it imposed a head tax of fifty cents an immigrant (not a serious burden!) and it barred idiots, criminals, and others likely to become public charges. Nine years later the category of excluded undesirables was extended to take in as well believers in anarchism and in polygamy. These minimal controls reflected no disposition to check the total volume of immigration. Indeed the hostility to any restraint was so strong that Congress, pressed by the Californians to shut out the Chinese, would do so only in a way that seemed tempo-rary and conditional.

The readers of the Irish and German and Yiddish news-papers accepted this legislation without resentment. But among the readers of the native press in Boston and New York was a growing body dissatisfied with the liberal policy. A famous geologist who spoke often on public questions, a respected social scientist, and a widely read popularizer of history and philosophy were among those by now convinced that a radical departure was essential to protect the nation. The hordes of inferior breeds, even then pouring freely into the country in complete disregard of the precepts of the new racial learning, would mix promiscuously with the Anglo-Saxon and would inevitably produce a deterioration of the species. A limit on the number of admissions was necessary and also some device to select from among the potential applicants only the superior stocks related to the American Aryans.

The Immigration Restriction League formed in Boston in 1894 had long worked to translate these objectives into law. The leaders of this association were well known and commanded a substantial literary audience. But they were not at once able to command many votes. The membership was drawn largely from New England and from a group which was itself losing political power within its own section. For almost fifteen years the labors of the league seemed in vain.

Only after 1910 did all these efforts begin to bear fruit. Not that the problem was then any more pressing — the volume of immigration actually fell after 1907 — but the spread of racist thinking induced many groups in addition to the New Englanders to view restriction as the solution to their own difficulties. And the impetus of wartime hatreds after 1914 induced a large part of the population to reject all foreign connections.

The South had always been fertile ground for ideas of inherent differences among humans. But its own complex situation had deflected hostility away from the immigrant. The most influential leaders of that section had in fact hoped that enough white newcomers would reach it to replace the Negro as a laborer and to permit the industrialization that would create the New South. To attain that desired end the states had set up elaborate commissions to make the attractions of the region known in Europe and to draw to the South a share of the enriching tide that flowed to the North.

All these efforts had failed when, in 1907, a federal edict had in any case outlawed them. The foreigner then joined the black as an object of fear and suspicion and Southern congressmen thereafter were among the most vigorous advocates of restriction.

Support from the ranks of the labor movement also strengthened the cause of those who wished to close the gates. Although immigrants made up the bulk of the country's industrial employees they were almost entirely unorganized. The A. F. of L., dominant since 1890, focused its attention entirely upon the skilled workers enlisted in craft unions which abjured any general reforms and concerned themselves entirely with improving the status of their own members. These associations had long regarded the newcomer with distrust; the addition of every new hand to the labor force was an unsettling element that threatened their own established position. Even before the opening of the new century, therefore, the A. F. of L. had expressed itself in favor of some form of control over admissions.

If the unskilled and the disorganized were a disturbing menace to the old union leadership, they were a challenge and an opportunity to the radicals who regarded the labor movement as a means toward widespread social change. The Socialists and the I.W.W., until the First World War intervened, sought to take under their own wings the mass of low-paid workers neglected by the A. F. of L. The effort came to nothing, for it failed to break down the stubborn conservatism of the immigrants. But it did succeed in frightening the entrenched organizations. The A. F. of L. responded not by reaching out to envelop the immigrants within its own fold but by rejecting them altogether. Restriction would bar entirely those who might listen to the blandishments of the revolutionaries.

The war of 1914 brought all the forces of xenophobia together and cast over them the aura of patriotic necessity. In the years when every citizen faced a running demand for proof of his "100 per cent Americanism," it was dangerous to champion the cause of the foreign-born. The restrictionists made capital of all the nationalistic fears stirred up by the conflict and also borrowed, for the measures they sponsored, all the arguments of national defense.

Under these circumstances, at last, the turn came; Congress took the first decisive step away from the long-accepted policy of free immigration. In 1917, over President Wilson's veto, the literacy test was enacted into law. Thereafter every newcomer would have to earn admission into the New World by demonstrating his ability to read.

The sponsors of this measure had not been interested simply in selecting the more intelligent and rejecting the less intelligent applicants. This test was rather a means of barring the southern and eastern Europeans without excluding those from the northern and western parts of the continent where the facilities for elementary education had become common by 1917. Such a differentiation was desirable because it conformed to the racist assumptions of the restrictionists. It was also strategic because it might earn the support of those foreign-born groups that would not be adversely affected.

The proponents of the new policy had long desired an alliance with some blocs of immigrants, preferably with those that seemed of kindred stock. The necessity for such an understanding accounted for the attempts by critics of the newcomers to distinguish between the old and the new migrations, between that before 1880 and that after. The virtue of the literacy test was that it would leave free the movement of natives of Great Britain, Germany, and Scandinavia and bar the subjects of Italy and of the Slavic East.

Their own faith defeated the restrictionists. They had expected that the test would cut down the flow from southern Europe because they had sincerely believed in the racial inferiority of the people of that region. The outcome was disappointing. Peasants, who until then had had no incentive to do so, now set themselves the task of learning to read, and succeeded. When commercial shipping resumed after the war, the volume of immigration began to mount once more and the proportion of Mediterranean and Balkan folk among the new arrivals proved no smaller than before.

The forces of exclusion would not now be denied, however. The very years that saw the Klan rise to a membership of almost five million and saw the League of Nations go down to defeat were not likely to see a softening of attitudes toward the foreigners. In the red light of the postwar scare all Slavs became "Bolsheviks," all Italians "anarchists," and all were alike plagues to be kept at a distance.

Back in 1911, Senator Dillingham had suggested as an alternative to the literacy test a new restrictive technique that would narrow the number of admissions from any country to a percentage of its natives already resident in the United States. The Reverend Sidney L. Gulick, long a missionary in the Orient, now gave this proposal fresh currency. In Japan Gulick had found potential converts unable to reconcile the Christian professions of the brotherhood of man with the policy of the United States which labeled the yellow people inferior and invidiously barred them. He hoped by a revised immigration system to abate the anti-American sentiment in the Far East. A new law that limited the admission of all nationalities in terms of their existing numbers would not discriminate against the Orientals and yet would satisfy the California racists, for only a handful of Chinese or Japanese would ever qualify for entrance.

Congress adopted the scheme, although ironically it still singled out the Asiatics for particularly harsh treatment and heightened rather than eased antagonisms in the Orient. For Europeans the acts of 1921 and 1924 set up quotas which sharply curtailed the volume of immigration and which assigned to each nationality a number of places proportionate to its contribution to the American stock as then constituted.

The new laws put an end to a century of free movement. They more than fulfilled the fondest hopes of their enactors;

even the tiny quotas were not taken up thereafter and there were years when the number of departures exceeded the number of admissions. England, Ireland, and Germany, which had the largest number of openings, by now had stationary or declining populations and no longer suffered from the displacements that had earlier set the peasants on the way. Italy, which felt most keenly the need for relief of its landless agriculturists, had a quota of 5800 a year. But even those five thousand would not come; the process of securing a visa and of meeting all the requirements of entrance was so hazardous that few would risk their lives on the chance of getting through.

To some extent the wanderers from Europe would be replaced by immigrants from the Western Hemisphere, exempt from the restrictive legislation for diplomatic reasons. Newcomers would move up north from Mexico and Puerto Rico and down south from French Canada. But taken all in all, these sources produced nothing like the earlier outpouring. Probably the whole twenty-five-year period after 1925 saw fewer newcomers to the United States than the single year 1907.

Now the moving men have come to rest. The last stragglers approach their destination. In a matter of years there will be the unaccustomed stillness of self-containment. Only then will the consequences of restriction emerge.

Americans will then face the question of whether the old expansiveness of their society will persist without the stimulus of an increasing population. The economy, once nurtured by an ever-available fluid labor supply, will now come to depend for development upon the extension of technology and will come to learn the inflexibility of machines as compared with hands; in the next depression it will not be so easy, by laying off employees, to contract production. Without the stream of newcomers who once by their simple presence at the bottom of the social scale had elevated every other element, social mobility will slacken. There will not be so much room at the top and the lines between economic groups will begin to harden. A society moving toward fixity will discover it cannot count on the assets of expansion. The citizens who have long been yearning for stability will come to realize that stability is not altogether compatible with growth. These effects will presently unfold and in their unfolding alter the lives of all Americans.

But for the immigrants the results of restriction were more direct and more immediate. As the purport of the deliberations in Congress became clear, the foreign-born could not escape the conclusion that it was not only the future arrivals who were being judged but also those already settled. The objections to further immigration from Italy and Poland reflected the objectors' unfavorable opinions of the Italians and Poles they saw about them. The argument that Greeks and Slovaks could not become good Americans rested on the premise that the Greeks and Slovaks in the United States had not become good Americans. In the halls of the Capitol they seemed to be saying, *We won't admit any more the strangers who came to strip our land of money; they have taken enough.* The assumption was that those who came from across the sea were strangers and would remain so.

Restriction involved a rejection of the foreign-born who aspired to come to the United States. It also involved a condemnatory judgment of the foreign-born already long established in the country. The end product of assimilation and racism, it confirmed and deepened the alienation those theories had produced. Restriction gave official sanction to the assertions that the immigrants were separate from and inferior to the native-born, and at the same time gave their isolation a decisive and irrevocable quality. The quota laws cut them off from contact with the sources of their culture in Europe and also marked the width of the division between them and the *truly American.*

[262]

The newcomers could not but feel estranged. In forty-two volumes, under the guise of science, the government had published the record of their shortcomings. Learned men had told them they were hardly human at all; their head shapes were different, their bodily structure faulty, the weight of their brains deficient. If they were Italians, they were not really like the Italians who had a claim to the mantle of Rome; if they were Greeks, they were not genuine Greeks descended from the Hellenes. The Armenians could not comprehend the jargon of the anthropologist who told them they were related physically to the Turks although the shortness and height and flatness of their heads were comparable only to the occiput of the Malays and Filipinos. Yet the derogatory intent of these inflexible classifications was plain enough.

Far from ending, restriction intensified the group consciousness of the immigrant peoples. The number of associations and the scope of their activity continued to increase. These still served the old functions of sociability and insurance. But in addition they became instruments of defense against the overt hostility of the society that rejected their members.

Indeed in some men the awareness of not being wanted stirred up the sentiments of offended pride into an inverted exclusiveness. Others had compassed them about with words of hatred and had fought against them without a cause. Well, they would accept the glaring ultimate result, that they were not wanted by, did not belong with the other Americans, and they would make a virtue of it.

The fixity now imparted to their separateness and the imputation of their inferiority drove some immigrants into a defiant nationalism of their own. Since they could not be 100 per cent Americans by the definition of the Klan, they contrived a patriotism of their own, found a refuge of sorts within their groups from the offensive rejections on the outside.

Usually it was those who had come closest in adjustment to native society whom the slurs of restriction shook most violently. Pride in their own stock compensated for the rebuffs. The vainglorious sentiments that now crept into the pages of the press and into the perorations of the orators were the products neither of the peasant heritage nor of the conditions of immigrant settlement in the United States. These sentiments were not of a kind with the older romantic glorification of folk heroes. Nor were they like the earlier nostalgic urge to extend the right of self-determination back to the European homelands. They were rather the equivalents of the narrow feelings that swayed the members of the Klan.

The new emotions found outlets in activities quite different from those that had arisen out of the fraternal, charitable, and cultural impulses that had formerly drawn the newcomers together. The old established organizations surrendered to the new tendencies only reluctantly, slowly, and incompletely. The nationalistic passions were the outcome of a repulse; they received their form by imitation of the closing social cliques active in the repulsion. Among many immigrants there appeared now associations that, in ideals and in action, mirrored the nativistic orders which, by their enmity, had evoked this sincerest tribute.

Thus, among some Italians in the New World, admiration for Mussolini implied not so much approval of Fascism as gratitude for the achievement of having earned the respect and fear of the great powers of the earth. When he stared out from the balcony of the picture in the local *Gazzetta* he seemed to laugh to scorn all those who here mocked the names like his; he seemed, by his boldness and in his strength, to justify those distant countrymen of his compelled in an alien land to accept the unmerited insults of strangers.

The Germans too had nursed their score of grievances since the hateful days of 1916 and 1917 when every symbol of the Fatherland had been besmirched with the mire of slander. Despite the professions of the President, the war had been fought against the German people and against German *Kultur* as well as against the Kaiser. Now, in the 1920's, the defense was as total as the attack then had been; to fail of support in any particular was to betray the old homeland to its vicious traducers. Not a few immigrants through this logic were led to uphold Hitler, after his seizure of power, as a rectifier of former injustices. If many others did not, they were in any case so confused by these issues as to allow a good part of the institutional life of the group to fall into the hands of the followers of the *Führer*.

Analogous sentiments drew some Jews into an invigorated Zionist movement. Bewildering onslaughts from the Klan, from Henry Ford, and from a host of lesser anti-Semites conjured up the fear that America might not be a permanent home for these immigrants. The terrifying example of Germany raised the persistent question of whether it could not also happen here. In the great uneasiness of being excluded, it was tempting to turn to the hope of a national state of one's own from which no exclusion would be possible, to which patriotic loyalties could adhere without question, a state which would justify the group in terms of the very standards of its critics.

Indeed it was a general result of restriction that the more acute awareness of their separateness drew many immigrant peoples into an intense nationalism of a kind with that of their native contemporaries. Perhaps these developments were to have been expected in a society that was settling down to a concern with place. They were none the less dangerous. Coming within a social context of contracting opportunities, the sentiments of exclusiveness supplied the emotional tinder of a major conflagration. With the slackening of population growth and of economic expansiveness, the competition for situations became keener, involved ever more tension. The men caught up in that competition were likely to conflate their personal and patriotic anxieties, to seek a common cause for their difficulties as individuals and for the national difficulties of the country. Particularly under the prolonged blow of depression in the 1930's they would sometimes turn to movements that held out some all-embracing panacea for the economic and ethnic ills of the country. This was the response to a situation that was general to the whole culture. Immigrants, and members of the second generation, and natives of the older stocks, to some extent, all participated in the drift. Not many individuals, by the time a new war threatened, could escape the broad implications of restriction.

The uneasiness was not confined to any particular sector of American society. Perhaps for that very reason there could be little consistency to the organizations that sprouted in the fertile soil of suspicion and fear. Some continued to wage war against all foreigners, others still reckoned the Pope their chief enemy, and still others directed their hostility primarily against the Jews. Some kept their ranks pure of all but Anglo-Saxon Protestants, others were made up largely of relative newcomers to the United States. Some were altogether indigenous, others had links to analogous movements abroad.

This was the saving element in the critical decade of the 1930's. Invariably the attempts to unite or co-ordinate these groups foundered upon the variety of their memberships and their objectives. The leaders had only to approach each other to recognize their essential incompatibility. The diversity, itself a product of America's immigrant past, that extended even into these organizations divided their energies and rendered them comparatively harmless until 1941. Few survived the war; the economic expansion that accompanied rearmament relieved some of the competitive tension and the recollection of the freedoms for which the struggle was waged subdued some of the hatreds at home.

Nevertheless, it was not the war that solved the immigrants' problems. The conflict removed the immediate danger from their situation and it discredited the racist thinking that had questioned their right to be in the United States. But it did not relieve their isolation; it did not settle the doubts as to how fully they belonged.

Those doubts were the larger products of a society that had moved to a restricted view of itself, of a culture that was beginning to think of itself as fixed rather than fluid, of a society tempted to prefer conformity over diversity. The newcomers, once the demand was made for a total choice between there and here, were incapable of tearing away either the one or the other part of themselves. They adjusted, as earlier, after their own fashion, only with the disquieting knowledge that no adjustment would earn them full acceptance.

The resolution of the immigrants' problems was approaching. But ingloriously. The simple operations of restriction yearly brought the number of the foreign-born lower and lower. The old people, growing older, could see the day ahead when there would be none of their kind left, when the country would be occupied entirely by natives, and when their own children or children's children would lose the very memory of immigrant antecedents. To the survivors the decline of their group was associated with their own aging. Thinking back over the long course of their settlement, it sometimes seemed to them that a young America had welcomed them in the power of their youth when their energies were serviceable, but now was discarding them to escape the pressing issues of its maturity.

They would never know, most of them, that there would be no evading those issues, which would only rise in other forms to confront the Republic.

TWELVE

Promises

WHEN A BOY had come, the friends had said, "Now you have a son and a successor."

But the son was no successor.

It might have been once on a cool evening that mercifully broke the summer's torpid grip, when they both leaned back suddenly refreshed in the chairs still sticky with the day's heat, it might have been then that the father thought, "Well, if only it were not so; if only he could walk a part of my way, enough to be sensitive to what emotions stir me, then I could tell him what this journey was, and in the communication that would make it ever of his heritage, I too could find the meaning of these turnings in my life."

The old man never tried. In the young American face was no hint of recognition. Fear of the bland, uncomprehending answer stilled the laboriously marshaled phrases that might have told the story. Silence filled the room as the moment passed. Only later, in some other connection, the inarticulate parent would complain, "We talk never seriously together." And he would thereafter pause often to rehearse the questions in the vain hope that the opportunity might return. Time and again, while the shovel grew loose in his hands, while the treadle rocked away beneath his heedless foot, while the load rested unfelt upon his shoulders, in his mind there was ever that asking.

WHAT WAS THE QUESTION, NEVER ASKED?

"For I was once a man, established; and had a place; and knew my worth, and was known for it. What of the hardships, if my situation then had a meaning in the wholeness of the community to which I belonged. But I was thrust away and carried cruelly to a distant land, and set to labor, unrewarding labor, for even the glittering prizes the few attained had little value in my eyes and came at a great price. Yes, I was plunged into an altogether foreign scene that yielded never to my understanding. Indeed, I made the effort, wished to be myself; but could not. Into all that was familiar, the New World introduced mutations; I built a church, then saw others fill it with strangeness; I drew close to my friend, then found our association develop toward an unexpected end. Power was cast into my hands which only slowly I learned to use, and never certainly.

"Indeed, in all that happened I was alone, although I did not wish to be. If I turned to those of my family I found them each confined to his own lonely round of concerns. I was separate while other men belonged. When there are none like me left, I shall be forgotten; there will be no successor to go on as I have gone. Such is the extent of my isolation. Were not then all my flutterings random, tricks of a meaningless circumstance?"

WHAT DOES THE QUESTION MEAN?

"I was pushed violently out from the nest of my birth. In the shattering fall and ever thereafter I longed to be back; my heart yearned for the security, for the familiar order of the warm feathery place. As I struggled in the effort to spread my wings and labored in the learning to bear my weight, as I

[269]

ventured to the far places and saw what never was seen before, I did not cease to dream of home. I did not cease to regret the lost safety that had been before — before the harsh winds of distance had bruised my body, before the impenetrable newness had shut light away from my eyes, before the vast aloneness had closed down around my spirit.

"Though a rest may come, end all these struggles, what shall I have gained thereby?"

The question never set to words never gains an answer. Locked in his own preoccupations, the unlistening son will not reply.

He might have. There was an answer, had he but known how to speak it. In the meaning of his father's life was a meaning of America.

THE ANSWER.

"No, you may long for it, but you will not take the steps to lead you back; the nest abandoned will never see its brood again.

"And what is this security of which you dream? Its warmth is that of many bodies crowded into a small place; its order is that of the rigid constriction that leaves no room for action; its safety is that of the binding fetter. The security of the nest is a huddled restraint.

"No, the blow that tossed you out, that forever snapped the ancient ties, that blow was an act of liberation. You had not much latitude in your choice of a destination; you knew only you would come to America. But America was not the British colonies or Brazil or Argentina where the governments lavishly held forth inducements to attract you. America was this country which was most hostile to your old way of life. Was it not that separation was also a release? Were you not tempted by a break as complete as possible?

"You long of course for the safety, you cherish still the

ideals of the nest. But danger and insecurity are other words for freedom and opportunity. You are alone in a society without order; you miss the support of a community, the assurance of a defined rank. But you are also quit of traditional obligations, of the confinement of a given station. This is no less a liberation because you arrived at it not through joyful striving but through a cataclysmic plunge into the unknown, because it was not welcomed but thrust upon you.

"No longer part within some whole, you mourn the loss beyond all power of repair and, blinded, fail to see the greater gain. You may no longer now recede into the warm obscurity where like and like and like conceal the one's identity. And yet, exposed, alone, the man in you has come to life. With every hostile shock you bore, with every frantic move you made, with every lonely sacrifice, you wakened to the sense of what, long hidden in that ancient whole, you never knew you lacked. Indeed the bitter train of your misfortunes has, in unexpected measure, brought awareness of the oneness that is you; and though the separation pains now will not let you know it, the coming forth endowed you with the human birthright of your individuality."

THE MEANING OF THE ANSWER.

The life of the immigrant was that of a man diverted by unexpected pressures away from the established channels of his existence. Separated, he was never capable of acting with the assurance of habit; always in motion, he could never rely upon roots to hold him up. Instead he had ever to toil painfully from crisis to crisis, as an individual alone, make his way past the discontinuous obstacles of a strange world.

But America was the land of separated men. Its development in the eighteenth century and the Revolution had set it apart from Europe; expansion kept it in a state of unsettlement. A society already fluid, the immigrants made more fluid still; an economy already growing, they stimulated to yet more rapid growth; into a culture never uniform they introduced a multitude of diversities. The newcomers were on the way toward being Americans almost before they stepped off the boat, because their own experience of displacement had already introduced them to what was essential in the situation of Americans.

A LARGER MEANING, AND SOME PROMISES.

This answer never was delivered. Perhaps it could not have been while the son was too engrossed in his own distinctiveness to recognize the paternity of his father.

Retrospectively now, with the movement ended, the son may begin to make out its meaning. A time came for many men when the slow glacial shift of economic and social forces suddenly broke loose in some major upheaval that cast loose the human beings from their age-old setting. In an extreme form this was the experience of the immigrants. It was also in some degree the experience of all modern men.

They did not welcome the liberation, almost any of them. Its immediate form was always separation. Its common incidents were the painful transitions from the tried old to the untried new. To earn their bread in novel fashion, to adjust their views of the universe to a new world's sights, to learn to live with each other in unaccustomed surroundings, to discover the uses of power, and to uncover beneath the inherited family patterns intimate personal relationships, these were the adventures all people in motion shared with the immigrants.

To the son now looking back it seems the movement comes untimely to a close. The ideals of the nest, remembered even at the height of flight, have triumphed. Men weary of a century and more of struggle, impatient of the constant newness, more eagerly than ever hunger for the security of belonging. Restriction becomes a part of their lives — and perhaps it must be so.

Yet looking at the old man's bent head in the chair, who came so far at such cost, the son knows at once he must not lose sight of the meaning of that immigrant journey. We are come to rest and push our roots more deeply by the year. But we cannot push away the heritage of having been once all strangers in the land; we cannot forget the experience of having been all rootless, adrift. Building our own nests now in our tiredness of the transient, we will not deny our past as a people in motion and will find still a place in our lives for the values of flight.

That also must be so. In our flight, unattached, we discovered what it was to be an individual, a man apart from place and station. In our flight, through the newness, we discovered the unexpected, invigorating effects of recurrent demands upon the imagination, upon all our human capacities. We will not have our nest become again a moldy prison holding us in with its tangled web of comfortable habits. It may be for us rather a platform from which to launch new ascensions that will extend the discoveries of the immigrants whose painful break with their past is our past. We will justify their pitiable struggle for dignity and meaning by extending it in our lives toward an end they had not the opportunity to envision.

THIRTEEN

After Two Decades

ETHNICITY WAS NOT a word of common currency in 1950. The Second World War, only recently over, had left Americans a vague optimism about the prospect that the whole world would become one in the immediate future. The United Nations, embracing all men in common discourse about common concerns, was a symbol of the universalistic assumptions of the times. Neither forebodings about Soviet intentions nor recollections of Hiroshima diminished the faith that men everywhere would steadily draw together in recognition of their common humanity.

Unifying tendencies were also in the ascendant within the United States. Divisive elements receded under the pressure of wartime collaboration against an enemy and for a purpose shared by all. Nationalizing forces rapidly gained strength; everyone read, watched and participated in the same experiences. Immigration, a dimly remote memory, generations away, had influenced the past but appeared unlikely to count for much in the present or future. The internment of the Japanese-Americans a few years earlier and the situation of the Negroes, North and South, left fewer grounds for complacency about the problems of race. Yet Harry Truman's call in 1948 for integration and equality sparked a glimmer of hope so that the Supreme Court decision soon to come in 1954 would seem a giant step toward unity. Increasingly then Americans considered ethnicity a fading phenomenon, a quaint part of the national heritage, but one likely to diminish steadily in practical importance. At most, pluralism might remain a sentimental cultural monument to the past.

Memories of diverse antecedents could then unify rather than separate. The millions who moved about the country had only this in common, that — a few generations back, or many — their ancestors had all been strangers in the land and had all passed through the trials of being uprooted.

Hence the not unrealistic affirmations with which *The Uprooted* concluded. Even then, the weary longed for the security of the nest, for the huddled warmth of the little community in which neither strangers nor strangeness intruded. Yet it seemed then appropriate to call attention to the values of transience; in flight, painful though it had been, the immigrant had discovered what it was to be an individual, casting off the comforting support of habit to test his human capacities against the shifting currents of the unfamiliar. There were still promises in that pitiable struggle for dignity and meaning which had been so much a part of the experience of all Americans.

Were the promises still valid in 1971?
Much had changed.

In the spring of that year, a committee of the United States Senate held hearings on an amendment to the higher education act. In the parade of witnesses, there were no dissenters. From many different parts of the country, representing many different organizations, they reiterated an identical woeful refrain.

We have been made victims!

The tone varied, from undiluted bitterness to a plaintive awareness of offsetting gains. But unfailingly the complaints expressed a sense of deprivation which was also a sense of emptiness, the ache of which required stilling. America had created the void by the theft of their ancestors; now the victims needed the healing pride of ethnicity.

The yearning to belong was already evident two decades before; the goal then however was a place in the gray-flanneled ranks which offered marchers the illusory security of homogeneity. Disabused, the ache not stilled, the men and women of 1971 were more likely to choose ethnicity as an anchor for life styles, values and tastes. Hence the firm determination to discover what were believed to be inherited characteristics. The tendency was most visible and most dramatic among disadvantaged Americans — blacks, Chicanos, and Puerto Ricans who thought they needed an ethnic explanation of their situation. But other elements in the population also felt the pull. The Jews, though less so now than in the recent past, had also been the victims of discrimination. Relatively new groups like the Cubans and older ones — the Italians and Poles, the Germans and Irish — also felt a revival of sentiments linking them to their ethnic origins.

There now seemed an advantage to identification, just as earlier there had been an advantage to assimilation. In part the advantage was economic. Formerly, preferences had gone to individuals who conformed to a favored type in dress, speech, manners, and family connections. Now the term, WASP, bore a slightly negative connotation; and some other identity was an asset in a society which was discovering the expediency of assigning places in education and employment by ethnic quotas.

But the source of the pull toward ethnicity was not simply economic in origin. All the cultural and social pressures of life in the 1960's also generated an inner desire for the security that such identifications brought. Therefore they huddled together, narrowed in upon one another, seeking in the nest of the familiar the security lacking in the wide open spaces.

Emphasis steadily shifted toward separatism — cultural as well as social. The far-out demands, with time, gained currency and respectability and the trend toward inwardness and separatism acquired a personal as well as an ethnic dimension. Only blacks could really understand the black experience, only the Chicanos, the Chicano experience. These half-truths spread: only Catholics, only Jews, only Poles, only Italians. Then spread still further: only women, only youth. And so on, perhaps till finally: only I, ME.

Yet the immigrant experience reveals the dangers of restriction, insidious because not visible on the surface. In times of shrinking expectations, 1971 as 1921, everyone feels a victim and pushes away outsiders to defend his own corner. The definition of the insider tightens. Communication breaks down. No one perceives a common purpose. And in the end, the individual is left, more isolated than ever. Then the self-fulfilling fear of being alone sucks people toward the all-encompassing unity of nationality or race in which the self submerged may at least be stilled.

The immigrant experience also throws light on the source of the self-destructive sense of alienation.

Americans who remained much in motion — and never more so than in the 1960's — often longed for loyalty, given and received, for the sense of being part of a group they could support and be supported by. Frequent changes in styles and in manners as well as in status and place of residence weakened the force of habit and destroyed the security of behavior at the dictates of custom. Almost everyone who lacked roots — and almost everyone did — sought the safety of a surrogate community to compensate for that they believed they had lost.

Those who remembered an ethnic past strove to recapture it; those who did not, sometimes invented one or else enviously suffered from deprivation of the glow that warmed the more fortunate. The passage of time therefore did not dull the longing to be part of a group. Through places dense with bodies in casual encounter, the one in the crowd stepped anxiously, fearful of losing the way, fearful too of following — unaware — paths prescribed by the stealthy trickery of others. The crowd ever threatened the ability or even the desire to exercise the will — either by obscuring the landmarks or by closing off the space for motion or by sweeping everyone along in response to some unseen pressure, distant and uncontrollable. Each wary one in the crowd was a stranger to the others. Alienation, formerly the penalty of migration, was now the lot of many people whose whole existence passed anonymously in impersonal communities, so massive that they assured no one recognition, so fluid that they held no one in place.

Irony — with the flow of foreigners ended, the sense of being strangers that once shaded lives begun in distant lands now casts a universal shadow, the penalty of existence among the large entities which dominate government, the economy, education, and the arts.

Instructive irony — now as then, the being alone does not damage the outsiders, so much as the frantic scratching to get in. Those chilled by loneliness who exhaust their energy seeking the radiance of some imagined hearth, neglect the choices isolation offers. However painful be the effort, now or then, to stand alone or walk the unfamiliar path, only thus do humans discover the power to try the will, only thus discover themselves. Will they accept the consequences, then alienation exalts them. Will they deny the reality, then it drags them down.

Them?

The precursors from distant lands; their descendants now.

Who?

Males and females; the full-grown and the young.

The thought comes in the crowd: does the clutched hand help or hinder? Parents and children; husbands and wives?

[278]

This was the immigrant calculation: could the family endure the crossing, then would its members sustain each other against the strangeness. Soon they tested the fragility of inherited ties. Strains on the transplanted European family were not new to American experience. The intruders upon the seventeenth-century wilderness had, upon arrival, begun the subtle adjustments which reshaped the household to new conditions. Wrenched away from the cohesive communities that supported it in Europe, the family could not hold its members to their expected roles. Well before Independence, they were not behaving as they should be — children, parents, husbands, wives.

Into this spongy ground the nineteenth-century immigrants tried to sink the foundations for their rebuilt homes, tried with much labor and only partial success. In the United States, they learned, personal gratification was the measure that regulated obligations, to kin as to strangers. It was not simply that the newcomers had left a native for a foreign place; a rural for an urban life; a family-centered, traditional, and agrarian economy for an impersonal, calculating and industrial one; but that, in addition, the dominant values of the New World were those of the individual. The paramount claim of each for self-fulfillment was a constant challenge to solidarity, breeding tension in repeated tests of will and purpose. And the bruises of the contest were the more painful in the absence of communal authority powerful enough to establish unquestionable norms.

In 1951, the tension seemed to have peaked and subsided, just as the flow of immigrants had. For somewhat more than a decade before that date and for more than a decade after it, relationships within the American family eased to the point of coziness. Depression and war left many rugged individuals emotionally as well as physically helpless; the shift of attention to the problems of survival emphasized mutual dependence. Mom, Pop, and the kids learned to cling together, pray together, stay together — if possible in split-level sub-urban security, otherwise, on whatever soil would hold roots struck by the children of the uprooted. Here the school was an ally, not a rival source of authority.

The child-centered home was however only an interlude, not the end of the story. In the 1960's, the center ceased to hold; the fragments flew apart. Divorce, desertion, plummeting birthrate, wandering children, the fading of all agreed-on codes of behavior, the abandonment of all accepted roles were the consequences of a change that amplified the claims to gratification of the ME to the point at which no other obligation could be heard.

The compilers of statistics provided antidotes to headlined exaggeration. Headcounts showed that the monogamous nuclear family still existed in America. Most children of the 1970's did not regard their oppressive parents with hatred. Some men and women remained together in matrimony through the whole of their contented lives. While half a million marriages ended in divorce each year, the rate was not rising significantly.

Then too, count the old-fashioned audiences for *Love Story* and *The Godfather*.

But the numbers obscured the true nature of the transformation. What formerly had been aberrant, unusual, illicit, now fell within the range of behavior regarded as usual. The alteration in the shared understanding of what a family should be had come through a decided shift in social norms and values. And the surrounding community was too weak to stay the change.

More than affluence was responsible for the change. The luxuriant security of the 1960's certainly quieted the concern for survival of earlier decades and permitted the resumption of the long trend toward liberating (that is, isolating) the individual from the bonds (that is, the supports) of kinship. But renewal of the drive toward Everyone's Lib, late in the 1950's, also coincided with a total transformation of the cultural setting. The leisurely paced family life of *The Saturday Evening Post* vanished, along with its derivative versions in movies, radio, TV. The dream substitutes that took their place flashed fast in the message; quick exposed, they bid up the shock — skin, blood, crash of bodies — in the grab for emotions hardening under repeated assault.

Formerly those emotions had established the identity of man and woman. Involved through matrimony in forming the family, through procreation in renewing the generations, those emotions had suffused the homes in which children were reared.

Love stories, 1970's. Turned on, turned off — easy responses to a machine's bidding. Feelings come, feelings go. The cast of characters may be the same or it may not. Choose.

So that it is not merely, as in the first half of the twentieth century, that ever more persons regarded the family as a means of individual gratification, but that after 1960 ever more of them identified gratification with the commonplace sensations readily available everywhere about them. One used others when convenient.

There is little direct connection between the family life the immigrants knew and that which emerged in the United States after 1960. Yet the men and women who came from the Old World to the New also suffered when familiar relationships collapsed beneath the weight of unanticipated burdens. What had always been ceased to be; what was never done, now was done. And he and she acted in fashions beyond any previous imagining.

Yielding to circumstances when need be, but not totally yielding, the immigrants learned that they could contain but not deny change. The posture of frozen immobility was futile but little retreats could win big victories. The effort was worthwhile because these people knew, too, the waste of making always a fresh start, of jettisoning the wisdom of experience and discovering each generation anew what earlier generations had already learned. Migration for many had a tragic outcome. Their loss was permanent, the remembered sweetness of family life left behind, unrecoverable. Yet others responded to the shock of shattered habit. The strange setting and unfamiliar tasks brought a new awareness of the partners in the home, partners not simply playing defined roles but each a person, individual, to love and be loved for self, not for position occupied in the family.

So that the most fortunate perceived through the pains of adjustment, healing glimpses of personality unfolding as custom cracked, unfolding not in sterile isolation but in pulsing contact with the life of others. The family then became a network of connections, exposing to each within the circle the uniqueness of each one among the several.

To the extent that the circle no longer holds, people seek other more difficult ways to know the self and to find kinship with some wider group.

They remain social beings. Not so clear, however, is the character of the society in which they are beings.

American society in the 1970's did not attain the stability observers anticipated two decades earlier. The transformation in which the immigrants had been involved had stretched over much more than a century and, in 1950, seemed to be drawing to a close. In the process, society had ceased to consist of small homogeneous communities, such as peasants had known, within which all life's concerns were the face-to-face responsibility of the whole group. Men and women in motion — here today, gone tomorrow — shuttling between job and home, between factory and flat, and equally unknown at either end, sought out those closest to them for mutual assistance and clung to one another in fellow feeling. The improvised associations sometimes had roots in the Old Country but they spread because they met the needs of the New. They were the voluntary, generally spontaneous, responses of people in a strange setting, driven to provide for themselves what existing communal agencies did not.

The end of free immigration after 1924 did not simplify the social pattern. Memories of foreign antecedents subsided in the decades that followed; and the mass media then created a powerful force toward cultural uniformity. Nevertheless enough differences persisted — regional and religious as well as ethnic — to sustain a vast array of organizations through which Americans acted as groups. The New Deal's extension of governmental concern to social security, unemployment relief and public welfare, matters formerly left to self-help, did not diminish the impulse toward association, but rather shifted it to other areas. In 1950, the pluralism and voluntarism which had furthered immigrant adjustment still was a vibrant feature of American society. Smaller groupings within the larger society took account of the actual differences among the population and encouraged the nation of joiners to operate in freedom toward whatever ends any of them wanted.

Furthermore, at mid-century the newcomers had mastered the techniques of democracy. Through the decades they had gradually learned to exercise political power, first as aldermen, then as mayors and governors. They had learned too that the State — which in the Old World had been a tool others used for oppression — could in the New be an instrument that served the welfare of the people. The Truman victory of 1948 was the culmination of a trend of almost fifty years duration not only because it was the occasion for promulgation of a program it would take years to complete, but also because it cemented an alliance of the underprivileged first put together during the New Deal. The unifying goal was government action to advance the equal rights and opportunities of all.

Enough had occurred between 1950 and 1970, however, to leave the situation uncertain both in the activities conducted through private associations and in those carried on through government.

The intellectual case for pluralism and voluntarism was as attractive as ever. In the rhetoric of statesmen, the freedom to choose received ample acknowledgement. Yet the old associations lost strength and new ones did not take their place. In the 1960's interest drained away from many a lodge or fraternal order as the founders died off and their children forgot what purpose it served. And despite the affluence of the decade the flow of contributions to sustain philanthropy diminished significantly in volume. In some places, the old forms persisted, either out of institutional inertia or out of the devotion of surviving members or out of the inability, as yet, to find substitute services. But there was reason to wonder whether people really wished to pay the price of voluntarism, whether decision was a burden or a privilege.

A tendency to thrust problems into the hands of the government hinted that Americans were not willing to shoulder this responsibility. The costs and the responsibility of educating the young, sheltering the dependent, curing the ill, and providing for the needy had grown beyond the point at which neighborliness, kindness and self-help were effective. It seemed plausible to let the State take over. It alone commanded the resources to cover the massive expense.

The immigrants of the past had set aside pennies out of meager laborers' wages to build schoo˙ and hospitals. Their affluent descendants could not. Or would not.

Despite the sentimental value set on ethnicity, fewer differences among the groups seemed worth preserving. Distinctive religious and ethnic characteristics faded and technically trained professional bureaucrats took charge, so that one institution was very similar to another. The more alike Beth Israel and Saint Elizabeth became, the less reason there was to preserve their separateness, the more reason to mingle their services under the auspices of the government that could pay for all.

And even comprehensive associations without ethnic

affiliations failed to hold the loyalty of their members. Retrenchment hit agencies supported by community funds as contributions failed to match the rise in costs or actually shrank. The will to voluntary action atrophied. Having ceased to think as members of groups and having lost the habit of giving or doing out of free will, people acquitted their social obligations by paying taxes; what remained was for the self. They preferred to let government act rather than to do the task voluntarily. Equitable common efforts were those made under compulsion — by force of law, by the collector's assessment.

The change, if permanent, will have profound implications for Americans. The involvement of the State in the most intimate decisions of existence will certainly increase the bureaucratic impersonality of life. It is not unthinkable now that papers shuffled across a remote desk will some day control the resources, services, and information that will license a marriage, permit a birth, and ordain a death. Always in the past, much in the individual personality hinged upon the way in which men and women dealt with these issues. A public interest has already infused the critical passages in human experience. Only the novelists have dared imagine the kinds of beings whose impulses the State will wholly regulate.

Political uncertainties further cloud the future. The alliance of the minorities that elected Truman has failed to hold on into the 1970's. To the extent that the government passes beyond negative action against discrimination, in which all have a stake, and undertakes to assign places to the least privileged, the political cement dissolves, for each group must now fight to enlarge its own share. Now too, the party structure bends beneath the pressure of new ideological issues and of divisive generational conflicts. The New Politics pushes aside the mediating boss and minimizes the effect of job patronage. The lack of some person to go to, of a dependable organization with which to deal, heightens the sense of individual helplessness against the bureaucracy. Although the calls made upon the State steadily expand, the system is less able than formerly to achieve accommodations among the numerous elements of a large and complex society.

When power was the product of compromise and negotiation, it drew minorities together in alliance. Now that power increasingly emanates from confrontation, it pulls each group apart in the quest of its own quotas.

The interdependence of individuals in modern society leaves no alternative; the tasks must be done, if not voluntarily then politically. The habit of relying upon government feeds upon itself.

Yet the State recognizes no differences among the citizens/clients/patients with whom it deals; each social security number has a similar array of digits and each must be treated alike. Variations are minimal and should be. And the uniform standards increase the pressure toward conformity. As all social relationships become relationships to the polity, the individual — one among many others — loses consciousness of his own unique qualities, of the importance of being the child of such parents, the native of such a place, the communicant in such a rite, the believer in such a faith. Only the number remains evidence of identity. And all numbers issue from the same accounting machine.

The jobs get done because they must — health, welfare, and schooling. But there is little satisfaction in the impersonal doing or the impersonal being done for.

Then, too, the withering away of all the little associations makes people, who wish to belong, yearn the more intensely for the large encompassing community of which to be part. And which they also lack.

Without the human associations through which their life-blood had once coursed, the ghettos died. The spirit fled.

The unpropitious physical setting and the external restraints remained, resented alike by residents and strangers.

In 1950, railroad passengers coming in on the New Haven could still glimpse, before the plunge underground toward Grand Central, scenes that brought back memories of ghetto life two decades earlier when the El on the Broadway-Brooklyn or the Myrtle or Third Avenue lines trundled by the rows of open windows at which heavy-breathing mamas caught drafts of summer air as they watched their kids at play below. The sight and sound of walkers — carrying, pushing, pulling, talking, hawking, bickering — mingled with the clatter of carts and wagons to keep the street in constant animation, while a succession of animal and cooking smells reflected the character of each district.

In 1970, the passenger coming down the same tracks or, more likely, taxiing across the Triborough from LaGuardia, observed a different panorama. Already the plane on a northeast approach had passed across the high-rise Bronx projects. Now the river ride revealed the jutting towers planted in jagged rows among the blank expanses of concrete. Thousands of people lived there, filed away behind locked and numbered doors. Only the sight of distant dots in hurried motion, the sound of voices muffled by the traffic hum, now and then gave notice of their existence.

The projects which housed these people were great achievements, not merely in the engineering and planning but also in the hopes of reform that impelled their construction. A whole generation of humanitarian activists had devoted its efforts to creating public concern with the problem of adequate shelter and to persuading the government to do something to remedy past shortcomings. And by the measure of the blueprints, these structures were far superior to those they replaced. Space, ventilation, sanitation — all the comparisons pointed in the same direction.

Nevertheless, the passing observer's uneasy sense of some

definite if not precisely definable loss was one the residents themselves shared. The swift dilapidation of recently completed units, the pervasive air of drab neglect, and a general shabbiness were the visible manifestation. Less perceptible was the lack of neighborliness, the absence of any developed relationship among the persons who entered and left the various doors that lined the long hallway, as if each had been put there by some bureaucratic decision that had little reference to any personal attributes, as indeed each had. Few felt any deep involvement with the lodgings in 14-D; or felt a compulsion to preserve or improve it; or considered it home.

Those who lived there resented being there, locked in, imprisoned, with hope only in some unforeseeable escape. Resentment of place in these districts engulfed not the poor alone, or the colored, or the disadvantaged ethnics; it spread among the integrated flats and crossed the streets to middle-income projects. A setting unpropitious for life evoked in people of every origin and of whatever status a sense of confinement, a desire to break away.

The immigrants who had once populated the slums of American cities had not occupied superior quarters — far from it. A harsh environment had taken a heavy toll in wasted bodies and had nurtured damaging social pathologies. But the dense blocks, stinking in the summer heat, frozen in the winter cold, had housed homes, had been the focus of communal lives, and had generated a loyalty to place that even in the 1970's survived in the vestigial ethnic enclaves of many cities, whether locked into old districts or transplanted to some gilded suburban ghetto.

The new environment of the projects lacked life. Cubic-feet and running-water comparisons with the past were irrelevant. It was not simply that expectations had risen, fed as they were by the ubiquitous blandishments of consumer-oriented media. More important, the project tenants had not come but had been put there by a scarcely comprehensible process. The machines that had determined they should lodge in one place could well be asked to locate them in another.

In any case, the family felt no loyalty to one set of cubicles rather than another. No particular address was associated with personal or group identitv. No purpose attached to the specific space occupied. No past, no future. No belief.

Aimless watchers. Only the flash of a contest across the tube involves them deeply. The drama of the football field or rink makes them care. Otherwise there is no equivalent in their lives for the culture that brought illuminating wonder, awe, and irony to the immigrants. Vast audiences sit in passive acquiescence to what the waves bring them, the ability to respond dulled by disuse. Sporadic rebellions sputter themselves out; acceptance takes less effort.

In 1950, the return to religion was in full swing: and it would endure for a decade more. The books promised peace of mind and delivered power in positive thinking. New structures clothed in contemporary concrete displayed the same modernity as schools or shopping centers or office blocks. As always, statistics were unreliable; but the numbers seemed to reveal a rise in membership, though not in attendance or participation.

The admen's ubiquitous plea greeted the hesitant, on car cards and radio announcements — *visit the church of your choice!* Why not? The selection of a house of worship was entirely voluntary and rarely made any creedal demands upon the entrant. Increasingly, intolerance was frowned upon and particularly that form which required the individual to subscribe to a defined article of faith.

That acquiescent temper tended to blur the differences among the churches. The propositions over which zealous believers had once slaughtered one another now took on a quaint, antique aspect, certainly not one serious enough to divide people into the saved and the damned. Adherents of any religion, or of none, could equally well lead a good life. The assumption that ethical behavior alone was significant disposed of the need for uncomfortable or even embarrassing choices, exemplified, for instance, in the growing number of intermarriages. A toss of the coin would decide; one alternative was as good as the other.

With the passage of the decades memories faded of old controversies in remote places which had formerly set one sect off against another. The times called for accommodation, for the resolution rather than the preservation of inherited causes of separateness.

There were still important differences among the churches, especially in enclaves where solid old communities held the loyalty of their members to unbroken tradition. But the fate of more general efforts to retain some standard of exclusiveness was already manifest on Boston Common in the pathetic figure of Father Leonard Feeney; stripped of his priestly function and his Center placed under interdict, he preached in the open to the mockers-by. His error, disobedience; its ground, insistence against the will of the Archbishop that there was no salvation outside the true Church. In 1953, the Pope for whose absolute authority Father Feeney fought condemned him to excommunication.

The rising church memberships of 1950 were not measures of the number of conversions to one faith or another. The urge to join responded to needs that were basically social. The young heads of families, mobile, frequently lacking other affiliations, reached out through the churches for a setting ordered by respectable values in which to locate suitable friends for themselves and for their children. They sought, that is, to attach their homes to an institution which involved in its activities people of all ages, and which, in addition, validated an ethical code governing the behavior of all.

Discontent after 1950 first took hold among the younger

clergy, not satisfied with the roles of social counsellors and teachers of morality. The ease of changing careers in a period of prosperity stimulated the increase in the number who put aside their vocations or at least found some alternative to pastoral work. By 1970, the trend had developed ominous proportions. Meanwhile the advanced theologians of the 1960's discarded the gloomy traditional view of man and rejoiced in the certain goodness of all authentic intuitive impulses.

Among the laity the shift was less perceptible, because it less often took the form of open revolt and more often was expressed in a growing laxity of observance, a gradual shedding of patterns of conformity and more frequent disposition to make decisions by internal personal judgments rather than by the standards of the faith. Church membership often dropped away not in some great crisis of the soul, but in the languid abandonment of an outworn habit long since empty of purpose.

During the earlier years of religion's revival, when membership figures rose, the soil lacked the fertility to sustain future growth. Cut off from any sources in tradition, attuned to serving an immediate social purpose, the American churches were not prepared to compete successfully for attention after 1950, when family structure, social relations, and cultural interests changed rapidly. Even before that date, the churches had rarely involved people in an esthetically satisfying ritual and had become peripheral rather than central to their communicants' way of life. Later, when respect for established authority faded, when the sovereign individual demanded that institutions shape themselves to each person's convenience, the concept of a religious imperative all but vanished.

An emptiness remains. Downtown, rain stains the saffron robes, but paratroop boots protect the feet of one of the acolytes. *Hare krishna!* He tinkles the little bell in monotonous ecstasy. Other searchers take other routes — to some fundamentalist faith, or to astrology, to witchcraft, to Manson, or to the private pursuit of sensation. It does not occur to many to explore the churches until the Jesus people appear.

To these developments, the immigrant experience has only the relevance of contrast. Instability, voluntarism, pluralism, and an emphasis on ethical precepts had always characterized American religion. Old World peasants and dissenters had alike felt the corrosive pressure of those traits upon the transplanted churches. But a faith reinforced by links to the past offered them at least the consolatory rewards of the future, a sense of involvement in a meaningful drama, and a coherent explanation of their place in the universe. With these supports they could face even the defeats of the New World encounter.

Without them, what was man? And who was mindful of him? And to what purpose did he strive?

The past had receded. The links snapped.

Unsettling thoughts intruded.

Objects created by a technology which was the product of science surrounded the Americans of the 1970's. But science was far from having molded their thoughts. The flick of a switch, the turn of a dial, put mechanisms of marvelous complexity at everyman's command. Yet the organized bodies of knowledge which generated the skills of contrivance had not supplied people a coherent picture of the world they inhabited. Lacking any whole vision of the universe, the users of the physics in the TV tube and of the chemistry in the pills and powders lacked also the reference points by which to understand their daily acts.

With some questions came answers.

Space? From the capsule the lens conveys an image: blue

sphere against the gray light. Beyond lies indefinite emptiness through which the rays reach.

Time? Genesis dated in exponential figures fixes the late
arrival of sun, earth, and the little span of man's tenancy.
Which has yet how long to run?

Why?

With that question no answer, only vague, ambiguous
impressions. *2001,* for instance. Shiny in its gadgetry, the film
makes a show of science, but retells the old Adam story — out
of the primitive unto death and redemption. The fiction
which clings to science usually retells old stories, because
imagination cannot transcend a reality the mind has not yet
grasped.

The intellectual implications of the knowledge science had
assembled were as remote from the American of the 1970's as
were the dominant ideas of the country to which the immigrants came a century earlier. They too could not locate
themselves for they had left a world that corresponded to
their understanding and had entered one that did not. The
conformity of concept with observable reality had developed
through centuries of peasant experience. Visions thrown suddenly out of focus could not adjust at once to the new shades
and shapes. Hence, to the pervasive optimism, the certainty
of progress, and the haste for change of the Americans, the
newcomers opposed a pervasive pessimism and a resigned
conservatism, resistant to novelty.

The intellectual disorientation of the 1970's evoked a similar, though not the same, response. A pessimistic unwillingness to change swept the country, but not so much out of
resignation as out of a furious loss of nerve, a desire for
insularity, a hesitation about new risks, a fear of an environment turned hostile — evidence of the inability to find meaning in it.

Furthermore, the immigrants had carried with them from
one world to another an unshakable meaning of life, one not

known to some Americans of 1970: sweat of brow was the price of survival.

It had become ever so fashionable to condemn material things. The sneers with which European aristocrats had once condemned the vulgar middle classes now were the habitual smart expression in the United States, and particularly among those so dulled to possessions they took them for granted.

The competitive impulse also fell into disfavor, at least in the talking about. The ability to move upward in occupation or status, having narrowed during the depression of the 1930's, broadened dramatically after 1950. No one ever expected rags to riches; but the hope of a climb, step by step, increasingly was open to fulfillment by all. Now, however, the value of striving to rise came under question. A society affluent enough to have outgrown meritocracy, could assign places by quota or lot.

Work, then, was an outmoded superstition somehow insinuated into the Protestant ethic by Calvin. Many people were now getting over the compulsion.

Making every allowance for their unreliability, the statistics told a dramatic story: a majority of Americans in the 1970's spent most of their lives not working. Count. More numerous than the dropouts who never took any job, were the professionals who did not slip into their posts until almost the age of thirty and then slipped out to long years of retirement. Add those who lived without labor on the income of others — contented heirs, decorative wives, miscellaneous pensioners and dependents. Add the intervals of unemployment that spotted the careers of those who did work. Add vacations and other times off. The sum — most lives devoted less time to earning a livelihood than not.

Worklessness had deeper implications than an accounting of years revealed. The farms and workshops of an earlier era had always provided something for everyone to do; the line between work and not-work was not rigid. Modern economy, however, abolished chores so that idleness was the alternative to labor. The little tasks of the children or grandparents, the big household tasks of the father or mother, had mostly disappeared; so that to be without a job was literally to be idle.

Yet the idle survived. The daily bread appeared whether sweat dampened the brow or not. Undoubtedly, nutritional deficiencies blemished the diet of the poor, as it did the diet of many others. But the assurance of being fed extended to all. American society had dissolved the immemorial connection between the obligation to work and access to the necessities of life. Be they rich or be they poor, Americans of the 1970's did not have to labor in order to survive.

That assurance was not a source of satisfaction. If the work, upon which survival was not dependent, was work not needed, then it followed that the people whose work was not needed were people not needed.

A long process neared completion. Work and life, once knotted into one, now separated. When the peasant entered the factory, one strand slipped apart: he produced inert bits of things that became goods for others to use. But the pay envelope then linked his work to food and shelter. So it still was in 1950. Two decades later, an increasing number of Americans could not guess the origin of the objects they consumed; nor could they in any sense connect the cans, cars, coats, clothes, coins, the numerous or few possessions about them, with their own efforts. Work and life were apart.

Yet what was life without work? Play. A sensual purposelessness oozed from the fold-outs to all activities and all walks of life.

Inevitably, however, the *Playboy* readers sank into miasmic discontent, exhausted in the relentless quest for ecstasy. At whatever level of the social system they stood, they were not needed; activities without purpose or function brought them goods without savor, left them dissatisfied as producers and as consumers.

And they, not knowing it, felt the need to be needed, felt the need to be self-sustaining, which alone provided humans the assurance they were not simply replaceable parts, but unique, individual. They had lost the ability to relate their lives meaningfully to an entity larger than themselves. They had lost also that immortal soul, eternally one, which sustained the peasants and other immigrants in their initial encounter with industrial experience.

The world lost, of the village and the town, had had deficiencies of its own, measurable in the rule of rigid habit, in low life expectancy, and in murderous famine years. But that world had accommodated the desire to be someone known and needed.

In 1950, one could hope that men and women released from want, their labor eased, would develop equivalent — perhaps better — ways of knowing and needing.

Two decades later, the want diminished, no equivalent had yet taken work's place in giving purpose to human life.

Perhaps the transition was too easy. The historian, surveying the twentieth-century's third quarter, is impressed with the velocity of change, with the abrupt transitions from style to style, with the casual discard of age-old practices. The stepped-up tempo is due in part to boldness in experiment, in part to a disregard of consequences, and in part to a lack of commitment — to faith or policy or fashion.

Changes of the same magnitude came less readily in an earlier era. The consequences therefore unfolded on the way. Immigrants gradually discovered the pattern of the new life they could lead in the successive stages of the crossing from the Old World to the New, from the initial village departure to the ultimate settlement across the ocean. Hence, though the voyage was painful and costly, there was time for the effect to sink in. Those who survived, inured to hardship, also learned the full meaning of the crossing.

Speed in the 1970's dulls the awareness of the distance traversed. The mountains lose their heights, the oceans their depths; and all earth's configurations vanish as we rocket through space. So too the jet through time obscures the duration of the voyage; when we scarcely bother to buckle and unbuckle belts, it becomes difficult to distinguish point of departure from destination.

Those peasant progenitors who made a different and more difficult crossing remind us of the direction of our own continuing journey. They left the closed communities which had once enclosed the whole of their lives. They left reluctantly, more often out of the pressure of circumstance than out of the lust for adventure or novelty. They arrived in a society of strangers which frustrated every effort to rebuild according to an old model. They discovered a setting that compelled them to improvise and imposed upon them the obligation to act the risky role of individuals. In doing so, they and their children revealed a potentiality for achievement unimaginable in the village.

Departure separated each one from the others; arrival forced all to remain apart. In painful flight, their thoughts turned to the America never seen, land of promise, sweet land of liberty — which would redress all grievances, reward all sufferers. America, soon to be resented, for its remoteness, for its failure as a dream substitute, for its resistance to rest, its insistence on further striving — that country 'tis of thee which then they would come to love not for its streets paved with gold, but perversely for the very pain it caused in thrusting upon them the obligation of learning in the loneliness to be an individual.

Some descendants forget. Weary, they seek safety. Loss of nerve in the loneliness converts their resentment into hate. Their thoughts turn, as their ancestors' had, to America —

land of failure, a mad, mad, mad world corrupting Spencer Tracy with the gaudy blandishments of success; behold here the country of the great betrayals approaching the last flickering of its picture show. Bad as its past was, the future threatens to be worse. Faith in visions of a future that worked — in Europe, the Soviet Union, or Mao's China — had once sustained Utopian hopes. Loss of that faith left only a bitter anti-Americanism to justify dreams of an earthly paradise beyond the horizon.

These repeated whimperings achieved a mawkish popularity among those who forgot what the actual promises had been. People sustained neither by a firm sense of their relations to others nor by confidence in the ability to stand alone could not bear appraisal. Drenched in pity of the self, unidentified because untriangulated, they shifted all blame to the nation which owed them the debt of happiness.

The 1970's can hardly fail to be a decade of reckoning. It will reveal how many Americans still find the immigrant story valid, not simply as a testament from the past but for what it says about the country migration built.

To those made faint by doubt of self, to those in quivering withdrawal, the millions who once made the crossing address an insistent reminder — that their movement led outward not inward, that it carried them from the known to the unknown, and that the promise of the shore they reached was not contentment but exploration. Here in the wilderness of the forests and the cities, which remained wilderness as long as it remained open to change, men and women ventured the boldest of discoveries, which in other times and places was the privilege of a fortunate few — what it was like to act and feel and think as individuals. As the crust of habit flaked away to expose the raw dermatic nerves, they discovered the glory and the grief of being free. Their successes and failures, above all the challenges to which they responded, long kept American culture on knife-edge between exhilaration and panic. And it may not yet be all over as the century nears its last quarter. While a taste for violence suffuses life, while military regimes clamp their holds across the earth's surface, and while nationalisms divide its population, the record of the immigrant adventure may still be worth pondering.

FOURTEEN

Encounters with Evidence

EARLY ON I understood that this book would not fit the forms prescribed by historical science, the forms which had sustained my previous writing. Problems of exposition sounded the warning. I weighed the evidence and reached the conclusions; I arranged the data and marshaled the documentation. But the sentences followed a pattern of their own: they begged for the alteration of tenses in quotations or for the substitution of one pronoun for another. I caught myself in the measure of meter, in the balance of shades of meaning, in the contemplation of the color, the tone, the feel of words. These were symptoms I discovered of strain as the imagination beat against the confining limits of the evidence.

In the end I cut loose. The footnotes went: they could demonstrate my ability to copy accurately from the sources, but I could not pretend that they proved the validity of what I had to say. Reaching back to a seventeenth-century convention, I italicized the phrases lifted from documents, thus evading the literal constraints of quotation marks. I abandoned chronology as an organizing principle and gave the material coherence through the employment of another logic. Thus I sought the means of utterance for what I thought the evidence said to me.

The hazards of a narrative that did not ride securely on rails of steely references demanded controls, although of a sort different from those historians conventionally employed. I relied upon precision — of fact, concept, and language — to guide imagination along the path the evidence directed. So that now, many years later, the effort to appraise the accuracy of what I then wrote called not only for scrutiny of what others had since written on related subjects but also for a retracing of the process of composing the book. And the latter task was by far the more difficult, requiring as it did an effort of the memory to sort out which steps research guided, which reading and reflection, and which the resonance of personal experience.

First had come a monograph pieced together from numberless hard bits of information; then the strain of envisioning the relation of the single instance to the whole; and finally the struggle to put words to the meaning.

The monograph was an accident. The day this graduate student came in to discuss a thesis subject, Arthur M. Schlesinger glanced at a letter recently arrived and handed over a title someone else had just released: a racial history of Boston. As simple as that! And why not, since the historian was a scientist who could focus his investigatory gaze on one area as well as upon another? I was a stranger to the city and knew nothing of the people who lived in it, so that month after month without ever perceiving an outcome I simply amassed vast quantities of data and only later and with much pain wrestled some sort of shape of it.

Well then, *Boston's Immigrants* taught me something about one city and something about the Irish and something about the more general forces at work in America at the middle of the nineteenth century. But the effort to project to a wider scale the insights derived from one place and one time called for comparisons with other places and other times; and, alas, the necessary books were not then written. No historian had treated another city or another immigrant group with competence or with sensitivity to the right questions. The resources for comparison grew somewhat thereafter, although not as much as might have been expected from the repeated calls for attention to urban and ethnic history.[1]

Nor were existing comprehensive studies of immigration helpful. The more important works, while competent in detail, fell into a defensive tradition that emphasized the contributions to American life of notable men.[2] Only the fragments left by Marcus L. Hansen revealed a comprehension of what the larger processes of migration meant to the masses who participated in it.[3] There were then no equivalents of the useful general surveys which appeared later and which revealed the broad outlines of the subject despite the limited fund of monographic information upon which they rested.[4]

The scattered clumps of information developed by students of social history for almost a half century suggested some sense of the background. Edward Eggleston's *The Transit of Civilization from England to America in the Seventeenth Century* (1900) had long before stated a central theme of the New World experience; and *The History of American Life Series* contained a great deal of information not fully appreciated in its own time or later. But no one had followed up on Eggleston's observations; and for all its merits the *American Life Series* was uneven in quality and conceptually unsystematic.

Hence it was tempting to look toward the analytical social sciences for an organizational framework. The common hope of historians that others would absolve them of the necessity for original thought had already led me through MacIver, Marx, Durkheim, Sombart, Weber, Mannheim, and Pareto; and I had at the time of writing enlisted in an experiment to create a new, unified department at Harvard. The senior members were Talcott Parsons, Gordon Allport, and Pitirim Sorokin. My assignment, to compile a canon of social science classics (i.e., books written before 1920), forced me to review a large and stimulating body of theory in the areas the nascent Department of Social Relations took as its province. Yet it is a simplification to imagine, as some commentators have, that I applied social science theory to my data.[5] I never declared allegiance to a coherent system. Nor did I test hypotheses. My debts were of another sort. From this reading I absorbed the awareness of certain problems; I got to understand how certain concepts could aid in the organization of information; and I learned something about the depth of meaning of certain terms that otherwise slipped all too casually into current usage. However, this reading did not remain apart from, but rather was assimilated with, reading of other sorts. So that in some way that I do not pretend to analyze, the literature that enriched me encompassed all the words that added to my vocabulary whether they had previously been used by poet, novelist, or scholar. And when I came to an immigrant letter or turned the pages of an old newspaper and tried to know, then describe, who'd written, then read, the sentences, I reached for what support I could in getting over time's gap.

There was the evidence — paper. It was evidence of at least this reality — that it had once actually rested in the hand of some living man or woman. And here, totally removed in time and place, another ventured to know, then describe, what those other beings had done, thought, felt.

Evidence and past reality; imagination, straining to leap the gap, called upon reserves of personal experience. Every question — what was it like to have felt, thought and acted as they did — was a call to empathy. In the end, the author, who was very different from his subjects, had to search himself to understand them.

My first published book announced the theme of this inquiry: I wished to explain "the intimate lives and deepest feelings of humble men and women who leave behind few formal records."[6] Not the great leaders, but people in the mass were the characters of my story. Yet reality, I knew, consisted of aggregations of individuals, each unique and different from others. As the letters took form on the line, the struck keys produced *Bostonians* and *Irishmen,* pale abstractions of the beings my pages sought to describe. How much more so was that the case with the immense variety of humans summed up in this volume in such terms as *peasants* or *immigrants!* A perceptive reviewer noted the device which coped with the problem, the creation of "an ideal type," the European peasant, and the analysis of its life history on both sides of the ocean.[7] A later, more systematic, generation might have referred to the procedure as model-building.

The way of writing *The Uprooted* immediately encountered adverse criticism, which has echoed through the years. Most commonly, the charge was that the generalizations applied only to immigrants from central and southern Europe who were stranded in eastern cities, notably New York, and perhaps not even to that group.[8] How about northern nationalities and the notable succeeders — Mellon, Carnegie, Giannini? What of the fortunate West, and California? Did their settlers share the lot of the dwellers in urban slums? Embedded in such questions were scarcely conscious preferences — for the "old" as against the "new" immigration, for rural as against urban life. More important, those questions reflected habits of looking at the evidence developed by the traditional historiography of the subject.

The first chroniclers of immigration were defensive. Mostly devoted amateurs who resented the slurs of restrictionists, they sought to demonstrate the legitimacy of a group by compiling the record of its contributions to American civilization. They stressed the achievements of notable newcomers, their ease of assimilation, their patriotism, and their cultural closeness to their hosts.[9]

Much of the writing about immigration therefore fell within a nationalistic mold. A good many books about specific groups already occupied library shelves in 1950 — some of them useful compilations of information.[10] The Scandinavians, as of that moment, had received clearly the most comprehensive and most judicious treatment.[11] In the years that followed, these studies were joined by works of varying degrees of excellence on the Irish, the Welsh, the Cornish, the Greeks, the Italians, and the Jews, as well as by valuable biographies, family histories, and collections of letters and memoirs.[12] The more recent volumes were temperate in judgment and generally scholarly in approach; but they still emphasized the coherence and distinctiveness of the particular national element described.

The authors of the decades after 1950 certainly avoided the gross apologetic errors of their predecessors but still exaggerated the national cohesiveness of the migrating populations. The consciousness of national identity, powerful as it was among the intellectuals and middle-class elements, had not seized hold of the laboring masses in the period of the great displacements. Only by jumbling together casual travelers, adventurers, priests, and merchants, with hardly a reference to peasants, could a writer discern a characteristic Italian group in the American West of the nineteenth century.[13]

Now, of course, there were ways in which the Irish differed from the English and the Germans from the Poles, just as there were differences between the natives of Cork and Galway, or Yorkshire and Cornwall, or Pomerania and Posen. In the last analysis, the passengers, in whatever ships they came, were individuals not abstractions, no two precisely alike. And just as it was possible to write appropriately of the Irish, the Italians, the Jews in some respects, so it was possible, in others, to write of the peasants, the immigrants.

This was common to all — Norwegians in Brooklyn, Italians in Louisiana, Finns in Maynard, and Greeks in Omaha; the maintenance-of-way laborer and factory hand, the prairie farmer, the peddler, the shopkeeper and contractor; the successful and the failures — that torn away from whole communities, they were thrust into an unstable new environment which compelled them to make unexpected adjustments. The process all shared was the subject of *The Uprooted.*

To what extent other peoples passed through the same experience remains speculative, because few have been studied from this point of view. It is tempting to seek points of similarity and difference among those who entered the United States from parts of the world other than Europe, with the black minority of the United States for instance. But practically nothing is known of the great transfer of Africans in the century after 1660.[14] And there are only suggestive indications of analogy in the handful of books on the French-Canadians, Orientals, Puerto Ricans, and Mexicans.[15] Yet migration and the subsequent juxtaposition of diverse cultures was an aspect of their personal and social development, as it may still have been of the Appalachian mountaineers who moved to Chicago or Cincinnati after 1950.[16] All modern human migrations display some of the same features because all involve the stress of adjusting to one culture the traits developed in another. And the universality of the migration experience was certainly characteristic of people who shared a European heritage.

Perhaps a reconstruction of the intellectual path actually followed will strengthen the case for describing an ideal type.

About the peasants, I was totally unknowing when I began the research for *Boston's Immigrants.* I learned something about the Irish in doing that book, then extended the inquiry to the natives of other countries.

From earlier reading in medieval history, I recalled vague figures in a faded economic panorama; and I had picked up something about agriculture from Marc Bloch, something about rural Russia from G. T. Robinson, and something about the concept of self-sufficiency from Sombart.[17] But of the situation of these people in modern times I had read little, and indeed I discovered there was little to read on the subject except for Arensberg's rather formal anthropological studies. Nor has much of interest been written since.[18]

Still the notes piled up as I read through newspapers, pamphlets and letters; and the little piles demanded understanding which I sought as best I could in the surviving evidence of peasant culture. The nineteenth and early twentieth centuries had produced batches of books on the folklore of many parts of Europe.[19] These I devoured, partly because to thumb their pages was less demanding than to take notes on old newspapers; partly because they left me a residue of impressions, not readily documented, but important nonetheless. Valuable as the compilations and studies were, they and their counterparts published since 1950 had a defect frustrating to a historian — the absence of a time sense. Whether they focused on regional and local variations or stressed universal themes, they disregarded chronology and created a sense of the changelessness of peasant culture that perhaps was not entirely valid. Nor did they draw class lines with precision or adequately set off specific incident from broad theme.[20]

In ways that are, again, difficult to document, I gained also from the most perceptive, although far from dispassionate, observers of the modern peasantry — the novelists, drawn by a variety of literary needs to examine the populace about them. Unfortunately, there was no pattern to my browsing among these books so that while I read George Moore on the Irish and Ladislas Reymont on the Poles, I devoted more time to Maupassant, to Zola's La Terre and to Jean Giono than the number of French immigrants would have justified.[21] Fiction, unsystematically absorbed, somehow expanded my understanding of the notes I shuffled.

How? The answer is not clear to me. By a process that was not purely intellecutal, through a linkage that was personal, I learned to feel with . . . enough so that the abstraction, peasant, corresponded to a real being. City bred, having never heard Old World family talk turn in that direction, I made myself physically present in the village and moved among its people.

I must early have sensed the importance of personal exposure to the setting. Why else did I choose to investigate Boston in Europe? Yet I had no precise research design as I discovered from R. H. Tawney's amiable bewilderment when I tried to explain what I was up to. Only in Dublin did I discover something and that not what I expected — not the documents in the libraries, not the sight of Bloom's city, but the lilt of Irish language everywhere adding a magical intonation to the words, so that never again could I read a line of the writing without hearing the resonance of actual speakers' voices, without knowing the presence of persons long gone-by but real.

It must have been accident, however, that exposed a glimpse of the peasant village in its isolation. Missed trains, fascist visa requirements, impasse at the border, and a chance encounter left us in dead midwinter in *Haute Savoie,* alone in the inn. Walking nowhere, the roads deep in snow, we entered communities not changed since the nineteenth century or earlier. That white Alpine world suddenly conveyed a visual impression that brought fragments of possessed information into focus.

The picture of peasant society here presented may be askew since it passed not through a scientifically precise lens but through an eye with a range of perceptions defined by limited personal experience. Max Beloff, for instance, noted critically the tendency to exaggerate "the stability and continuity" of that society.[22] He was correct, how correct I discovered some years later during an extended stay in another Alpine village. By then I had read the neglected novels of Charles F. Ramuz and thought I knew what to expect.[23] Perched high on the slopes of a steep gorge, linked to the valley below by a perilous road which twisted down through fifty-six hairpin curves in seven kilometers, the place possessed not a beast of burden — everything was carried, pushed or pulled. A dense local patois, as well as the monotonous repetition from family to family of a common surname, left an impression of resistance to time and of a life ingrown and isolated. The quiet stranger, tolerated because to all intents and purposes non-existent, after months was acknowledged by the police, the *poste,* the children, and the peasants (in that order) so that at some point the expression of an interest in the past produced a book. Here were the records and it turned out that no family had been there from time immemorial. The Coquoz had drifted up from the Val d'Aosta, probably in the sixteenth century, and the Fleutry, from Bern; and Fournier the butcher sprang from an outlander from Lyons.[24] And that evidence conformed to the larger European pattern, which showed frequent thrusts to all the marches and a steady eastward drift of peasant population through the centuries.[25]

Yet the impression of sameness was not merely the product of distortion through the observer's eye. Nor did it spring simply from the romantic fancies of folklorists. The villagers themselves believed that they had always been there, always worn the same costumes, made the same lace, sung the same music and danced the same figures. That belief was not evidence that they and their ancestors had actually done so, but it was evidence that the community possessed institutional devices for absorbing the effects of change and preserving stability over very long periods.

Peasant society therefore accommodated numerous variations. The evocation of an ideal type was not intended to deny the existence of variations. Indeed the text (Page 8) made plain the marked difference of Irish and Norwegian from most West European villages. There were other differences as well — between Baltic and Mediterranean communities, or eastern and western, or large or small ones. But the inference did not follow, as an article in a learned journal would have had it, that because the villages differed in some respects they were not similar in others and the same as a type.[26]

I wished when I wrote that more had been written on the history of the modern peasant; I still do. No one doubts the past importance of this social group. But its pattern of daily life in the nineteenth century has escaped the attention of scholars, and curiously those who have turned to the subject have emphasized the moments of crisis — riot, rebellion, or ultimate disappearance rather than the evolution of a distinctive social environment.[27]

To describe the communities which existed in that environment is not to express a preference for them. That comment seemed superfluous twenty years ago; and few readers failed to understand that *The Uprooted* celebrated the departure from the village. At the risk of laboring the obvious, I make the point explicit for the benefit of the handful so habituated to abstraction that the subtleties of actuality escape them.

I rested my discussion of the factors influencing the size of the European population upon the work of demographers of the 1920's and 1930's. More recent valuable studies have significantly increased the range of detailed information and the precision of statistical analysis of the problem. A good deal more is also now known about the nature of the food supply and about the nineteenth-century famines. But the new evidence requires no change in my discussion. Thus the quantitative data on the influence of subsistence crises and on fluctuations in marriage patterns confirms in a more exact fashion what was already known from other sources.[28]

The land and sea crossing to America remains in 1971, as it was in 1950, a promising subject of investigation. The student at the later date would not find much more on the subject than I did at the earlier. Conceivably, a study of mortality statistics would show a record not as grim as that locked into immigrant memories. There may have been more movement by whole communities than I allowed for. Melville's description of Liverpool in *Redburn* recently reminded me how fascinating would be a study of the European exit ports and heightened my regret that the task has not been done. The roster of unwritten books could be lengthened almost indefinitely.[29] As it was, the voyage meant to me what it seemed to mean to the immigrants, a traumatic transition to life under new conditions.

Upon arrival the immediate, critical problem was earning a living. Abundant evidence marked the steps by which the newcomers did so — statistical, literary, governmental and business. Yet it took more effort than I could afford to trace the route.

A misleading theoretical premise at first led me astray. My initial subject was nineteenth-century Boston, hub of New England, seat of the industrial revolution, American model. The men off the boats who took the lowest paid jobs should have been factory workers. They were not. I knew that they were not because I looked for and could not find them. A hot summer in Washington thumbing through the manuscript census schedules among the lady genealogists revealed that where there were factory workers in 1850, they were not usually immigrants and not residents of urban places. The immigrants lived preponderantly in cities like Boston but the most common occupation ascribed to them was laborer.

What was a laborer? Unfortunately there was no account of the structure of the commercial city to which I could turn for an answer, so that it was necessary patiently to piece together the elements that shaped the economic role of the great mass of the urban population. Analysis revealed that industrialization entered the city later than the immigrants, with effects different from those commonly imagined.

The resources for treating these issues have not expanded substantially in the intervening decades, in part at least because economic historians have focused their attention on numbers not people. Whatever the merits of the new quantitative techniques, they have not addressed such subjects as the employment patterns in cities which served primarily administrative and distributing functions; or the development of the building trades; or the operations of the construction industry; or retail entrepreneurship.[30]

More surprising was the survival of the concept of the solidarity and unity of the laboring classes. The idea, exemplified in the nineteenth century by the willingness of the Knights of Labor to open membership to all, became fixed in historical thinking through the influence of John R. Commons and his school. The word laborer in their usage was pliable enough to include the steel worker and the craftsman, the ditchdigger and the locomotive engineer, the printer and the sharecropper.[31] For a considerable period I, too, thought in this way, despite the evidence I was gathering.

Another aspect of the laborer's condition pressed upon my consciousness as I reached for the persons behind the numbers. Accustomed to a way of thinking in economics that identified people by their relation to the productive system — merchants, manufacturers, farmers, artisans — my mind kept turning, in the case of the immigrants, to their role as consumers. At first, I resisted this perversity, which ran counter to what the formal lessons had taught. Then I let the old mind turn where it would. For many of my subjects, the daily bread upon which they utterly depended was a sufficient goal, how they earned it far less important. Any job would do for them.

Their dependence was a shadow of the ever overhanging threat of hunger. Yet it was difficult to make out or understand their plight, for the documents did not bear upon it directly even when it drew the attention of social workers and novelists toward the end of the nineteenth century. Sympathetic observers, often driven by reformist zeal, tended to sentimentalize their descriptions.[32] That there was nothing ennobling about hunger I could remember from a desperate mother's assurance to a crying younger brother that there would be more bread tomorrow when papa came home. And the leaping awareness of how long the absence had been, and what if he did not come, and there was again nothing.

There had to be some way other than the abstract numerical way to describe earning a livelihood in America. I sought that way in the description of the quest for daily bread.

The great issues connected with labor as a nexus of social relations remain unexploited; and the conclusions suggested in *The Uprooted* have therefore scarcely been tested. Among these issues are the effects upon the human personality of involvement in the impersonal factory environment, the relationship to work not attuned to natural rhythms like that on the soil, and the modes of association through trade unions and otherwise. A few recent works have pointed clearly enough in the direction of what could be done, enough to excite but not satisfy the appetite.[33]

More attention has gone to the argument, rather sterile from the point of view of the historian, about whether industrialization produced an over-all decline in the standard of living of large classes of the population. The discussion, pursued mostly in England, had political overtones and, although the participants valiantly mobilized interesting statistical evidence, the outcome largely followed upon the premises given. Comparisons across the centuries did not really measure the difference between the peasant and the factory worker because gains and losses were not simply economic. People left the land for the city because they expected that the increment in benefits would more than balance the losses, though both were real; and the balance between the two can only artificially be reckoned in statistical terms.[34]

Nor am I content with the scholarship of the past two decades on the fascinating analytical questions connected with social mobility in the United States. Was success simply a myth or did it have a relationship to reality? Why could some people become entrepreneurs and not others? Was it easier to get ahead earlier or later? Did some groups move faster than others? Were some environments more congenial than others? My own conclusions emphasized the importance of the cultural variable, of the difference between people reared in a peasant milieu and those, native or immigrant, brought up as dissenters, outsiders, in cities or apart from the land. Only a very few studies have assembled the evidence to bear upon these points.[35] On the other hand, individual works of value treat various isolated aspects of the immigrants' place in the economy.[36]

New Worlds, New Visions — title of a book never written, appropriated for another purpose.

Long talks with Hans Rosenberg turned my thoughts to the history of ideas; and I read with absorbing interest the authors of whom he spoke, Meineke, Dilthey, and Cassirer. I projected for some day a work in the grand style on the enlightenment that would treat the new intellectual horizons eighteenth-century man's enlarged perceptions revealed. Meanwhile I turned the dreary newspaper pages, searching for meaning in the stories the immigrants once read. Through the window against which the bound volume rested, I watched the shadows pass across the gray renaissance courtyard of the Boston Public Library and copied ineffectual passages for later decipherment. Often then I yearned for a different subject that would sparkle with the great thoughts of great men. Instead I grappled with the ideas of the inarticulate.

It was one thing to deal with the minds of those who wrote, another to probe the minds of the silent who read or listened.

The evidence fortunately was more abundant than I originally believed it would be, embedded in a great fund of literature by, for, and about the immigrants.[37] It presented considerable problems of judgment and interpretation and it called for a dangerous stretching of the imagination.

How could I know what happened in the long dead night of the peasant winter who had never laid eyes upon the drooping trees and looming crosses of the churchyard? The clusters of words drawn from the printed or written pages remained inert; until once, the effort to imagine what it was like shut in with the beasts against the cold night evoked the memory of a shivering boy hastening up the pitch-dark stairwell of the tenement on Columbia Street under the bridge. At each landing, the grip of fear; then the burst of light at the kitchen door and the relief, having once again come past the dread mystery for which the name was death and the certainty suppressed that he was destined again and again to make the passage until that future day when the sun's rays on the high skylight above would dissolve the dark. Some gift of feeling then linked memory to words.

It was not so remote from experience, after all, to conceive of being alone, to find equivalents of the chance occurrence that altered the direction of a life's journey, to discern the conservatism that hardened around people who appraised the limits of their power realistically.[38]

The relationship of migration to American religious life presented fewer problems of interpretation. The distinction here drawn between peasants and dissenters was not out of accord with the differentiations established by other scholars. After 1950, an impressive array of talent focused on the history of the churches in the United States, stimulated no doubt by the current concern with faith. For the most part, the works produced in those years were congruent with the conclusions of *The Uprooted*.[39]

Again the issue of uniqueness was troubling. Students who probed the history of one denomination or another tended to stress its distinctive attributes above those it shared with other groups. Again, the response is that while each was different — and not only Catholics from Jews, but also Irish Catholics from Italian, and Galician Jews from Lithuanian —

it remains possible to discern meaningful common features among them and above all in the impact upòn them of migration and of the New World environment. From that point of view, the analyses of republican religion with which the traditions of the newcomers clashed are particularly helpful. The accounts of American beliefs at the opening of the nineteenth century offset the inclination of some writers to overemphasize the closeness of traditional immigrant faith to that of natives and to minimize the importance of internal conflicts within each group.[40]

The burst of interest in urban history produced some helpful monographs after 1960 which assembled a good deal of useful information and threw light on developments scarcely understood a quarter century before. The preference of scholars continued to rest on the smaller, more manageable communities. New York, Los Angeles, and Chicago received little attention; Baltimore, Detroit, and San Francisco practically none at all.[41]

Furthermore, the eagerness to transpose to materials from the past techniques developed in modern economic analysis or survey research caused serious problems, especially in discussion of the question of whether the immigrants lived in ghettos. The early studies of residential distribution, like my own, were primitive in method; they simply traced and plotted on a map the addresses of individuals of foreign birth. Social scientists who had to treat the much larger numbers of the twentieth century developed a useful statistical tool to do so; the index of dissimilarity compared the degree of concentration of various ethnic populations among the census tracts of the city. Historians later applied the same device to eighteenth- and nineteenth-century communities.[42] The more sophisticated procedures were not, however, fully the equivalent of the laborious process of counting, house by house, for the boundaries of the ward or district usually concealed its local character and, in any case, the unit often was small — a single block could form a ghetto without ever showing up in the measurement of dissimilarity.

Many important problems remain unexplored. We know little about movement into, out of, and within the city. We do scarcely more than guess whether some groups shifted about more swiftly than others. We only speculate about the forces that made some enclaves resist change, held their residents against the temptation of the suburbs, and fended off intrusions by outsiders. We are equally in the dark about the substantial numbers in the nineteenth century who drifted from place to place without ever settling down.

Occasional accounts of immigrant life and institutions demonstrate what can be done and also how much yet remains to be done. There have been some efforts to examine political leadership; but it is by no means certain that the relationship of the mayors and congressmen to the voters was the same as that between the spokesmen and members of social, religious, cultural, and economic organizations. Very few individuals whose prominence was a product of position in such associations have been the subject of study, a circumstance which increases the difficulty of making meaningful comparisons with black or native-white migrants.[43]

The explosion of interest in popular culture during the 1960's produced numerous books on American music, movies, and theater, in addition to some serious treatments of games and athletics. The materials thus assembled could certainly amplify the interpretation of the adjustment of immigrant culture advanced in *The Uprooted*. Regrettably few of the recent works have been sufficiently analytical to have traced the distinctions among folk, popular, and mass forms of expression. The emphasis on anecdote and appreciation has generally focused attention on the artistic intentions of the performer or creator rather than upon the audience and its needs.[44]

An analogous bias warped the study of the social disorders

into which many immigrants fell. Poverty, criminality, and intemperance were subject to well-developed communal controls in the peasant villages of the Old World and were less visible to outsiders than they would be in American cities. Migration probably increased the range of deviant behavior and certainly magnified the consequences. Yet recent studies have concentrated on the reform response, on methods of treatment and cure, rather than on the meaning of the condition examined in the lives of its victims. The books, that is, have dealt with the temperance movement rather than with the causes that drove men to drink, with penology rather than the impulse to theft or violence.[45]

The most fruitful research of the decades after 1950 examined the immigrant involvement in American politics. The consolidation of the minority alliance during the postwar period sensitized scholars to its antecedents as did the tendency to look for the influence of ethnic and other blocs in shaping the use of power. Furthermore, the application to these problems of statistical tools of analysis was particularly rewarding. State and local studies, biographies, and formal party histories threw light upon the election process, officeholding, patronage, and the formulation of legislation.[46] There were also some useful examinations of ethnic involvements in foreign policy.[47] The drastic shift in emphasis from the 1930's, when class and section were the only terms of reference, deepened the understanding of American politics.

The scholars of the 1960's made a promising start in the study of a theme of central importance to *The Uprooted*, the history of the family in the United States and in Europe. Numerous pitfalls still surround this difficult subject, but at least some basic data offer guidance to its comprehension.

A good deal of thought went into defining the types of family structure — stem, nuclear, or extended. The discussion seemed to shake down to the rather sensible conclusion that much depended upon time, place, and circumstance.[48] The strains of migration therefore were not the product of a shift from one type to another, from extended to nuclear, for instance. The family structure and habits were adaptable to either variant. Tensions emanated rather from the altered relationship to the community, from the removal out of the village context to the environment of the isolated farm or the city.

Much about the transition remains still unclear, as does much about the experience of the American family in general. We know nothing, for instance, about the life of the individuals who lived alone in nineteenth-century cities, massive numbers of lodgers and boarders without connections. The immense outpouring of publications on twentieth-century education has included few histories, and those mostly studies of the policies of schoolmen rather than of the experience of children. We have such information about wives, mothers, and children as efforts to improve their lot generated in the women's rights or child labor movements. We know less about husbands and fathers, since they were not the beneficiaries of any liberation effort. And what we know is by way of views from the outside, perceiving the family more as an institutional structure, less as a human group.[49]

A critical, but fair, review of *Boston's Immigrants* commented on the absence of any systematic discussion of the family in that book.[50]

Later, I puzzled over the omission. There was material. Reviewing the boxes of unused notes, some of which would serve me later, I found all sorts of interesting information that I had not been able to fit together in any meaningful way. Often and again, I wondered why.

Another failure of omission came to mind, also puzzling. The boy who had been a voracious reader and had prided himself on his swift progress among the library shelves had been no better able than anyone else to speak up when the class turned at last to the subject of books. This was not a matter usually discussed in a school, the main business of which was drill. But the substitute — a man there for one day only and perhaps bored or unknowing — wandered into a discussion of what I would later recognize as literature.

What were most books about?

Our fumbling efforts at response he fended off with negative smirks until, having had enough, he gave us the answer. *Love,* he said, *ahava, amor.*

The dismay at having been trapped in period-long talk about THAT mingled with perplexity at the inability to produce the simple word. Love was after all busting out all over in the 1920's. It was not only that the books were full of it, but also the movies, the magazines, and the *American, News,* and *Mirror.* Love as a literary stock-in-trade I knew well enough. Why had I not produced the word?

Partly the reticence reflected a running uncertainty about what was and was not proper as a subject of discourse in school. The language used and the range of concerns expressed in the classroom were entirely different from those of the playground or the street or home. The demand that we draw upon language not in the lesson was unexpected and disconcerting.

But the inability to speak had more complex sources also. Or so it later seemed to me. Love was the familiar idiom of movies and novels. But I could not translate it into the terms of the life I knew. Fairbanks, D'Artagnan, Gilbert, Ivanhoe blurred in an image that after all had nothing to do with me. Nor did it have anything to do with the starched older cousins of the weddings at Willoughby Manor. Nor with the family.

On great occasions, the aunts and uncles assembled all in their pairs, each with its reputation, each respected, pitied, or envied. "Oh, that one"; and "remember when"; and "who would think." The talk swirled, evoking a distant landscape against which the familiar figures of the old people incongruously moved. They?

The couple, for instance, notorious for incessant bickering, ever dragging quarrels into the open in eternal worrying over wrong decisions, children, money, spending, saving. Now he spoke over the steaming glass of tea. Was it memory's trick or in the white wisps slipping from her bun did some enduring perception preserve the sight of dark hair streaming through the meadow's breeze? As when in winter, the wisps of snow along the lilac's brittle twigs will not efface the fragrance cast forever in the air?

And she, hustled into betrothal at the age of sixteen by an impatient father of too many younger ones, she had acquiesced out of faintness, not daring to depart the home as her older sister had at the same age. Some errant image at that moment softened the usual hard thin line of her lips.

When I reflected upon the relationships within the family, which gave each member a knowledge of the others, and therefore of the self, I understood why so many notes for *Boston's Immigrants* went unused. Riffling through the cards, as I put together "Generations," I sought the connections between remote numerical abstractions and historical reality.

The concept of alienation was already in the air of 1950, put there by the rediscovery of the early Marx, by existential philosophy, and by widely read novels. While aware of these intellectual influences, I made every effort to ground my own discussion in the evidence.[51]

The concern in the years after 1950 with problems of group prejudice and discrimination produced some significant studies of the immigration restriction movement, of its sources in American nativism, and of the social, economic, and cultural forces which shaped governmental policy. The most useful works were monographic and dealt in depth with the context of changing attitudes. The least useful were those which took for granted an easy schematic link between the views of people and their interests or else simply regarded prejudice as a constant in the national experience.⁵²

No doubt, into the summation I brought a need to say something to an audience of one.

His life's adventure might have run its course near Mukden when the sniper paused one second more to shift the sight, then released the stock as startling steel ripped forth and spurts of blood. He never learned whose lunge then drove a friendly bayonet through the limp assassin's body so that he did not die there, wearing the Czar's coat, but returned to the gray Ukrainian town which was not of his birth and would not be of his death.

Drops of dextrose now sustained his life, and draining tubes. In weekly drives of futile piety, we crossed to Whitestone, hit the parkway and approached, knowing again there would be nothing to say, knowing too the demand for meaning in that wasting frame.

No doubt, too, my own commitment to the meaning I then discerned influenced the reactions in the aftermath to the developments of the decades after 1951. The revived interest in ethnicity, the pride and petulance that seeped into group life, the fears of the future, the aversion to risk, and even the rejection of the New World heritage were predictable.⁵³

I will nonetheless not turn away from the hope that there will be no forgetting the meaning of the America he and the millions more expended their lives in making.

NOTES TO CHAPTER FOURTEEN

1. Robert Ernst, *Immigrant Life in New York City, 1825–1863* (New York, 1949) ; Moses Rischin, *The Promised City. New York's Jews 1870–1914* (Cambridge, Mass., 1962) . See also note 41.

2. George M. Stephenson, *A History of American Immigration, 1820–1924* (Boston, 1926) ; Carl Wittke, *We Who Built America: The Saga of the Immigrant* (New York, 1939). I leave altogether apart earlier works of less value, written in the heat of controversy over immigration policy.

3. Marcus Lee Hansen, *The Atlantic Migration, 1607–1860* (Cambridge, Mass., 1940) ; Marcus Lee Hansen, *The Immigrant in American History* (Cambridge, Mass., 1940).

4. Maldwyn A. Jones, *American Immigration* (Chicago, 1960) ; Philip Taylor, *The Distant Magnet* (London, 1971) ; Oscar Handlin, *Race and Nationality in American Life* (Boston, 1957) ; Oscar Handlin, ed., *Immigration as a Factor in American History* (Englewood Cliffs, N.J., 1959) ; Oscar Handlin, *Pictorial History of Immigration* (New York, 1972) ; Oscar Handlin, *American People in the Twentieth Century* (Cambridge, Mass., 1954).

5. M. A. Jones, "Oscar Handlin," Marcus Cunliffe and Robin W. Winks, eds., *Pastmasters* (New York, 1969), 240, 245.

6. Oscar Handlin, *Boston's Immigrants: A Study in Acculturation* (Cambridge, Mass., 1941), vii.

7. Richard Hofstadter, "West of Ellis Island," *Partisan Review*, XIX (1952), 252.

8. Karen Larsen in *American Historical Review*, LVII (1952), 703.

9. Edward N. Saveth, *American Historians and European Immigrants* (New York, 1948) ; Oscar and Mary F. Handlin, "The New History and the Ethnic Factor in American Life," *Perspectives in American History*, IV (1970), 9ff.

10. Examples include: Albert B. Faust, *The German Element in the United States* (2 vols., New York, 1927) ; Henry J. Ford, *The Scotch-Irish in America* (Princeton, 1915) ; William I. Thomas and Florian Znaniecki, *The Polish Peasant in Europe and America* (2 vols., Chicago, 1918–1920).

11. Theodore C. Blegen, *Norwegian Migration to America* (2 vols., Northfield, Minn., 1931, 1940) ; Florence E. Janson, *The Background of Swedish Immigration, 1840–1930* (Philadelphia, 1931) ; Carlton C. Qualey, *Norwegian Settlement in the United States* (Northfield, Minn., 1938). For other groups, the best works were by economists or sociologists, among them Robert F. Foerster, *The Italian Emigration of Our Times* (Cambridge, Mass., 1919) ; Emily G. Balch, *Our Slavic Fellow Citizens* (New York, 1910) ; and Phyllis H. Williams, *South Italian Folkways in Europe and America* (New Haven, 1938).

12. Arnold Schrier, *Ireland and the American Emigration 1850–1900* (Minneapolis, 1958) ; William V. Shannon, *The American Irish* (New York, 1963) ; Carl Wittke, *The Irish in America* (New York, 1970) ; Edward G. Hartmann, *Americans from Wales* (Boston, 1967) ; A. L. Rowse, *The Cornish in America* (New York, 1969) ; A. William Hoglund, *Finnish Immigrants in America, 1880–1920* (Madison, Wisc., 1960). Grazia Dore, *La Democrazia italiana e l'emigrazione* (Brescia, 1964); and her "Some Social and Historical Aspects of Italian Emigration to America," *Journal of Social History*, II (1968), 95ff. make interesting comparisons with other parts of

the world. *See also* Silvano M. Tomasi and Madeline H. Engel, eds., *The Italian Experience in the United States* (Staten Island, New York, 1970). The detailed research of Charlotte Erikson, *American Industry and the European Immigrant 1860–1885* (Cambridge, Mass., 1957) disposes of the old belief that manufacturers recruited labor in Europe; and the quantitative analysis in Lowell E. Gallaway and Richard K. Vedder, "Emigration from the United Kingdom to the United States: 1860–1913," *Journal of Economic History*, XXXI (1971), 885ff. confirms earlier conclusions about motivation. Among the interesting collections of source materials are: Alan Conway, ed., *The Welsh in America: Letters from Immigrants* (Minneapolis, 1961); Theodore C. Blegen, ed., *Land of Their Choice: The Immigrants Write Home* (Minneapolis, 1955); Stepas Zobarskas, *Lithuanian Folk Tales* (Brooklyn, 1958); and Harriet M. Pawlowska and Grace L. Engel, *Merrily We Sing* (Detroit, 1961), a collection of Polish immigrant folk songs. Richard D. Brown, "Two Baltic Families Who Came to America," *American Jewish Archives*, XXIV (1972), 39ff. is a good example of family history.

Information by way of "oral tradition" I found of little value, however. I recall talks with the seminarians at St. John's while doing the research for *Boston's Immigrants* and, after the appearance of that book, hour-long conversations with the descendants of its subjects, among them notably John F. (Honey) Fitzgerald. Later, too, I was the recipient of confidences from other immigrants and their children. Apart from the distortions caused by the lapse of time and by the passage through the prisms of several memories, I was discomfited by the eagerness of the narrators to make their stories relevant, that is, to tell me what I wished to know.

13. Andrew Rolle, *The Immigrant Upraised: Italian Adventurers and Colonists in an Expanding America* (Norman, Okla., 1968). Regrettably most accounts of nationalism simply take the phenomenon for granted: those which treat Europe rarely touch on peasant attitudes; and those dealing with the United States fail to examine the forces which shape group loyalty.

14. There is a useful summary of available information in chapters 4–10 of John Hope Franklin, *From Slavery to Freedom* (New York, 1967). But the great African forced migration to America in the century after 1660 has not as yet been adequately treated; and less has been written on the mainland, than on the island, colonies, there being no equivalent for the former of Elsa V. Goveia, *Slave Society in the British Leeward Islands at the End of the Eighteenth Century* (New Haven, 1965); or Horace Orlando Patterson, *The Sociology of Slavery: An Analysis of the Origins, Development and Structure of Negro Slave Society in Jamaica* (London, 1967). There are interesting comparisons with the twentieth-century black migration to northern cities in Orlando Patterson, "On the Fate of Blacks in America," *The Public Interest*, No. 27 (1972), 51ff.

15. Jacques Ducharme, *The Shadows of the Trees; the Story of French Canadians in New England* (New York, 1943); Gunther P. Barth, *Bitter Strength* (Cambridge, Mass., 1964); Oscar Handlin, *The Newcomers* (Cambridge, Mass., 1969); Manuel Gamio, *Mexican Immigration to the United States* (Chicago, 1930); Pauline S. Kibbe, *Latin Americans in Texas*

(Albuquerque, 1946) ; Carey McWilliams, *North from Mexico* (New York, 1961) ; Paul S. Taylor, *Mexican Labor in the United States* (3 vols., Berkeley, 1928–1934).

16. Robert Coles, *Migrants, Sharecroppers, Mountaineers* (Boston, 1972) ; Robert Coles, *The South Goes North* (Boston, 1972) ; Todd Gitlin and Nancy Hollander, *Uptown: Poor Whites in Chicago* (New York, 1970).

17. I was fortunate in that A. P. Usher, with whom I studied economic history, expected his students to read French and German.

18. Conrad M. Arensberg, *The Irish Countryman* (New York, 1937). Hans Günther's sociological study, *Das Bauerntum* (Leipzig, 1939) was far too idyllic. Most of the old historical accounts emphasized legal and administrative issues, for example, Alfred Babeau, *Le Village sous l'ancien régime* (Paris, 1879). Even Emile G. Léonard, *Mon Village sous Louis XV d'après les mémoires d'un paysan* (Paris, 1941), based on eighteenth-century notes by Pierre Prion, dealt largely with such matters. There is material for interesting comparisons with later Polish village life in the memoirs of Jan Slomka, *From Serfdom to Self-Government: Memoirs of a Polish Village Mayor 1824–1927* (W. J. Rose, transl., London, 1941). For more recent works, see note 27.

19. For example, Christina Hole, *English Folklore* (London, 1940) ; G. Pitre, *La Famiglia, la casa, la vita del popolo siciliano* (Palermo, 1913) ; Joseph Schopp, *Das Deutsche Arbeitslied* (Heidelberg, 1935) ; Eduard Hoffmann-Krayer, *Feste und Brauche des Schweizervolkes* (Zürich, 1940).

20. Among the more recent and more interesting studies are: Hermann Strobach, *Bauernklagen: Untersuchungen zum sozialkritischen deutschen Volkslied* (Berlin, 1964) ; Richard M. Dorson, *The British Folklorists* (Chicago, 1968) ; Richard M. Dorson, *Peasant Customs and Savage Myths* (2 vols., Chicago, 1968) ; Arnold van Gennep, *Le Folklore des Hautes-Alpes* (2 vols., Paris, 1946–1948) ; Giuseppe Bonomo, *Scongiuri del popolo siciliano* (Palermo, 1953) ; *La Religiosità popolare nella valle padana* (Firenze, 1966) ; Maria Brandon-Albini, *Midi vivant, peuple et culture de l'Italie du Sud* (Paris, 1963).

21. George Moore, *The Untilled Field* (London, 1903) ; Wladyslaw S. Reymont, *The Peasants* (4 vols., New York, 1925) ; Émile Zola, *La Terre* (Paris, 1887) ; Jean Giono, *The Harvest* (New York, 1939).

22. Max Beloff, "The Uprooted," *Encounter*, I (December, 1953), 78ff. On the issue of peasant stability, see also Laslett, *World We Have Lost* (note 48), xi, 148.

23. Available in English are: Charles F. Ramuz, *When the Mountain Fell* (New York, 1946) ; *The End of All Men* (New York, 1944) ; and *Terror on the Mountain* (New York, 1967).

24. Louis Coquoz, *Histoire et description de Salvan—Fins-Hauts* (Lausanne, 1899).

25. For example, Karl Stumpp, *Ostwanderung* (Leipzig, 1941).

26. Rudolph J. Vecoli, "Contadini in Chicago," *Journal of American History*, LI (1964), 404ff. The assertion that the Italian peasant of the nineteenth century lived in a "rural city" is misleading. On the size of the villages

and the pattern of life, see Giovanni B. Bronzini, *Vita tradizionale in Basilicata* (Matera, 1964) ; Brandon-Albini (note 20) .

27. Eric J. Hobsbawm, *Bandits* (London, 1969) ; Eric J. Hobsbawm, *Primitive Rebels: Studies in Archaic Forms of Social Movement in the 19th and 20th Centuries* (Manchester, England, 1959) ; and Eric J. Hobsbawm and George Rudé, *Captain Swing* (New York, 1968) treat violence. John G. Gagliardo, *From Pariah to Patriot: The Changing Image of the German Peasant 1770–1840* (Lexington, 1969) deals with aspects of the agrarian problem; and W. M. Williams, *Gosforth: The Sociology of an English Village* (Glencoe, Ill., 1956) and Henri Mendras, *The Vanishing Peasant* (Cambridge, Mass., 1970) are the analyses of contemporary sociologists, while S. H. Franklin, *The European Peasantry: The Final Phase* (London, 1969) is the work of a geographer. Even some of the excellent studies of popular associations and of rural life in France pay little attention to the *gens de la terre* — e.g., Maurice Agulhon, *Pénitents et Francs-Maçons de l'ancienne Provence* (Paris, 1968) , 81ff.; Anne Zink, *Azereix* (Paris, 1969) .

28. Edward A. Wrigley, *Population and History* (New York, 1969) ; David V. Glass and David E. C. Eversley, eds., *Population in History; Essays in Historical Demography* (London, 1965) ; Michael Drake, *Population and Society in Norway 1735–1865* (Cambridge, England, 1969) ; William L. Langer, "Europe's Initial Population Explosion," *American Historical Review*, LXIX (October, 1963) , 1ff. There is a helpful review of recent literature in Franklin F. Mendels, "Recent Research in European Historical Demography," *American Historical Review*, LXXV (1970) , 1065ff. *See also* Cecil Woodham-Smith, *The Great Hunger: Ireland, 1845–1849* (New York, 1962) ; Robert D. Edwards and Thomas D. Williams, eds., *The Great Famine: Studies in Irish History, 1845–1852* (New York, 1957) .

29. Vilhelm Moberg, *The Emigrants* (New York, 1951) contains a graphic fictional description of the crossing. The eighteenth-century account in Gottlieb Mittelberger, *Journey to Pennsylvania* (Cambridge, Mass., 1960) remained valid well into the nineteenth century.

30. The view of industrialization then conventional was ably expressed in Edward C. Kirkland, "Economic Ferment," Caroline F. Ware, ed., *The Cultural Approach to History* (New York, 1940) , 252ff. On cities, see Ralph E. Turner, "The Industrial City," *ibid.*, 228ff.; Robert G. Albion, *The Rise of the New York Port, 1815–1860* (New York, 1939) .

31. Henry Pelling, *American Labor* (Chicago, 1960) ; J. R. Commons, et al., *History of Labour in the United States* (4 vols., New York, 1918–1935) . The loose usage was far from Marxist although it crept into the writings of the 1930's oriented in that direction.

32. Leo Fishman, *Poverty Amid Affluence* (New Haven, 1966) ; Robert Hunter, *Poverty* (New York, 1904) ; Upton Sinclair, *The Jungle* (New York, 1906) ; Walter B. Rideout, *The Radical Novel in the United States 1900–1954* (Cambridge, Mass., 1956) .

33. Oscar Handlin, "Man and Magic: Encounters with the Machine," *American Scholar*, XXX (Summer, 1964) , 408ff.; Victor R. Greene, *The Slavic Community on Strike: Immigrant Labor in Pennsylvania Anthracite* (Notre Dame, Ind., 1968) ; David Brody, *Steelworkers in America: the*

Nonunion Era (Cambridge, Mass., 1960) ; Gerd Korman, *Industrialization, Immigrants, and Americanizers: the View from Milwaukee, 1866–1921* (Madison, 1967) ; Edwin Fenton, "Immigrants and Unions, A Case Study: Italians and American Labor, 1870–1920," Ph.D. thesis, Harvard University Archives, 1958.

34. There is a useful general summary of the conflict of views on the whole subject in Brian Inglis, "The Poor Who Were With Us; Old Myths & New Views," *Encounter*, (1971) , 44ff., which, however, accepts the conventional formulation of the issue.

35. Stephan Thernstrom, *Poverty and Progress: Social Mobility in a Nineteenth-Century City* (Cambridge, Mass., 1965) ; Oscar and Mary F. Handlin, "Ethnic Factors in Social Mobility," *Explorations in Entrepreneurial History*, IX (October, 1965) , 1ff. Stephan Thernstrom's forthcoming study of the process of mobility in Boston, 1880–1970, which I was able to read in manuscript, breaks totally new ground in showing the persistence of mobility in the nineteenth and twentieth centuries.

36. For example, Rowland T. Berthoff, *British Immigrants in Industrial America, 1789–1950* (Cambridge, Mass., 1953) on immigrants from other than peasant backgrounds; and Joseph Brandes, *Immigrants to Freedom: Jewish Communities in Rural New Jersey* (Philadelphia, 1971) on agricultural settlements.

37. I am far from certain that I solved the problems connected with the use of this literature. Two, in particular, are important. It is difficult to tell how representative the exceptional work of genius is: for example, Ole E. Rølvaag's *Giants in the Earth* (New York, 1927) . To pass judgment on that point calls first for comparison with a large number of fictional accounts of the same genre, such as Dorothy Burton Skørdal's *The Divided Heart* (in press) will soon provide. It calls also for examination of such related folk materials as are assembled in Robert L. Wright, *Swedish Emigrant Ballads* (Lincoln, Nebraska, 1965) . The same difficulty arises with the exceptional writers of other immigrant groups.

The other problem is more complex still. It arises out of the fact that immigrants read and found their ideas reflected in the writings of authors who were not members of their own group. The link between the author and his audience can neither be neglected nor taken for granted but must be assessed in each particular case.

38. The conservatism referred to in *The Uprooted* involved habits of thought and social attitudes and was not always expressed in political or economic terms. It did not, for instance, restrain immigrants from joining labor unions which served their interests or from voting for liberal candidates who promised to do so, although radical social experiments and efforts to tamper with family life remained suspect. See, Greene (note 33) ; Handlin (note 46) ; Huthmacher (note 46) .

39. Notice, for instance, the congruence with the categories of Jensen (note 46) . There is a useful guide to the material on the history of the churches of the United States in the essays and bibliographies in James Ward Smith and A. Leland Jamison, eds., *Religion in American Life* (4 vols., Princeton, N.J., 1961) .

40. Sidney E. Mead, *The Lively Experiment: The Shaping of Christianity in America* (New York, 1963); Martin E. Marty, *Righteous Empire: The Protestant Experience in America* (New York, 1970) ; Robert D. Cross, *The Emergence of Liberal Catholicism in America* (Cambridge, Mass., 1958) ; Thomas T. McAvoy, *The Americanist Heresy in Roman Catholicism, 1895–1900* (Notre Dame, Ind., 1963) ; Thomas T. McAvoy, *The Great Crisis in American Catholic History, 1895–1900* (Chicago, 1957) ; Thomas T. McAvoy, ed., *Roman Catholicism and the American Way of Life* (Notre Dame, Ind., 1960) ; Colman J. Barry, O.S.B., *The Catholic Church and German Americans* (Milwaukee, 1953) . On the period since 1950, *see* Jeffrey Hadden, *The Gathering Storm in the Churches* (New York, 1969) .

41. Robert M. Fogelson, *The Fragmented Metropolis: Los Angeles, 1850–1930* (Cambridge, Mass., 1967) ; Humbert S. Nelli, *The Italians in Chicago 1880–1930* (New York, 1970) ; Sam B. Warner, Jr., *Streetcar Suburbs: The Process of Growth in Boston, 1870–1900* (Cambridge, Mass., 1962) ; Herbert J. Gans, *The Urban Villagers: Group and Class in the Life of Italian-Americans* (New York, 1962) ; Roger Lane, *Policing the City: Boston 1822–1885* (Cambridge, Mass., 1967) ; Peter R. Knights, *The Plain People of Boston, 1830–1860: A Study in City Growth* (New York, 1971) ; James F. Richardson, *The New York Police* (New York, 1970) ; also notes 1, 42, 43, 46.

42. Sam B. Warner, Jr., *The Private City; Philadelphia in Three Periods of Its Growth* (Philadelphia, 1968) ; Stanley Lieberson, *Ethnic Patterns in American Cities* (New York, 1963) , 30ff. See also the discussion reported in *Journal of American History*, LVIII (1971) , 698.

43. Mary Antin, *The Promised Land* (Foreword by Oscar Handlin, Boston, 1969) ; Charles Reznikoff, ed., *Louis Marshall: Champion of Liberty; Selected Papers and Addresses* (Introduction by Oscar Handlin, 2 vols., Philadelphia, 1957) ; Morton Rosenstock, *Louis Marshall, Defender of Jewish Rights* (Detroit, 1965) ; Milton Hindus, ed., *The Old East Side. An Anthology* (Philadelphia, 1969) ; Ronald Sanders, *The Downtown Jews: Portraits of an Immigrant Generation* (New York, 1969) . There are useful insights on the development of ethnic consciousness in the United States in Edward C. Banfield, *The Moral Basis of a Backward Society* (Glencoe, Ill., 1958) . *See also* note 46.

44. For the discussion of gambling and the theater, there are interesting insights in the typology of Roger Caillois, *Man, Play, and Games* (Meyer Barash, translator, New York, 1961) . See also Oscar Handlin, "Notes on Mass and Popular Culture," Norman Jacobs, ed., *Culture for the Millions? Mass Media in Modern Society* (Princeton, N.J., 1961) ; Albert F. McLean, *American Vaudeville as Ritual* (Lexington, Ky., 1965) ; Marvin L. Felheim, *The Theater of Augustin Daly: An Account of the Late Nineteenth-Century American Stage* (Cambridge, Mass., 1956) .

45. Andrew Sinclair, *Prohibition. The Era of Excess* (Boston, 1962) ; James H. Timberlake, *Prohibition and the Progressive Movement, 1900–1920* (Cambridge, Mass., 1963) ; Robert Bremner, *From the Depths: The Discovery of Poverty in the United States* (New York, 1956) ; David J. Rothman, *The Discovery of the Asylum: Social Order and Disorder in the New Republic* (Boston, 1971) .

[328]

46. Oscar Handlin, "The Immigrant in American Politics," David F. Bowers, ed., *Foreign Influences in American Life* (Princeton, 1944) ; J. Joseph Huthmacher, *Massachusetts People and Politics, 1919–1933* (Cambridge, Mass., 1959) ; J. Joseph Huthmacher, "Urban Liberalism and the Age of Reform," *Mississippi Valley Historical Review*, XLIX (1962), 231ff.; J. Joseph Huthmacher, *Senator Robert F. Wagner and the Rise of Urban Liberalism* (New York, 1968) ; Lee Benson, *The Concept of Jacksonian Democracy: New York as a Test Case* (Princeton, 1961) ; John M. Blum, *Joe Tumulty and the Wilson Era* (Boston, 1951) ; Seymour J. Mandelbaum, *Boss Tweed's New York* (New York, 1965) ; Arthur Mann, *LaGuardia* (2 vols., Philadelphia, 1959–1965) ; Oscar Handlin, *Al Smith and His America* (Boston, 1959) ; Paul Kleppner, *The Cross of Culture: A Social Analysis of Midwestern Politics, 1850–1900* (New York, 1970) ; Walter D. Burnham, *Critical Elections and the Mainsprings of American Politics* (New York, 1970) ; John M. Allswang, *A House for All Peoples: Ethnic Politics in Chicago 1890–1936* (Lexington, Ky., 1971) ; Richard J. Jensen, *The Winning of the Midwest* (Chicago, 1971) ; Robert L. Buroker, "From Voluntary Association to Welfare State," *Journal of American History*, LVIII (1971), 643ff.; also note 41. On the other hand, Michael P. Rogin, *The Intellectuals and McCarthy: The Radical Specter* (Cambridge, Mass., 1967) makes the dismal mistake of assuming the constancy of election units over a long period.

47. Finis H. Capps, *From Isolationism to Involvement: The Swedish Immigrant Press in America 1914–1945* (Chicago, 1966) ; Thomas N. Brown, *Irish-American Nationalism* (Philadelphia, 1966) ; Louis L. Gerson, *The Hyphenate in Recent American Politics and Diplomacy* (Lawrence, Kansas, 1964) ; Joseph P. O'Grady, ed., *The Immigrants' Influence on Wilson's Peace Policies* (Lexington, Ky., 1967). Brian Jenkins, *Fenians and Anglo-American Relations during Reconstruction* (Ithaca, N.Y., 1969) is written from the point of view of the diplomatic historian.

48. L. K. Berkner, "The Stem Family and the Developmental Cycle of the Peasant Household: An Eighteenth-Century Austrian Example," *American Historical Review*, LXXVII (1972), 398ff.; Philip J. Greven, Jr., *Four Generations: Population, Land, and Family in Colonial Andover, Massachusetts* (Ithaca, 1970) ; John Demos, *A Little Commonwealth: Family Life in Plymouth Colony* (New York, 1970) ; Peter Laslett, *The World We Have Lost* (New York, 1965) ; Peter Laslett, "Size and Structure of the Household in England Over Three Centuries," *Population Studies*, XXIII (1969), 199ff. Ware, *The Cultural Approach* (note 30), 95–139 contained a suggestive section on the history of various types of peasant families; but no one pursued the suggestions.

49. Richard Sennett, *Families against the City: Middle Class Homes of Industrial Chicago, 1872–1890* (Cambridge, Mass., 1970) does not do justice to the subject. Other aspects of the problem receive attention in Marvin Lazerson, *Origins of the Urban School* (Cambridge, Mass., 1971) ; Oscar Handlin, ed., *Children of the Uprooted* (New York, 1966) ; Oscar and Mary Handlin, *Facing Life* (Boston, 1971) ; and William B. Whiteside, *The Boston Y.M.C.A. and Community Need* (New York, 1951).

50. William F. Whyte, *American Journal of Sociology*, VII (January, 1943), 288.

51. The parallels are drawn in Richard E. Ruland, "A View from Back Home: Kafka's *Amerika*," *American Quarterly*, XIII (1961) , 33ff.

52. On restriction, see Barbara M. Solomon, *Ancestors and Immigrants* (Cambridge, Mass., 1956) ; and John Higham, *Strangers in the Land* (New Brunswick, N.J., 1955) ; on socialist attitudes, Ira Kipnis, *The American Socialist Movement 1897–1912* (New York, 1952) ; on eugenics, Mark H. Haller, *Eugenics: Hereditarian Attitudes in American Thought* (New Brunswick, N.J., 1963) ; and on social workers, Roy Lubove, *The Professional Altruist* (Cambridge, Mass., 1965) .

53. Some expressions of ethnic pride follow a quite usual filopietistic form which stresses contributions to America. See, for instance, Ellen Taussig and Paul Price, "The Polish Community," *Buffalo Evening News*, November 13, 1971; Lou Lepis, "Al Smith Was Italian," *The Challenge*, II (October, 1971) , 1. Others are bitter and implicitly hostile to the United States. See, for instance, U.S. Senate Subcommittee on Education of the Committee on Labor and Public Welfare, *Hearings on the Education Amendments of 1971* (Washington, 1971) ; *Washington Post*, November 21, 1971; Michael Novak, *The Rise of the Unmeltable Ethnics* (New York, 1972) . See also Andrew M. Greeley, *Why Can't They Be Like Us? America's White Ethnic Groups* (New York, 1971) ; Ben Halperin, *Jews and Blacks* (New York, 1971) . The most popular of the panic statements was Alvin Toffler, *Future Shock* (New York, 1970) . For anti-Americanism in popular culture, see Lewis H. Lapham, "What Movies Try to Tell Us," *Harper's*, CCXLIII November, 1971) , 106ff.

Acknowledgments

I HAVE NOT FOUND it in the nature of this work to give its pages the usual historical documentation. I do not, however, wish the reader to lay the book aside without some indication of the kind of sources upon which I have drawn.

I found the material for this volume entirely in the writings of the immigrants and of sensitive observers who witnessed their adjustment at first hand. The most valuable repositories of such data throughout the nineteenth and early twentieth centuries were the newspapers published by and for the various groups of newcomers. These journals chronicled the affairs of the immigrants, gave voice to their points of view, and provided media for the record of their thoughts in literature. They are an inexhaustible mine of information that historians would do well to continue to exploit.

To a surprising degree the newcomers themselves set down accounts of their own experiences. In addition, a good fund of immigrant letters has survived. Supplemented by the writings of members of the second generation and of sympathetic Americans who watched the difficulties of acculturation, these are also useful bodies of material. Among the more important published collections are Edith Abbott's *Immigration* (Chicago, University of Chicago Press, 1924) and her *Historical Aspects of the Immigration Problem* (Chicago, University of Chicago Press, 1926), and W. I. Thomas's and Florian Znaniecki's *Polish Peasant in Europe and America* (Boston, Badger, 1918). In the successive volumes put forth by the historical societies that commemorate the part in American history of the various immigrant groups may often be found further records of this sort.

Finally, I found most enlightening the insights of observers who gave their observations fictional expression. I am particularly indebted to Ladislas Reymont's *Peasants* (New York, Knopf, 1924), and Ole E. Rølvaag's *Giants in the Earth* (New York, Harper, 1927), to Helena Frank's collection of *Yiddish Tales* (Philadelphia, Jewish Publication Society, 1912), and to Pietro Di Donato's *Christ in Concrete* (New York, Bobbs-Merrill, 1939). For those who wish to pursue such material further, there are helpful bibliographies in David F. Bowers, *Foreign Influences in American Life* (Princeton, Princeton University Press, 1944), and William C. Smith, *Americans in the Making* (New York, Appleton-Century, 1939).

The italicized passages in the body of the book are taken from direct immigrant accounts or other contemporary sources, but are not quoted verbatim.

I should like at this point to acknowledge the stimulating assistance of the students who worked with me in successive seminars at Harvard University in the history of American immigration, and to express my gratitude to Provost Paul H. Buck and to my colleagues in the Department of History who encouraged me to pursue my investigations in the subject. At a critical point in the preparation of this study I profited greatly from grants in aid from the Social Science Research Council and the Clark-Milton Fund of Harvard

University. For the contents and the form of the volume I am, of course, alone responsible, except in so far as the constant collaborator to whom it is dedicated bears the onus of having inspired it.

O. H.